Not in *My*
Library!

NOT IN *MY* LIBRARY!

"Berman's Bag" Columns from The Unabashed Librarian, *2000–2013*

SANFORD BERMAN

Foreword by Maurice J. Freedman

McFarland & Company, Inc., Publishers
Jefferson, North Carolina, and London

ADDITIONAL WORKS BY SANFORD BERMAN AND FROM MCFARLAND
Prejudices and Antipathies: A Tract on the LC Subject Heads Concerning People (1993)
Worth Noting: Editorials, Letters, Essays, an Interview, and Bibliography (1988)

SANFORD BERMAN AND JAMES P. DANKY TOGETHER EDITED THE SERIES
Alternative Library Literature: A Biennial Anthology. THE VOLUMES COVERED
1984–1985 (Oryx, 1986)—AND FROM MCFARLAND: *1986–1987* (1988); *1988–1989*;
1990–1991; *1992–1993*; *1994–1995*; *1996–1997*; *1998–1999*; and *2000–2001* (2002)

ALTERNATIVE CATALOGING-IN-PUBLICATION DATA

Berman, Sanford, 1933–
Not in my library! : "Berman's bag" columns from the Unabashed
librarian, 2000-2013 ; foreword by Maurice J. Freedman.
Jefferson, NC: McFarland, copyright 2013. Includes
material on book-burning, weeding, genocide, government
secrecy and repression, cataloging, indexing, Banned Books Week,
commercialization, classism, self-censorship, and free speech for library staff.
1. Critical librarianship.   2. Critical cataloging.   3. Subject headings.
4. Library of Congress cataloging.   5. Libraries—Self-censorship.
6. Intellectual freedom.   7. Classism in libraries.   8. Poor people's
library services.   9. Information access.   10. Libraries—Commercialization.
I. Title.   II. Unbashed librarian.   III. Freedman, Maurice J., 1939–
Foreword.   IV. Title: "Berman's bag" columns.

LIBRARY OF CONGRESS CATALOGUING-IN-PUBLICATION DATA

Berman, Sanford, 1933–
[Essays. Selections]
Not in my library! : "Berman's bag" columns from
the Unabashed librarian, 2000–2013 / Sanford Berman ;
foreword by Maurice J. Freedman.
p.   cm.
Includes bibliographical references and index.

ISBN 978-0-7864-7822-4
softcover : acid free paper ∞

1. Library science—Moral and ethical aspects.   2. Library science—
Political aspects.   3. Libraries and society.   4. Censorship.
5. Libaries—Censorship.   6. Cataloging.   7. Subject cataloging.
8. Subject headings, Library of Congress.   I. Title.
Z665.B525 2013   020—dc23   2013022273

BRITISH LIBRARY CATALOGUING DATA ARE AVAILABLE

© 2013 Sanford Berman. All rights reserved
Foreword © 2013 Maurice J. Freedman

*No part of this book may be reproduced or transmitted in any form
or by any means, electronic or mechanical, including photocopying
or recording, or by any information storage and retrieval system,
without permission in writing from the publisher.*

On the cover: Sanford Berman in his home office, 1999
(photograph by Tony Nelson); quotations from Sandy; hand painted
tempera background (iStockphoto/Thinkstock)

Manufactured in the United States of America

*McFarland & Company, Inc., Publishers
Box 611, Jefferson, North Carolina 28640
www.mcfarlandpub.com*

To the memory of these inspiring
and supportive friends and colleagues:

Fay Blake
Bill Katz
Noel Peattie
Marvin Scilken
Celeste West
Charles Willett

Table of Contents

Foreword by Maurice J. Freedman 1

Introduction (Counterpoise *Interview with Kristin Hoyer, 2005*) 10

Why Catalog?
    (U*L 116, 2000) 19

Must "The Poor" Always Be Among Us?
    (U*L 117, 2000) 21

The Top Censored Library Stories of 1998–2000
    (U*L 118, 2001) 27

Updates and Additions
    (U*L 119, 2001) 31

Updates and Additions
    (U*L 120, 2001) 35

No More Shushing: Library Staff and Users Speak (Part 1)
    (U*L 121, 2001) 42

Harry Potter Imperiled, Keyword Searching as Panacea, Robin Hood's
    Noble Liege, and Other Foolishness
    (U*L 124, 2002) 46

"Not in My Library!"
    (U*L 125, 2002) 52

Updates and Additions
    (U*L 127, 2003) 57

Cuba Libre!
    (U*L 128, 2003) 62

No More Shushing: Library Staff and Users Speak (Part 2), More on Cuba
    (U*L 129, 2003) 65

Table of Contents

King County Responds, "Banned Books Week" Deconstructed, Cataloging Blues at LAPL, Loompanics' Mike Hoy on Censorship, Deep-Sixed Afghan Atrocity Film, Cuba Again
(U*L 130, 2004) 71

Access Denied
(U*L 133, 2004) 77

Squelched Letters, More Access Denied
(U*L 134, 2005) 81

Fighting the USA PATRIOT Act, Updates and Additions
(U*L 135, 2005) 86

UCLA Cross-Refs, AACR3, Library Openness
(U*L 136, 2005) 89

Cataloging Zines and Widgets
(U*L 137, 2005) 92

Questions
(U*L 138, 2006) 95

"Genocide" or Merely "Massacres"?—The Politics of Subject Cataloging
(U*L 139, 2006) 98

Darfur Revisited, GLBT Access Denied
(U*L 140, 2006) 101

LC Subject Cataloging (Part 1)
(U*L 143, 2007) 103

LC Subject Cataloging (Part 2)
(U*L 142, 2007) 105

LC Subject Cataloging (Postscript), Self-Censorship
(U*L 143, 2007) 108

Obsessions
(U*L 144, 2007) 111

Huh?, Fines and Fees, Self-Censorship (Continued)
(U*L 145, 2007) 114

"Controversial" Cataloging
(U*L 146, 2008) 117

Flawed Indexing, Erotica Selection, Subject Heading Currency, Undercataloging
(U*L 147, 2008) 121

Table of Contents

Darfur Redux, LC Cataloging Rescue, Subject Heading Currency
  (U*L 148, 2008) 124

One Book, Many Missed Opportunities, or Why Cataloging Matters
  (When It's Done Right)
  (U*L 149, 2008) 127

Cats, Cataloging, Fines, and BBW (Banned Books Week)
  (U*L 150, 2009) 131

More Classism in the Stacks
  (U*L 151, 2009) 134

Cataloging Stink, Truth in Materials Selection, CEO Pay
  (U*L 152, 2009) 138

Liberated Foreword, Unrequited LC Letters
  (U*L 153, 2009) 141

Nation Gets It Wrong, More Unrequited LC Letters, LCSH Currency
  (U*L 154, 2010) 144

More (Attempted) LCSH Input, Geopolitics Versus Historical Truth
  (U*L 155, 2010) 147

LCSH Currency (Continued), Libraries and Politics, Retiring the
  R-Word, Celeste West Tribute
  (U*L 156, 2010) 151

The Kids Are Not All Right
  (U*L 157, 2010) 154

Remembrance of Things Past, Interview Excerpts
  (U*L 158, 2011) 157

More Interview Excerpts, Atheist Deficit, What Rosa Said
  (U*L 159, 2011) 161

No to Government Secrecy and Repression!
  (U*L 160, 2011) 165

Word Peeves, "Content-Enriched Metadata," No "Sexting" Allowed
  (U*L 161, 2011) 168

Really Banned Books, Another Word Peeve, Clint's Fantasy, OWS
  Library Trashed, PFC Manning's Gift
  (U*L 162, 2012) 171

Post Office Crisis, LC Letters
  (U*L 163, 2012) 175

TABLE OF CONTENTS

Another Real Banning, the Trashing of Both Hypatia and Her Library,
Not-So-Funny Cataloging
 (*U*L 164, 2012*) 178

Laureates Support PFC Manning, Self-Censorship Affirmed, J'Accuse
LC of Untimeliness and Sloth, Let's Hear It for Robin Hood!
 (*U*L 166, 2013*) 182

Index 187

Foreword
by Maurice J. Freedman

I first met Sanford Berman via his letters from Africa that were published in *Library Journal* in the late 1960s and early 1970s. They were strongly political — if memory serves me right — and most especially they were critical of Library of Congress cataloging practices.

I personally became involved with him later. In 1972, I was head of technical services at the Hennepin County (Minnesota) Library, which at the time had its headquarters in the third and fourth floors of the Minneapolis Public Library. The HCL head cataloger left for California and I needed to replace her. I called two close friends of mine for recommendations, Art Plotnik and Patricia Glass Schuman. At the time Art was editor of the *Wilson Library Bulletin* (now defunct) and subsequently editor of *American Libraries* prior to his retirement. Pat had an editorial position at R.R. Bowker (a vastly changed company now, which also dropped the R.R.); more recently Pat sold Neal-Schuman Publishers (of which she was president and co-founder) to the American Library Association (ALA).

I asked both of them if there was anyone they knew or could recommend to help me fill the vacancy. Surprisingly, they each, quite separately and without any mutual consultation, recommended Sandy. I said that I knew his politics were good from the letters he sent to *LJ*, but I wondered if he knew anything about cataloging. I pretty clearly remember Pat saying that he was brilliant. I know both gave him a strong recommendation.

In January 1972, computing was mainframe-based and required people with strong systems and programming abilities to make them work. At Hennepin I was fortunate enough to have Jerry Pennington, formerly of the Library of Congress MARC Project, a great programmer as well as librarian, who was the HCL computer maven, and assistant head of technical services. Back then the big annual computer conference was the Joint Computer Conference, which was held in Anaheim, California, that year. I asked Jerry to meet with Sandy in Los Angeles while he was at the conference to see if Sandy was qualified for the cataloging position. When Jerry, a relatively taciturn guy, returned from the conference he told me that Sandy would be fine. I don't remember getting much more from Jerry, but knowing him very well, I knew that that was a strong recommendation.

Foreword by Maurice J. Freedman

I subsequently called Sandy to see if he'd be interested in the position. I was pretty sure he would be, having been told by Pat or Art that Sandy was unemployed, and that he and his wife, Lorraine, and their two children, Jill and Paul, were living in someone's basement in L.A. We chatted a while. He said that he was interested in the job. I told him I'd get back to him. I called him back and offered him the job. I asked him how much he wanted. He said $10,000 or $11,000, maybe. I told him that I would hire him but it had to be for $12,000+ dollars. I made that decision because I didn't want him to be paid any less than someone in the public services department in a comparable position. His response was something to the effect of, "When do I start?"

Fast forward to my meeting him at the airport in the middle of winter on the Minnesota tundra. He and his family were dressed in clothes that were L.A.'s best approximation of what winter apparel should be in Minnesota. They all moved into my house until they could find a place of their own. It worked out very well. My children, Jenna (now Director of Research & Instruction services and Zine Librarian, Barnard College Library) and Susan (a psychiatric social worker at Hunterdon [N.J.] Medical Center), were roughly the age of his children and our families became lifelong friends.

Getting back to library matters, I had sent Sandy the *Anglo-American Cataloging Rules*, and Jean Weihs' book, *Non-Book Materials: The Organization of Integrated Collections*. I asked him if he could begin working on rules for cataloging non-book materials. The Hennepin County Library in the early 1970s was undergoing a revolution in library buildings, collections, and service, which included a major commitment to audiovisual materials. I was surprised when Sandy showed up with a completed set of rules specifically applicable to the cataloging and classification of non-book titles. These rules were instituted and applied virtually at once.

There was so much that was done at HCL during the early 1970s. (My tenure was 1969–1974; Sandy stayed on much longer.)

Robert H. Rohlf, a world-class library buildings consultant, was the director of HCL from 1969 through almost all of my tenure (I started a couple of months before Bob arrived, but he was there many years after I left for the New York Public Library), and a good chunk of Sandy's time. To Bob's credit, he encouraged the "hundred flowers to bloom." In technical services, I was the division manager; Jerry Pennington was the assistant division manager (and also immediately responsible for systems and programming); Sandy was the head cataloger; and, elsewhere, Don Roberts, the great librarian media advocate, innovator, and practitioner, was responsible for the introduction and use of a broad range of media equipment, collections, and services. (Don was the guy who coined the phrase regarding the worship of library buildings: the *edifice complex*.)

Bob Rohlf was supportive of what we did, much of which had never been done before and probably has never been done since. Of particular note, the automated book catalog we produced was a complex effort that was innovative in a variety of ways. Originally, HCL was going to use the series of programs that were being developed at the University of California's Institute of Library Research (ILR) for the purpose of

Foreword by Maurice J. Freedman

converting all of the university's campuses' catalogs to the MARC format and then producing from that database a printed book catalog.

John Knapp, one of the three authors of the original MARC II Communications Format during his Library of Congress tenure, was head of systems at the University of California at Santa Cruz and affiliated with ILR; he recommended that the ILR conversion and maintenance programs would save HCL a tremendous amount of money and simplify data entry and record maintenance. The reason for the savings was that the few libraries actually creating MARC records and manipulating them had to fill out *on paper* the equivalent of an OCLC online cataloging template. Except for the college libraries of Ohio that were the only OCLC members at the time,[1] there was no online input to MARC available to HCL or any other U.S. library with the possible exception of Stanford University's BALLOTS system.

An ILR staffer with an MIT Ph.D. in linguistics, Don Sherman, noticed that random samples of the millions of catalog cards in the collective UC card catalogs shared similar formatting. Noticing that such elements as the main entry came first, the title paragraph followed after a carriage return and indent, subject headings were preceded by Arabic numbers followed immediately by a period, added entries were introduced by Roman numerals, etc., he decided that rather than manually coding data on worksheets it would be so much faster and cheaper to write a program — Automatic Field Recognition (AFR) — so that the data entry person need only enter the bibliographic information in the sequence and with the spacing and punctuation found on the actual catalog card. In the beginning Sherman created a few simple codes (e.g., the "¢" sign) to separate some of the data elements. But the codes selected could readily be learned and inserted by the keyboarder as part of the data entry process. This eliminated the tedious process of handwriting (or typing) code sheets for subsequent input by the typist.[2]

We also made the decision to hire University of Minnesota library school (now defunct) students to proofread the MARC records created with the ILR programs.

Seemingly a major digression from Sandy's work at HCL and our relationship, this automation background is relevant to what ultimately became Sandy's great achievements while at HCL.

Automation projects then, and today IT projects, virtually always missed multiple deadlines. One systems designer would estimate how long it would take to get a piece of software written, double the estimated time, and still found that the predicted deadline was missed.[3] Of consequence here was that HCL had an enormous building program underway. The point of the book catalog was to eliminate the need for card catalogs

---

1. Hence OCLC's original name, Ohio College Library Center.
2. Incidentally the ILR staff member primarily responsible for creating the MARC record maintenance program was Stephen Silberstein, co-founder and co-owner of Innovative Interfaces, Inc. He stayed at my house in 1973 when he came to Minneapolis to install the FIX program, i.e., the ILR program for correcting errors in MARC formatted records.
3. Based on my experience of having worked on such projects beginning in 1968, I came up with the adage, "We always meet our last deadline."

in the newly constructed branches. The problem was that ILR was massively behind in the development of its predicted completion of the two major programs needed to create the formatted data as it was to appear on the pages of the book catalog. Consequently, we had created a MARC database but it could not be used for the creation of a book catalog. Sort of "all dressed up and no place to go."

In January 1972, Jerry and I attended the MARC Users' Group meeting at ALA Midwinter. Making a presentation were the head and assistant head of the New York Public Library Systems Analysis and Data Processing Office (SADPO), James A. Rizzolo and S. Michael Malinconico. They distributed sample pages from the automated system that NYPL would soon be using to produce book catalogs for NYPL's Research Libraries and Branch Libraries, respectively. Aside from state-of-the-art photocomposition that effectively displayed catalog entries with letterpress quality, it introduced automated authority control to the machine-based cataloging process. This was revolutionary, and had especially important implications for HCL.

What made it unique and of such importance was that its goal was to automate the cataloging process, whereas the increasingly successful OCLC (then spreading to networks beyond Ohio, slowly but surely) was designed to facilitate data entry or transcription of cataloging information and the subsequent production of catalog cards.[4]

Together, Jerry and I decided that we should approach NYPL to see if we could use their system to create a book catalog for HCL from the MARC database HCL created using the ILR programs. Without going into the gory details, a deal was struck. HCL contracted with NYPL to have its MARC records processed through the NYPL system. As part of the process, HCL received a printout of all of the authorities (authors, subjects, uniform titles, and series titles) in its database. NYPL used the authority system to ensure that its catalog records were rigorously consistent with the Library of Congress names, subjects, etc. The system displayed erroneous terms and permitted simple (and not so simple) corrections. It also automatically flipped names or subjects that were cross-references to the established forms. The system permitted global changes to terms when LC updated some of its many outmoded headings— if LC changed "automatic calculating machines" to "computers," all of the records with the former heading could be converted to the latter by simply changing the authority record. Of course, for LC to change a heading, it had to reprint and then file every catalog card in three separate catalogs in which the outmoded term appeared.[5] NYPL also provided with the system

---

4. The catalog card production process developed by OCLC left the Library of Congress catalog card service in the dust. While OCLC used a degraded type font — degraded only by letterpress standards — it produced catalog cards from OCLC line printers alphabetized in filing-ready order with tracings and call numbers in place exactly to the specifications of the individual library — virtually overnight. This was effectively the end of the LC card service although it didn't shut down till much later. It must be added that OCLC, despite its poor quality control, created the most extraordinary interlibrary loan tool in history.

5. This was the harsh economic reason why LC wanted to avoid changing its terms. The cost of reprinting the catalog cards and filing them, and of removing the outdated cards, was the primary reason LC was so reluctant to make changes. We also know that LC avoided changes that (cont.)

for the embedding of public notes and cataloger notes in the authority records. The cataloger notes only were displayed for the cataloger.

As stated, NYPL did not want to change LC cataloging to meet some other standard; it used the system to be consistent with the LC name and subject authorities.

Hiring Sandy combined his brilliance, his seemingly Renaissance knowledge, and his strong political and social views with the capabilities of the NYPL authority control program. It was a collaborative effort. We suggested that Sandy could take advantage of the system to "correct" all objectionable or outmoded LC terms and to add appropriate terms where none heretofore existed — as Sandy saw fit. Prior to implementing this change in cataloging, i.e., moving beyond the slavish adherence to LC cataloging followed by virtually all libraries to this day, I recommended this policy to Bob Rohlf, who gave us the go-ahead. Bob was more conservative than we were, but his principled stance as a librarian made it possible for so many wonderful flowers to bloom at Hennepin — not just the cataloging and automation innovations.

With the policy now adopted and in place, Sandy led the cataloging staff in implementing the kinds of changes he had recommended in *Prejudices and Antipathies* (Scarecrow, 1971; revised and updated, McFarland, 1993) and whatever else made sense — because automated authority control made it possible!

Two major achievements took place:

1. The (probably) only time that a mainframe-based library catalog system was transferred and implemented at another location, and it was done twice by HCL: first with the University of California Institute of Library Research's book catalog system and second with the New York Public Library automated book catalog system.

2. The adoption of a cataloging policy and its implementation that broke with the automatic adherence to LC terminology and practice. When LC's terms didn't make sense, were wrong, outdated or nonexistent, Sandy and his staff could correct or innovate them because the NYPL system gave them the facility to readily do so.

The second would not have been possible without the first.

I can't proceed further without recognizing the enormous contributions of Jerry Pennington and Michael Malinconico. Jerry did the incredible work required to make that mainframe software transfer happen on the Hennepin end. From a systems standpoint it was an enormous achievement. Without Michael's help on the NYPL end the first HCL book catalog could not have been produced. He and his staff did all of the work necessary

---

had political implications inimical to government policy (e.g., Vietnam Conflict rather than Vietnam War) or represented cultural shifts which essentially made a stodgy LC uncomfortable. Sandy has written extensively about LC's intransigence when it comes to popular culture terminology replacing LC's outmoded terms or innovating new terms reflecting contemporary usage.

Henriette Avram, the "godmother" of MARC, put all of her effort into the development, maintenance and adoption of MARC internationally; this is why LC was quite late coming to the development and implementation of a cataloging and authority control system — hence LC's resistance to changes in headings, not just because they didn't like them politically speaking but also because of the enormity of the cost of implementing changes in withdrawing, printing, arranging, and filing cards from card catalogs.

to process the HCL database, get it run through the NYPL system, and then produce the first HCL book catalog. (The actual transfer of the system from NYPL to Hennepin occurred later.) The HCL MARC database could not have been successfully created without the contribution of Stephen Silberstein (of ILR at the time and future and past co-owner of Innovative Interfaces, Inc.) who came to Minneapolis and installed FIX, the complex program he wrote that provided the means to edit the converted MARC records.

One interesting story — of so very many — will be mentioned. It was an enormous job getting the master catalog card file converted to machine-readable form. We chose to use the IBM Magnetic Tape Selectric Typewriter (MTST) for the conversion. These devices were leased and very expensive. We started with two or three and added another one. We wanted to increase production so that a book catalog could be produced in the not too distant future. It occurred to me, why not put on a second shift. That would mean that we could increase productivity without adding more machines.

Two keyboarders were hired, one of whom was Myrna Harper, who had been taking one or more extension courses at the University of Minnesota that focused on Native American history. Myrna also read the information on the catalog cards as she was typing it onto tape. She came to me and said, "I see that you're changing the names of all of these African peoples to the way they want to be identified, why aren't you doing the same for the Native American tribes?" My response was simple. "You help us, and we'll do it." Myrna worked with Sandy — while still doing her keyboarding — and Sandy systematically changed the LC Westernized version of the tribal names to the names by which they preferred to be called. And that is how "Nimipu" became the name for the people that French settlers called "Nez Percé."

The last major innovation was the creation of the *Hennepin County Library Cataloging Bulletin*. I had suggested to Sandy that he create a newsletter for the public service staff that would inform them of the changes being made to the catalog. The idea was to help them better serve the patrons and guide their own research. It became a wonderful publication. Sandy listed the changes but also wrote explanations and mini-essays concerning cataloging policy and practice. *HCL Cataloging Bulletin* had an international circulation and was widely read and discussed in cataloging circles. In 1976, it won the H.W. Wilson Library Periodical Award.

I will move forward with a discussion of this collection of Sandy's columns in *The U*N*A*B*A*S*H*E*D^{TM} Librarian*, the *"how I run my library good"^{SM} letter* (U*L), but first a not-so-happy coda must be added to the Hennepin story. Once I left, many of the 100 flowers wilted.

As Sandy related, "Rohlf ... was so uncomfortable with our cataloging operation that I tried to get out.... [Rohlf] and [Lora Landers, a Hennepin division manager] censored the *Cataloging Bulletin*, banning all illustrations[6] and insisting that

---

6. The illustrations were created initially by the late Inese Jansons, the HCL staff artist, a warm, extraordinarily talented and joyous person filled with love for the people she liked, which fortunately included Sandy and me. The offending cartoons were drawn by Inese's successor, Jackie Urbanovic.

Foreword by Maurice J. Freedman

all copy be approved by them in advance. That's what reduced the mag to simply a bare bones report on new and changed headings." Don Roberts fell out of favor and, according to Sandy, "was ridiculed and humiliated in front of library staff by Landers."[7]

The retirement of Bob Rohlf led to his replacement by someone who had *no* respect for the work done by Sandy and his staff, nor for that matter did he see any value in the innovative audiovisual services introduced by Don Roberts. In a Stalinesque erasure of history, the HCL cataloging database was overlaid by OCLC's LC (or other) catalog records and all of the innovative work was destroyed. The director reassigned Sandy to a research position, thus relieving him of all catalog management responsibility. And that was the end of a creative era at the Hennepin County Library that had begun in 1969. With a prescience that I hadn't foreseen, Sandy, at a goodbye party for me, said about my leaving HCL, "That's the end of Camelot."

As Vonnegut would say, "and so it goes."[8]

Now let's pick up the U*L story. U*L began in 1973. It was the creation of Marvin H. Scilken, its *Founder* (Marvin's self-appellation) and one of the great and most underappreciated librarians of the 20th century. Marvin was an iconoclast, a public librarian who believed that public libraries existed to provide the best possible service to their patrons. His criticism and anger were directed at libraries and library practitioners who established practices and procedures that made things easier for the staff but frequently usually made things harder for the patrons. In the days before integrated library systems, Marvin had his circulation staff make a crayon hash mark in the back of the a book every time it circulated, changing the crayon color each year. In this way, by simply opening the back of the book he could tell how many times an item circulated each year with a simple glance, as well as the first and last time it was borrowed.

He had a seemingly infinite number of ideas to improve service to the public. He also had numerous criticisms of library practices, but always suggested user-friendly alternatives. U*L was the place to go for ideas, suggestions, procedures, and forms that would improve service to the public library users—and sometimes for a good laugh. Marvin also included in U*L similar material from libraries around the country that he characterized as *nifty*. Along with his wife Polly (now deceased), he produced four issues per year up until 2000, when he died suddenly of a heart attack while attending the ALA Midwinter meeting in January.[9]

My wife, Paula, and I came into the U*L picture when we purchased U*L from Polly in early 2000. The first 113 issues were edited and published by the Scilkens. Beginning with issue number 114, the first issue of 2000, Paula and I have published all subsequent issues of U*L.

Not being Marvin or having the veritable fountain of nifty ideas that flowed from

---

7. Quotations are from a letter sent to me by Sandy, dated May 17, 2013.
8. A favorite expression of Kurt Vonnegut that appeared countlessly in his writings.
9. It was the third consecutive Midwinter Meeting in Philadelphia at which librarians died. Harold Roth was the first, followed by Elizabeth Futas, and then Marvin. I was nervous about attending the next Midwinter scheduled for Philadelphia—fortunately, there were no mishaps.

him, we decided that having some regular contributing editors would be a positive addition to the kinds of material that characterized U*L from the outset. We asked Sandy to be a columnist for a couple of reasons. We knew that Sandy had an enormous following and would offer columns that always would be challenging and sometimes even controversial.

In addition we added Mark Hasskarl, a long-time public library director and also a published movie critic in Connecticut papers, and Bernadine E. Abbott Hoduski, probably the single most important advocate for government publications in the last several decades. Jenna Freedman at Barnard College Library has contributed articles on an occasional basis. Ben Ostrowsky contributed crossword puzzles for numerous issues; and Dan Stanton, government information librarian at Arizona State University, contributed a number of interesting articles.

At present, along with Sandy, Mark, and Bernadine, Adrienne L. Strock, a YA librarian recently appointed Manager of YOUmedia Chicago, Youth-Powered 21st Century Learning, at the Chicago Public Library; and Susan L. Polos, Library Media Specialist, Mount Kisco Elementary School, Mount Kisco, New York, have been regular contributors.

There are numerous articles of varying size and topics that are drawn from library newsletters, nonprofit journals, and miscellaneous sources including all that speak to best practices for public, academic, school, and other types of libraries, or as Marvin put it, articles about "how I run my library good."[SM] Occasionally some of them are in a more academic voice, but overall U*L has been practical and practice-oriented. Because of my extensive travels, there are at least a couple of photos each issue to do with libraries in a multitude of venues, foreign and domestic.

As a contributing editor, Sandy has had virtually complete license about what he chooses to write and its length. You'll see from the range of his contributions that there are a variety of topics, but his focus on the terminology of LC — going back to the 1960s — the de facto national library, has never flagged.

He also has been a pain in the ass.

All of Sandy's contributions are typewritten on a manual typewriter. When we worked together at Hennepin, I offered to get him an electric typewriter, but he declined the offer. An extraordinary typist — 80 to 90 words per minute — he said he likes to think with his fingers on the typewriter keys. Unfortunately his resting fingers are not always idle. Unintentionally a resting finger may trigger a keystroke. Which is why Sandy will only use his manual typewriter. I tried to buy him a PC for his columns. For the same keyboard-related issue, he rejected the offer.

Sandy sends me manual typewriter–produced copy. This means that there are shadowed letters, insertions of printed text of various physical size and type font, redactions, and a multitude of ink spots, all of which confuse the sophisticated — but not sophisticated enough — scanning/Optical Character Recognition (OCR) program, ABBYY® Fine Reader® 11. Photocopied information and cataloging information with all of its esoteric single and multiple indents, capitalizations, etc. all bedevil [not so]

Foreword by Maurice J. Freedman

Fine Reader. If Sandy had sent me a word-processed document of his article, I'd have little to do other than ensuring that it would be accurately placed into the desktop typeset publication.

The initially scanned output from his manuscript can look like a train wreck. The OCR program converts every shadow, redaction, smudge, etc. into something that makes no sense, a seemingly random series of characters, that otherwise bears little relation to what Sandy intended. It then is incumbent on me to use his manuscript as a reference in order to make the additions, deletions, and changes to the OCR output that will result in the U*L published article that Sandy intended it to be. Depending on the condition of Sandy's manuscript, the conversion process runs the gamut from extraordinarily tedious and painstaking to a little less tedious and painstaking. The beauty of it is that at the end of the process, the successfully converted column is yet another nugget of Berman gold.

It's a labor of love. I love Sandy, and I'm happy and proud to publish his columns—all of which have enriched U*L and its readers. (It should be noted that Sandy had occasionally submitted pieces to Marvin Scilken during the first 27 years of U*L's history.)

I'm also thrilled that having Sandy as a contributing editor of U*L has provided yet another reason for maintaining a friendship and a professional relationship that began 40+ years ago in Minneapolis, Minnesota, one I cherish to this day.

> Maurice J. Freedman, MLS, Ph.D.
> Publisher, *The U*N*A*B*A*S*H*E*D^{TM} Librarian*,
>   the *"how I run my library good"*^{SM} letter
> Past President, American Library Association

A Note from the McFarland Editors: The Unabashed Librarian *has been going since 1973. It's a terrific periodical, unique in coverage and wide-ranging in subject. Mitch Freedman is the publisher and may be contacted at editor@unabashedlibrarian.com or at PO Box 287, Mount Kisco NY 10549, for subscription information or editorial correspondence. Highly recommended!*

Introduction

I first wanted to call this collection *Making a Stink* or *Raising Hell*. Why such inelegant titles? This interview, conducted by Kristin Hoyer in March 2005 and originally published in the fall 2004 *Counterpoise*, may help explain.

Counterpoise (CP): Were you surprised when the American Library Association awarded you honorary membership, its highest award? Do you feel ALA has supported you in the work you have done?

Sandy Berman (SB): Not entirely, since I'd been forewarned about the nomination. I confess, though, that nearly every time I get an ALA envelope in the mail, I wonder if it's going to be an oops!-sorry-for-the-mistake-but-please-send-back-the-award message. While there was no chance at the award ceremony to make an acceptance speech, I wanted to say something like this:

You do me a great honor today. Yet an even greater honor, both for me and all of you — the whole association — would be to energetically promote and implement ALA's Poor People's Policy, which has essentially remained dormant since 1990, and to add to the "Personnel Practices" policy a clause affirming free speech for library workers.

Although happy for the recognition (especially when still fit enough to enjoy it) — and truly overwhelmed by the loud and loving ovation at the Orlando presentation — the truth is that a number of other people also deserve such affirmation and applause. Thus, without doing a humility trip, I want to now share the award with:

- The late Noel Peattie, *Sipapu* editor, UC–Davis librarian, poet, raconteur, reporter, printer, aesthete, social activist, philosopher, critic, publisher, sailor, cat-lover, and eccentric.
- Fay Blake, library educator, access-advocate, and unstoppable hell-raiser.
- Zoia Horn, the very embodiment of intellectual freedom and personal courage.
- Celeste West, *Synergy* and *Booklegger Magazine* editor, the most awesome, electric, and incisive voice ever in library literature.
- Five selfless citizen-activists who love books and libraries so much that they're willing to fight for them: Peter Warfield and James Chaffee (San Francisco), Fred Whitehead (Kansas City, KS), Fred Woodworth (Tucson), and Nicholson Baker (Maine).

Introduction (Counterpoise *Interview*)

Has ALA supported my work? Well, some of ALA has. Sometimes. SRRT colleagues have surely been supportive. So have people in EMIERT and GLBTRT. Once, for a brief, glorious period, the Subject Analysis Committee — under the leadership of an unusually responsive person — actually took important action on previously-ignored proposals to expand subject and genre access to fiction and other literary works, to expedite the creation and use of topical descriptors, and to eliminate remaining bias from Library of Congress Subject Headings. On the other hand, myriad letters to ALA executive directors and presidents, for instance concerning resuscitation of the Poor People's Policy, advocacy for workplace speech rights, and — most recently — support for the National Coalition for the Homeless-crafted Bringing Home America Act have gone either unanswered or without follow-up action. And my personal ALA history, of course, began with a disaster: the refusal of the Association's Publishing Services to print my *Prejudices and Antipathies*, a tract on the LC subject headings concerning people, without serious revisions in content and tone — even though ALA itself had commissioned the book!

CP: After your forced retirement from the HCL in 1999, you must have been angry. How do you feel about the Hennepin County Library now that the dust has settled? Do you feel they have disrespected your life's work?

SB: Angry? Yes (when I allow myself to think about it, which isn't that often). All I wanted subsequent to that forced retirement was two things:

- Rescinding the unjust reprimand that disciplined me for expressing my professional views on AACR2 and allegedly opposing Hennepin County Library's membership in OCLC (I didn't oppose it);
- An apology for the humiliation and punishment inflicted on me. I never demanded reinstatement or monetary damages. Just a clean record plus a "We're sorry." But they simply couldn't manage it, despite several requests. In fact, most later correspondence to HCL, typically dealing with cataloging, service, and collection issues (e.g., recommending local alternative press and ethnic, particularly Latino, publications for the magazine collection), were never answered. And three successive letters to a community newspaper simply asking about HCL's activities regarding the USA PATRIOT Act elicited no reply whatever.

Did they "disrespect" my life's work? Much worse than that: they literally demolished it. Perhaps two or so years ago, the authority file and bibliographic database carefully, innovatively, and lovingly built over 2.5 decades, were totally destroyed, being replaced by strictly "standard" OCLC records and LC terms. (A "snapshot" of our earlier labor was captured on a disc only after a public outcry and clamor. It has yet to be made available, perhaps through the University of Illinois Archives, in an easily searchable, interactive mode.) In the meantime, the director who presided over my expulsion and the later data-demolition left — voluntarily — for a warmer clime. And the cabal of upper-level managers who inspired and engineered the catalog destruction as well as my exile remain, to this day, secure in their positions. None of the three principals have ever, even privately, expressed any remorse or regret over what happened. On a less somber note, many frontline HCL staff, especially those who in the late '90s formed the first-ever librarians union at Hennepin, were and continue to be, firm friends and colleagues. Hell, I lunch with 3 or 4 of them every week! And their AFSCME local succeeded in getting a "free speech" clause added to their contract. That's gratifying.

Bottom line: I'm profoundly disgusted by HCL's administration (which, incidentally, I believe was complicit in the wholesale removal of some 6 books by and about me, plus their online catalog records, a few years ago), but I highly respect the dedicated and imaginative HCL workforce.

CP: You have long been associated with the Social Responsibilities Round Table of the American Library Association. How has it changed? How do you feel about having future involvement in SRRT?

SB: I've been a SRRTer, with only a few interruptions, since 1973. It's the only place to be inside ALA for those who oppose "business model" librarianship, replete with branding, naming rights, blockbuster-hyping, outsourcing, mindless weeding, endless management fads, and top-down governance, and who are actively concerned about the connection between libraries and democracy, social justice, and the environment. SRRT has historically functioned as ALA's, if not the profession's, conscience. Its *Newsletter* today, ably edited by Sally Driscoll, is better than it's ever been (including my own 2-year stint in the '70s). Some of its task forces have become so large and strong that they morphed into round tables themselves. That's the genesis of GODORT, EMIERT, GLBTRT, and, I think, IFRT. So SRRT has definitely been a prod, a beacon, an incubator. The one task force I founded, dealing with what I have increasingly felt is the paramount issue facing society and libraries, poverty, has seemed relatively inactive in the past several years (apart from a fine program in Toronto). It needs to spark interest in the long-aborning Poor People's Policy and provide desperately-needed counsel and information (e.g., on how people experiencing homelessness can get library cards and what libraries can do to better sensitize their staffs to poor people's rights and needs). With the recent advent of a new coordinator — John Gehner, a soon-to-graduate library student who has actually worked at a homeless shelter and is extremely principled, skilled, and creative, the Hunger, Homelessness, and Poverty Task Force is certain to fully revive and make a real impact on library practice.

There has always been some contention and even heated debate within SRRT. In the past few years, however, there appears to have developed an almost measurable rise in incivility, vituperation, and often vindictive, lacerating, ad hominem attacks. This trend contributes nothing to improving librarianship (or the world). It only wastes time and energy, embittering and alienating many erstwhile allies and comrades in the process. Someone last year described the AC Coordinator as a kind of "excrement." I've been savagely accused of doing things I never did (like deliberately excluding *Progressive Librarian* selections from *Alternative Library Literature* anthologies and somehow "giving up the fight"). I've been characterized as throwing a "hissy fit" over the

Introduction (Counterpoise *Interview*)

editorial mutilation of an article I submitted to *PL*. ("Righteous outrage" would've been more accurate.) I've been excoriated for labeling people "Stalinists," although I never did so. During an unsolicited phone call after I'd announced support for a draft ALA resolution praising the Cuban Revolution's health and literacy progress, but calling for the release of some 75 jailed dissidents, I was derided for not being a "deep thinker." Later I was termed "a foot soldier for Bush" (and worse)! (All because I took the very same position on the dissident-crackdown as Naomi Klein, Barbara Ehrenreich, Howard Zinn, Noam Chomsky, Cornel West, Amnesty International, and Human Rights Watch.)

Which brings me to two deeply troubling recent events concerning SRRT. The second I already alluded to. When ALA convened in San Francisco in 2001, the Hotel Workers' union declared a boycott against the Marriott Hotel, designated as ALA Conference Headquarters. Many ALA units accordingly arranged to switch their event-venues from the Marriott to other locations. SRRT's Coretta Scott King Task Force did not arrange to move its scheduled Tuesday morning award breakfast out of the Marriott. H.E.R.E. Local 2 planned to picket the Marriott that Tuesday morning. SRRT leaders vigorously tried to get the union to forego that demonstration, inasmuch as it would embarrass the CSK Breakfast attendees. Persons who resisted this pressure were dismissed as "racist." (Never mind that Local 2 is hugely multiracial.) The SRRT leaders may have sincerely wished not to discomfit the largely Black CSK Task Force. They may also have sincerely wished not to lose the considerable revenue that the breakfast ordinarily produces. Although alternative sites were proposed (probably involving the sacrifice of the $40-per-plate breakfast), none were accepted. Then the inevitable happened. Having been told of the CSK TF intention to meet in a boycotted hotel, Coretta Scott King herself issued a letter stating the obvious: that such an act would not harmonize with Martin Luther King's legacy and spirit. Once published, CSKers and SRRT cancelled the whole program. No alternative venue. No possibly donating the uneaten breakfast food to hotel workers or soup kitchens. Nothing. At the very least, the Marriott fiasco represented a case of paralytic inflexibility. At the worst, it was a betrayal of principle.

The second instance: Cuba. Frankly, it has shaken me to the very core that nearly everyone in SRRT, however intensely committed to Cuban sovereignty and pleased with its literacy and medical successes, could fail to understand that the 75 dissident journalists, teachers, and librarians were the victims of totalitarian repression. They were tried suddenly in remote locations. They were charged with such heinous crimes as mounting human rights posters and holding or disseminating "subversive" and "counterrevolutionary" materials. Yes, they may have received money and literature and communications equipment from the United States. (Sweden and Spain, too.) But dealing with books, posters, and faxes—not guns and grenades—hardly makes these people dangerous spies, saboteurs, or agents of American imperialism. Simply to invoke terms like "subversive" and "counterrevolutionary" is to give away the game: that the regime wants to suppress ideas, to restrict speech, to limit intellectual freedom. Of all people, librarians should instantly recognize that kangaroo courts and the confiscation, even destruction, of reading matter signifies thought control, censorship, and repression. Yet not many have recognized that, leaving me, at any rate, with a sickening feeling in my gut that our professional commitment to free speech is not universal and unequivocal, but rather circumscribed by politically convenient double standards.

CP: How would you update your comments in "Jackdaws Strut in Peacock's Feathers," which appeared in *Librarians at Liberty*, six years later?

SB: Of course, some specific examples might be dropped or revised, but I'd retain the overall complaint and indictment. Let me stipulate the continuing problem in a few pithy observations:

- Cataloging should unmistakably identify a given work, convey its nature, content, and thrust, and specify how it can be accessed: e.g., by subject headings and various added entries for title variations, editors, illustrators, notable contributors, translators, associated groups or agencies, and local, specialty, and alternative presses.
- Electronic tinkering and keyword searching do not compensate for rigorous, accurate, fulsome, and fair cataloging at the start: that is, the crafting of a functional bibliographic record.
- Most U.S. libraries rely on Library of Congress cataloging for the bib-records that will appear in their local OPACs. This is especially so for U.S. trade publications, which constitute the bulk of new acquisitions by public, school, and some college libraries.
- Increasingly, most libraries do not review "outside copy" (i.e., the LC or network-supplied data) in a constructively critical fashion. Too often, paraprofessionals or clerks may be assigned merely to check on call number suitability and verify such basic elements as main entry and title, nothing more.
- As demonstrated in "Jackdaws" and numerous other sources, LC-originated copy is often deficient in notes, subject tracings, and other access points. Further, despite some fairly recent improvement in the liberality of heading assignment and the topical and genre treatment of literary works, such assignments remain inconsistent and spotty. Moreover, much subject heading vocabulary is still biased, awkward, or absent.

The dilemma persists: libraries accept LC-like products and tools with an almost infantile faith that they're really useful. In fact, they are frequently imperfect and dysfunctional. What to do? Undertake more local enhancement and revision, realizing that poor cataloging may undo the considerable effort and expense of selecting and processing material. If the items can't be found, what's the point? Also, support LC's future requests for greater funding and staffing, providing they acknowledge what particularly needs repair, like the more timely establishment of topical headings and the accelerated inclusion of content-clarifying and keyword-searchable notes.

Introduction (Counterpoise *Interview*)

For recent examples of LC cataloging infelicities, see my column, "Berman's Bag," in UNABASHED LIBRARIAN, no. 132. Last week, I received a gift from students at the College of St. Catherine in St. Paul: *Shut Up Shut Down: Poems* (Minneapolis: Coffee House Press, 2004). It's by Mark Nowak, with an Afterword by Amiri Baraka. It consists largely of poems about work, workers, and the labor movement, punctuated by black-and-white photos, quotations, and reading lists. Coincidentally, it is a case study in what's wrong with standard cataloging. LC assigned a generous four headings: Corporate culture, Corporations—Corrupt practices, Business ethics, and Greed, all subdivided by—Literary collections. The sole added entry: I. Title. So what's amiss? No added entry (access point) for notable contributor Amiri Baraka. No turnaround title added entry for "Shut down shut up." No tracing for the alternative publisher: Coffee House Press. No note indicating the graphic dimension, the photo-documentary aspect. No genre heading for "Working class poetry." No topical headings for plant closings, downsizing, and labor movement. Nor for, say, "Employee resistance and revolts." And "Greed" is way too broad. This is emphatically about corporate greed, which demands an appropriate new heading. Also needed: "American poetry—21st century." Finally, Dewey classifiers placed this essentially verse collection in "American fiction." Not quite bibliocide-by-cataloging, but close.

For the record, over two years or longer I submitted suggestions and documentation regarding cataloging improvements and possible new or substitute headings to LC's Cataloging Policy & Support Office. No replies. Then, finally, after some 40 or 50 submissions, came a response, which I believe materialized only because the CPSO Chief was ordered to do so by her superior. Since that December 16, 2004 letter, more have arrived. I would dearly like to report that the "thaw" betokens a genuine responsiveness, manifest in concrete reforms or new-heading creation. Alas, that hasn't quite happened. Mostly, it's been perfunctory acknowledgments or tortured explanations about why they won't do what they should do.

Among other things, I've been trying to get them to introduce subject headings for CULTURE WARS, INFOSHOPS, STUDENT ANTI-SWEATSHOP MOVEMENT, PLUTOCRACY, and NATIVE AMERICAN HOLOCAUST, as well as either replacing FANZINES with ZINES or creating ZINES as a complementary descriptor. The latest LC communication was a full-page rebuke, dated 2-10-05, for daring to mention the inadequate Cataloging-in-Publication entry for Nan Levinson's *Outspoken: Free Speech Stories* in my upcoming *College & Research Libraries* review.

CP: You encouraged Charles Willett to start *Counterpoise*, and have been associated with it since the first issue. How has it changed or improved? How could the magazine improve?

SB: Rescuing *Counterpoise* from the clutches of a few SRRT Action Council members who sought to emasculate it was an accomplishment I'm genuinely proud of. I believe that the review-and-essay journal devoted to alternative media and socially responsible librarianship that Charles Willett had the vision to create and the expertise to produce qualifies as the most lasting, tangible, and useful product ever to emerge from the

Introduction

Alternatives In Publication Task Force — and SRRT itself. Indeed, the only other comparable achievement in recent AIP and SRRT history also owes much to Charles Willett's inspiration and guidance: the absolutely critical support provided to our island companions during the Hawaii Outsourcing Scandal. The advice, encouragement, and communication resources supplied by AIP's Hawaii Working Group to those beleaguered offshore colleagues absolutely enabled them to successfully resist the privatizing machinations of Bart Kane and Baker & Taylor. No other ALA unit came so quickly and committedly to their aid. For those two triumphs alone, Charles Willett should long ago have won the Jackie Eubanks Memorial Award. I nominated him more than once.

Counterpoise could improve in two basic ways: First, it needs to appear more regularly. And second, it should contain more reviews. Otherwise, it's terrific!

CP: What can and should librarians do outside of libraries and in their communities?

SB: Within the very real limits of available time and energy, tell community groups, publications, and activists about new (and even old) library resources likely to interest them and perhaps help in their work: from books, CDs, and videos to journals, databases, and web sites. Government documents, too. Do it by mail, phone, or computer. And don't wait to be asked. If you're comfortable writing, contribute letters, columns, and op-eds to the local press on library and information-access issues (e.g., "dumbed down" collections); Internet filtering; media bias and concentration; regional and out-of-the-mainstream news and opinion sources; the USA PATRIOT Act; censorship-by-copyright; adequate and stable library funding, perhaps through special tax districts, to prevent closings and cuts in hours; materials on urgent topics like peace, war, poverty, corporate greed and power, citizen action, GLBT rights, genocide, election reform, and environmental threats that can be reached online or found at libraries. If you'd rather speak, do the same on public access cable and community radio shows. Or arrange to talk or conduct panel discussions at meetings of civic, religious, labor, business, and political organizations.

CP: How long have you been sending out informative mailings? Where do you get the material, and to how many people do you send it?

SB: Forever. Well, almost. I did it while working. And I do it in "retirement." Admittedly, it's kind of a compulsion. An obsession. But my hope is that recipients find at least some of the material useful, perhaps even amusing or inspiring. What I typically send are newspapers, magazines, pamphlets, clippings, flyers, and — uh huh — web printouts. My object is to target the items to particular individuals and groups. Not everyone gets the identical mailing.

How do I assemble this treasury of stuff? Many things I pick up as freebies at shops or events. Some material comes through memberships and subscriptions. And a small but diligent network of penpals supplies the rest, most notably Steve Fesenmaier (West Virginia Library Commission), Jim Danky (Wisconsin Historical Society), Donny Smith (*Dwan/American Libraries/Library Journal*), Chris Dodge (*Utne*), Fred Whitehead, (*People's Culture/Freethought History*), Earl Lee (Pittsburg State University), and

Introduction (Counterpoise *Interview*)

John Gehner (ALA/SRRT Poverty Task Force). While there's no formal "mailing list," I currently have about 81 active address cards. If I don't mail out SOMETHING every week, I'm likely to sink into serious depression and self-rebuke.

CP: What print and Internet resources can you recommend for people who will be the Sanford Bermans of the next generation?

SB: Hey, the next generation of "revolting librarians" doesn't need ME to recommend Internet resources. They're all amazingly adept and knowledgeable concerning online communication. Some, in fact, maintain their own web sites and blogs. Others produce their own zines. Since there's occasionally a temptation among, ahem, senior members of our congregation to bewail how few younger colleagues seem to be carrying on the (let's call it) radical or progressive or ass-kicking tradition in librarianship, let me puncture that somewhat condescending contention by naming several committed, energetic, and independent colleagues I happen to know — all my juniors by about 30 years or more — who make me confident that the future's in very good hands: Jenna Freedman, Sean Stewart, Bruce Jensen, John Gehner, Jessamyn West, Katia Roberto, Donny Smith, Alycia Sellie, and Tatiana de la Tierra.

CP: What words of wisdom can you give to budding librarians and activists?

SB: At the great risk of being at once trite and obvious:

- As much as possible, try to harmonize your values and your behavior. (Your mental health may depend on it!)
- In the process of saving the world, don't stint on family and friends. (Indeed, they should come first.)
- Read *The Onion*. Laugh a lot. Sometimes do silly things. (If possible, hang out with toddlers and any kids up to 7 or 8 years old.)
- No matter how dismal or hopeless things seem, don't give up. Said Gandhi: "Even a single lamp dispels the deepest darkness." And Adam Hochschild has demonstrated in his *Bury the Chains* that even so clearly compelling a matter as ending the British slave trade took at least 50 years of effort.

Okay. End of interview. The fact is that "making a stink" or "raising hell" is sometimes the best — and perhaps only — way to raise otherwise overlooked issues (like self-censorship and such wanton government repression as the treason charges leveled against whistle-blower Bradley Manning and Mayor Bloomberg's destruction of the Occupy Wall Street library), change attitudes (for instance about treating poor people with respect instead of disdain), and actually get something done, whether cajoling the cataloging gods (at the Library of Congress and elsewhere) to variously reform antiquated and bigoted terminology (e.g., replacing WATER-CLOSETS with TOILETS and deleting YELLOW PERIL), vastly enhance subject access to fiction and other literature, provide more useful content data in bibliographic records, and abandon confusing Latinisms and abbreviations; derailing a major public library's ridiculous plan to increase revenue by hiking children's fines; finally enshrining free speech for library staff in

INTRODUCTION

ALA policy; or assisting colleagues at the Hawaii State Public Library System to reclaim their autonomy by overturning privatization of acquisitions and cataloging.

Finally, heartfelt thanks to Robert Franklin of McFarland, who for decades has fostered critical and contrary voices in librarianship. And my profound gratitude to Mitch Freedman, who unstintingly furnished the space to speak and most graciously dealt with my typewritten texts.

Why Catalog?
(U*L 116, 2000)

Issues of cataloging adequacy and reform can't be meaningfully addressed in a vacuum. So I propose this credo or "mission" as context:

> Cataloging should identify and make accessible a library's resources—in all formats. That identification and access should be swift and painless. The language and structure of catalog entries should be familiar and comprehensible. And catalogers should recognize that they do what they do not to please bosses and not to mindlessly adhere to rules and protocols, but to serve their information desk colleagues and the public. That's whom they're working for.

Given such a mission or function, which incidentally coincides nicely with Ranganathan's famous admonition to "save the time of the reader," how does today's reality stack up?

Libraries tend to trumpet how easily and helpfully their wares can be accessed. Some really seem to think that just because they have "push-de-button" online catalogs with keyword searching, everything is findable and the bib-records are invariably useful. Well, as I've argued and demonstrated in many writings (most recently, "Jackdaws Strut in Peacock's Feathers: the Sham of 'Standard Cataloging,'" in the June 1998 *Librarians at Liberty*), basic, national cataloging records—whether created at the Library of Congress or in the LC manner—provide too few subject and other access points, seldom include searchable and clarifying notes, and continue to employ abbreviations and other bibliographic conventions (like slashes, dashes and brackets) that most people don't understand.

What's more, many topics are still not recognized *by* LC (try searching for CORPORATE WELFARE, PSEUDOSCIENCE, SECULAR HUMANISM, WORKING POOR PEOPLE, CYBERCULTURE, MANAGEMENT FADS, CONSPIRACY THEORIES, CULTURE WARS, ANTIRACISM, NATIVE AMERICAN HOLOCAUST (1492–1900), or CLASSISM). Some subjects are rendered in such an arcane, unfamiliar form that almost no one would search for them that way (and too many libraries don't make necessary cross-references); as examples: ABNORMALITIES, HUMAN instead of BIRTH DEFECTS; CESTODA rather than TAPEWORMS; INTERVERTEBRAL DISK DISPLACEMENT for SLIPPED DISC; and, believe it or not—CANADA. TREATIES, ETC. 1992 OCT. 7 instead of NAFTA or NORTH AMERICAN FREE TRADE AGREEMENT.

Not in *My* Library!

Other topics are constructed in an indisputably biased or inaccurate fashion that may misinform or prejudice catalog users against either the materials or the subjects; for instance: MANPOWER, CRO-MAGNON MAN, and SWORDSMEN instead of the more inclusive HUMAN RESOURCES, CRO-MAGNONS, and SWORDFIGHTERS; GYPSIES rather than the self-preferred ethnonym ROMA; UNTOUCHABLES rather than the widely-accepted and nonpejorative DALITS; SIAMESE-TWINS for the medically-sanctioned and much more precise CONJOINED TWINS; and a distinct preference for Christianity in scores of religion-related forms.

A further actuality, perhaps spawned in part by increasingly reduced quality control in LC's Cataloging-in-Publication (CIP) program, is mistakes. Sometimes Big Ones. In classification and subject analysis. Like Chris Kreski's *Life lessons from Xena, warrior princess: a guide to happiness. success, and body armor* (Andrews McNeel, 1998), clearly denoted "a parody" on the cover, which got soberly classed in self-help psychology and assigned the single misleading descriptor, SUCCESS — PSYCHOLOGICAL ASPECTS.

Why catalog in-house? Why catalog locally? And why not outsource the whole operation? Because critical, creative catalogers within individual systems are the last and only bulwarks against the often error-laden, access-limiting, and alienating records produced by giant, distant, and essentially unaccountable networks and vendors.

Must "The Poor" Always Be Among Us?
(U*L 117, 2000)

As a donor to St. Stephen's Shelter in Minneapolis, I lately got a letter from the shelter director, Ed Murphy. He wrote, in part:

> It used to be that if a person worked in America they'd be able to afford a place to live. For many who worked cleaning offices, washing dishes, or any of a number of essential jobs, home was a room at a downtown hotel or boarding house. Some lived most of their lives there, while others stayed long enough to save up for something better.
>
> But in the past few years, things have changed.... Rapid downtown development destroyed hundreds of units of low-cost housing, leaving many workers with fewer options. Some people were able to double-up in apartments or find other housing. Others ended up in homeless shelters just to get off the streets and keep their jobs. A recent survey of homeless men at St. Stephen's showed that 810 are working, most employed full time. Yet they live homeless because there are so few low-cost apartments and wages aren't high enough to afford the available housing.
>
> As a result, shelters fill quickly, leaving many on the streets. At St. Stephen's alone, 80 or more sober, homeless men each night try for one of our 40 beds. That means too many are left to sleep outside or on the floor in downtown refuges. What's worse, the vulnerable mentally ill who most need shelters are unable to get in and left to fend for themselves on the streets, seeing their lives spiral further downward.

Despite an undoubted economic "boom" and much-vaunted "prosperity," one in five American children remains in poverty (42 percent of Black kids!), food shelf and shelter use rises, a third of the workforce makes less than livable wages, and some 45 million people have no health insurance. It's not widely reported, but many homeless people are murdered (29 last year), some also decapitated, and laws—for instance, against panhandling or loitering—frequently criminalize poor people just for being poor. So celebration of our collective "good times" seems a little premature.

By contrast, the very rich are becoming ever richer. Fortune 500 CEOs typically "earn" 400 times more than their lowest-paid employees, that pay gap being 5 times wider today than in 1990 and 10 times greater than in 1980. And the wealthiest fifth of the population receives more than half of the nation's income. In this context of persistent and growing inequality, class-based discrimination, and lack of such taken-for-granted basics as shelter, food, and health care, I propose as an analog to the well-established concept of "institutional racism" that we now start talking about "institutional classism." In libraries, we'd then be looking at policies, practices, and attitudes that either keep poor people out altogether or treat them as though they don't deserve equal, first-class service, and—in the realm of resources and bibliographic access—that banish or mute their voices and those of antipoverty allies.

To get specific: It may shock the innocent and idealistic among us to learn that fines for overdue materials are no longer collected to get the materials back or to promote responsibility among borrowers. They're levied to make money, to generate revenue. Indeed, if everyone returned materials on time, a library like Hennepin County in Minnesota would suddenly lose over $800,000 a year. What does that have to do with classism? Simply this: Fines demonstrably keep some low- and fixed-income people from using the library. When it's a question of putting milk on the table or paying an overdue fine (or paying for transportation to return materials on time), milk wins. As it should. But the result is often that folks then stay away from the library. Or keep their kids out. In short, fines are discriminatory. So are fees for core services like video borrowing. Three or more ALA policy statements unequivocally proscribe fees, yet libraries continue to assess them, in effect censoring certain resources and services for people without the ability to pay. (Bestseller and audiotape rental programs also exemplify services denied to persons strictly on an economic or classist basis. Jenna Freedman, incidentally, critically examined such programs in a recent *U*N*A*B*A*S*H*E*D Librarian*: "Express This—the Road to Ruin," no. 116 (2000), pages 28–31.)

Another form of institutional classism is the failure to provide catalog access to topics well represented in library collections but not yet sanctified by the Library of Congress, subjects like HOMELESS MENTALLY ILL PERSONS (explicitly mentioned by Ed Murphy), POOR PEOPLE—EMPOWERMENT, NONCLASSIST CHILDREN'S LITERATURE, LIVING WAGE LAWS (to complement the belatedly created LIVING WAGE MOVEMENT), FOOD SHELVES, STREET NEWSPAPERS (there are over 40 such tabloids—by, for, and about homeless people—in North America), and myriad "CLASSISM IN" forms, like CLASSISM IN EDUCATION and CLASSISM IN SOCIAL POLICY (which, as an example, perfectly fits such a work as Ruth Sidel's *Keeping women & children last: America's war on the poor* (Penguin Books, 1996).

The longstanding terms PUBLIC WELFARE and PUBLIC WELFARE ADMINISTRATION should be converted to the more readily findable WELFARE and WELFARE ADMINISTRATION. (Since not all catalogs furnish adequate cross-references, the most common and familiar version of a term ought always to be the primary form.)

And the Victorian-era descriptor, POOR, needs to be transformed into the more human, less objectified form: POOR PEOPLE. (Naturally, there's already a heading for *RICH PEOPLE*. In response to questions raised about the discrepancy between these two headings, an LC staffer explained: "'Poor' is an original subject heading, established in 1898, that followed a pattern, prevalent at the time, of referring to groups of people in this manner, similar to 'Blind' or 'Deaf.' 'Rich people,' however, was established in 1996 and follows the current pattern of including 'people' in the heading." So it seems that obsolete, dehumanizing terminology must be retained for the sake of historic preservation!)

Additionally, there needs to be more depth, breadth, and specificity in the cataloging of poverty and social policy titles. For examples of how LC typically under- or mis-catalogs such material and a comparison with Hennepin County treatments of the same works, have a look at my "Foreword" to Karen Venturella's *Poor People and Library Services* (McFarland, 1998), pages 7–13.

Still one more kind of institutional classism is the refusal to allow street papers to be distributed free in library foyers and entranceways. And there's the corollary failure to subscribe to, keep, and catalog local homeless and welfare rights periodicals, thus excluding the voices of the very people most affected by anti-panhandling laws, welfare repeal, and a host of other measures that further marginalize and oppress poor people, In the event there are few or no such local or regional publications, libraries should stock at least some representative titles from elsewhere, for instance:

- *Catholic Agitator*. 632 N. Brittania St., Los Angeles, CA 90033. 8 nos. $1.00/year. ISSN 0045-5970. The feisty, fervent product of L.A.'s Catholic Worker movement. Heading a recent full-page review of *Word on the Street: Performing the Scriptures in the Urban Context*: "Reader beware! This book could be dangerous. It may compel you to practice Christian compassion on the streets of your city and get you in trouble ... just like Jesus. You may depart from the comfortable confines of the safe seminary and quiet church to discover the reality that God dwells among the poor."
- *Long Haul: Speaking Out About Poverty*. End Legislated Poverty, No. 211, 456 West Broadway, Vancouver, BC, Canada V5Y 1R3, monthly. $30/year. Contains information on British Columbia policies and politics, and how poor people and antipoverty activists there agitate and mobilize to make life more dignified and fair for unemployed, homeless, and other low-income persons— together with Canada-wide and international reports, as well as spirited volleys against wealthfare and poor-bashing. Done with style, verve, and solid data, the whole paper's an inspiring example of powerless, downtrodden folks getting it together and fighting back. Also— like *Survival News* and *Welfare Mothers Voice*— it's an effective antidote to cynicism and despair.
- *Survival News*. Survivors, Inc., 95 Standard St., Mattapan, MA 02126. quarterly. individuals: $10/ year, organizations: $25, low/no income people: free. A jumbo tabloid, partly in Spanish, featuring much Massachusetts news and opinion, but also many articles of general interest (e.g., in the Summer 2000 issue: "YWCA's Nazi tendencies?," "Hunger in the U.S.," "Female poor getting poorer," "Which way welfare rights?" and "Taking back Mother's Day") plus abundant survival tips and resource-listings.
- *Welfare Mothers Voice: A Paper by, for, and About Mothers in Poverty*. Welfare Warriors, 2711 W. Michigan, Milwaukee, WI 53208. quarterly. individuals: $15, organizations: $25, mothers in poverty: free at distribution sites/$4 by

mail. A vital, spirited, outspoken panoply of letters, photos, cartoons, essays, and news with a Wisconsin accent but global reach, making important links between issues as apparently diverse as environmental protection, welfare rights, corporate crime, campaign finance reform, globalization, women's resistance, and the prison-industrial complex. Their mission: "We want to share our knowledge and strength with each other, to validate each other, and support each other until the poverty community is strong and unified with a VOICE in all systems that affect our lives. We are angry and bored with the lies and stereotypes about moms whose children receive government child support (TANF). We will no longer remain silent. We will unite and fight for the lives of all mothers and children in poverty. We demand dignity."

- *By What Authority.* Program on Corporations, Law & Democracy (POCLAD), P.O. Box 246, So. Yarmouth, MA 02664. 3 nos., $30/year (for newsletter & "contact kit"). "An unabashed assertion of the right of the sovereign people to govern themselves," POCLAD's organ contends that "a minority directing giant corporations privileged by illegitimate authority and backed by police, courts, and the military define the public good, deny people our human and constitutional rights, dictate to our communities, and govern the earth."
- *Dollars and Sense: What's Left in Economics.* Economic Affairs Bureau, 740 Cambridge St., Cambridge, MA. 02141. bimonthly. individuals: $22.95/year. institutions: $42. "Edited and produced by a collective of economists, journalists, and activists ... committed to social justice and economic democracy," *D&S* "explains the workings of the U.S. and international economies" in accessible prose "and provides left perspectives on current economic affairs." This is where to find understandable analyses of such issues and developments as drug policy, corporate welfare, Third World debt, the clean-elections movement, neoliberalism, multinationals' influence, labor militancy, privatization, and income inequality. A necessary complement to *Business Week, Time, Newsweek,* and *U.S. News & World Report*.
- *Kids Can Make a Difference Newsletter*, P.O. Box 54, Kittery Point, ME 03905. 3 nos. free (but $5/year contribution welcome). "A program of World Hunger Year (WHY)," its goal is to "help young people understand the root causes of hunger and poverty and inspire them to end hunger in their communities, country, and world." This is the sort of priceless nugget often found in such out-of-the mainstream sources, the first two paragraphs of Dan Zuckergood's "RESULTS Educators Network: Helping Teachers Empower Students" (Fall 2000, pages 1–2):

Before becoming a professor of education at Springfield College, I was a Jr. and Sr. High Social Studies teacher for twelve years. For the first few years, I taught about hunger as just another "world problem" that we all needed to solve. Like many other issues, it seemed like an issue "too big" and "too unsolvable" to do anything about.

This all changed after a local church hosted an "Ending Hunger Briefing," put on by the

Must "the Poor" Always Be Among Us?

Hunger Project. The speaker asked whether the crash of a plane carrying 400 children would make the headlines the next day. He then asked if the crash of two planes carrying 400 children would make the headlines the next day. After going through a few more "plane crash" scenarios, he informed us that on every single day, 40,000 children were dying as a result of hunger and hunger related diseases. That was the equivalent of 100 planes carrying 400 children! And this was happening each day! And no newspaper was carrying that as a headline!

(For more on the "street newspaper" genre, including details for several outstanding titles, see Terry Messman's "Dissenting Voices of the Street" and Chris Dodge's "Street Newspapers Create Lively Alternative to Establishment Media," both in *Alternative Library Literature*, 1998/1999 [McFarland, 2000], pages 239–245.)

Finally, if we're truly committed to helping, empowering, and liberating low income persons, rather than passively accepting the hoary shibboleth that "the poor must always be among us," we have to get political. ALA's "Poor People's Policy" mandates exactly that.

Stunningly absent from major-party election rhetoric in 2000 was an explicit commitment to genuinely aid low-income persons by fighting to eliminate low incomes, to dismantle poverty itself, to really achieve a more equitable "playing field." No citizen, no politician, no librarian can truly be neutral or passive about this, for within a context of inequity and injustice, neutrality and passivity invariably favor wealth and privilege, ensuring the continuing misery and hopelessness of the "less fortunate."

There's no mystery about what to do. Practically every social critic and antipoverty activist comes up with nearly the same "laundry list" of needed initiatives and policies, among them:

- A much greater public investment in affordable housing (in Minnesota, 43 percent of renter households can't afford the $591 Fair Market Rent for a two-bedroom unit — and nowhere in the U.S. is the minimum wage adequate to afford a two-bedroom dwelling)
- Universal health care or national health insurance (perhaps based on the excellent Canadian, Dutch, German, or Scandinavian models)
- A higher — or living — minimum wage, guaranteeing that no working person stays below the poverty line (almost half of male workers in Minnesota earn too little to adequately support a family of four, while over 72 percent of women workers make less than what's required to maintain a single-parent family of three)
- Provision of child care, educational benefits, and transportation subsidies to welfare consumers (the recent "welfare repeal" act actually forced many poor women out of college or vocational school, and in West Virginia, as merely one example, 80 percent of former welfare recipients annually make $10,000 or less, almost half of those trying to exist on incomes below $5,000)
- Ample welfare payments for people who need them and a moratorium on heartless, family-destroying time limits and sanctions

Not in *My* Library!

The real "trouble" with poor or homeless people isn't mental illness or physical disability or drug use or personal irresponsibility. It's that they don't have enough money. Or a network to support them. Affluent people with mental illness, disabilities, addictions, or bad luck get taken care of. The big difference is bucks. And readily available services. Thus the full challenge isn't simply to furnish temporary band-aid programs or goods to poor people. It's also to treat them with the same dignity and respect as anyone else, and to remove such barriers of "institutional classism" as—for instance, in public libraries—fines, fees, and unreasonable residence requirements for securing a library card. And ultimately the challenge is to work like hell to consign poverty itself to the dustbin.

Americans intent on "doing the right thing" might well emulate our Canadian neighbors, particularly the 160,000 individuals and 1,100 groups in Quebec who lately proposed legislation based on these three principles:

- The elimination of poverty is a priority
- Increasing the income of the poorest fifth of the population takes precedence over increasing the income of the richest fifth
- People living in poverty and their organizations must be involved in the creation, implementation, and evaluation of all future government initiatives.

Why not insist that every candidate, lawmaker, and public servant, including library boards and directors, embrace these sensible precepts—and act accordingly?

The Top Censored Library Stories of 1998–2000
(U*L 118, 2001)

Since 1976, Project Censored, founded by Carl Jensen at Sonoma State University in Rohnert Park, California, has diligently (and appallingly) identified critical public issues and events that mainstream media either underreported or failed to report at all. In that same spirit and format, these are stories that the orthodox library press—most notably *American Libraries* and *Library Journal*—altogether ignored or minimized, even though they dealt with clearly significant professional matters. And it's not that *AL* and *LJ* didn't know about these things. They did. Fortunately, other sources recognized the importance of these challenges and developments, but their reports and analyses hardly reached the substantial readership commanded by the two leading journals.

1. HEIGHT-SHELVING PROPOSED BY LIBRARIAN OF CONGRESS

Synopsis: James Billington, the Librarian of Congress, hoping to save space in LC's Capitol Hill collections, announced a plan to shelve books there *by height,* which would effectively eliminate useful browsing by reference librarians and scholars, and might well be disastrously copycatted throughout the library community. Billington apparently believes that everything will ultimately be digitized and available on the tube so why bother about shelving the physical volumes in any classified order? And he also seems to suffer from the delusion that standard, LC-type cataloging is so adequate, so functional, that relevant, wanted materials can be easily and confidently discerned through the catalog. Every LC professional organization openly opposed this potentially precedent setting, wrong-headed idea. And critiques appeared in several "alternative" media, resulting in the proposal being put "on hold."

Sources: Thomas Mann, *Height Shelving Threat to the Nation's Libraries* (Washington, DC: Library of Congress Professional Guild, AFSCME 2910, 1999), reprinted in *Counterpoise,* v. 3, nos. 3/4 (July/Oct. 1999), p. 1938, and *Alternative Library Literature, 1998/1999* (Jefferson, NC: McFarland, 2000), p. 338–56; Sanford Berman, "Keep It Classed!," *ibid.,* p. 337; Grace Palladino, "Out of Sight, Out of Mind: Shelving by Height at the Library of Congress," *Chronicle of Higher Education,* v. 45, no. 40 (June 11, 1999), p. B6–7; "Good Reasons to Oppose Height-Shelving at LC," *Bulletin Board: the Voice of the Library of Congress Professional Guild, AFSCME 2910,* December 6, 1999, p. 3, reprinted in *The U*N*A*B*A*S*H*E*D Librarian*™, no. 114 (2000), p. 13;

Robert Anderson, "Research Collection Shelved by Subject — an Endangered Species?," *LG Communicator*, v. 33, nos. 4/5 (July/October 1999), p. 16–17.

2. THE WEEDING EPIDEMIC IN AMERICAN LIBRARIES

Synopsis: Discarding damaged or truly obsolete library materials is a practical necessity, but lately — in part flowing from a reigning mentality that deemphasizes print and AV in favor of purely digital resources— there's been a virtual epidemic of trashing, hiding, or selling arguably historic and valuable items without proper review or consultation. At San Francisco Public Library, for example, an expensive new downtown building was constructed with ample accommodation for computer terminals but hugely insufficient shelf space for books, resulting in thousands of volumes (some estimates suggest half-a-million!) being unceremoniously and often secretly pulped or remotely stored. Variations of this frequently appearance- or circulation-driven practice are now so common that a Midwest library user was even prompted to write a scorching poem in California's *Anderson Valley Advertiser*.

Sources: Fred Whitehead, "'To Thine Own Shelves Be True': a Call for a Working Group in Defense of Library Collections," *People's Culture,* no. 37 (1997), p. 1–2, reprinted in *Alternative Library Literature, 1996/1997* (Jefferson, NC: McFarland, 1998), p. 180–81; Fred Woodworth, "Report from Arizona," *People's Culture,* no. 37 (1997), p. 3–5, reprinted in *Alternative Library Literature,* 1996/1997, p. 182–83; Clark Dissmeyer, "Public Library, R.I.P.," *Anderson Valley Advertiser,* v. 47, no. 26 (June 30, 1999), reprinted in *Alternative Library Literature, 1998/1999* (Jefferson, NC: McFarland, 2000), p. 86; Fred Whitehead, "Update on Library Collections," *People's Culture,* new series no. 42 (1997), reprinted in *Alternative Library Literature, 1998/1999,* p. 87–89; Bill Witherup, "The Burning of the Books: 2000 A.D.," *People's Culture,* new series no. 42 (1997), reprinted in *Alternative Library Literature, 1998/1999,* p. 90; Fred Woodworth, "One of the Strange Features of Life and Civilization," *Mystery & Adventure Review,* no. 34 (Summer 1998), p. 4–7, reprinted in *Alternative Library Literature, 1998/1999,* p. 91–94; Mark Campos, "The Wishing Ring" (comic strip), *Exapno Mapcase,* no. 2 (1998), reprinted in *Alternative Library Literature, 1998/1999,* p. 95–99.

3. FREE SPEECH FOR LIBRARIANS

Synopsis: Early in March 1999, hoping to prevent other colleagues from undergoing the same denial of on-the-job intellectual freedom that I was experiencing at Hennepin County Library, I proposed this resolution to the American Library Association Council:

WHEREAS the American Library Association is firmly committed to human rights and freedom of expression (Policies 53 and 58.4.1); and

WHEREAS candid, robust debate is essential to the making of sound policy; and

WHEREAS library staff do not universally enjoy the right to openly discuss library and professional issues without fear of reprisal;

THEREFORE BE IT RESOLVED that ALA Council amends the Library Bill of Rights (53.1) by adding:

7) Libraries should permit and encourage a full and free expression of views by staff on professional and policy matters.

On Tuesday, June 29th, in New Orleans, ALA Council overwhelmingly voted to refer the amendment to its Committee on Professional Ethics. As I feared, that referral effectively killed any possibility of amending the Library Bill of Rights. Indeed, the

Ethics Committee subsequently determined that workplace free speech was already addressed by ALA's Code of Ethics, opting simply to draft a clarifying document, "Questions and Answers on Librarian Speech in the Workplace," presumably to be presented to Council for approval. In a "brief reply" (12-18-00), I remarked that "while it may be a reasonable statement (with certain noted reservations) on how things are, it does not ringingly declare — as only an amendment to the Library Bill of Rights could — how things should be, unequivocally establishing as professional philosophy and principle that library staff ought to enjoy the right to full and free expression of views on professional and policy matters." I concluded that "despite the admonition to library administrators (pages 3–4) to encourage staff input and discussion, the document frankly appears to be a manifesto supporting 'managerial prerogatives,' not free speech." Neither *AL* nor *LJ* traced or commented upon the tortured history of the original resolution and its abject fate, even though the issue is central to librarianship itself.

Sources: Sanford Berman, "Rights or Ethics?" (letter), *American Libraries,* September 1999, p. 40, reprinted as "An Open Letter to ALA Members," *Alternative Library Literature, 1998/1999,* p. 85; letter from Sanford Berman to Charles Harmon, 5-3-00; "Draft ALA Committee on Professional Ethics Minutes, 2000 Midwinter Conference, San Antonio, TX," p. 7–11; letter from Charles Harmon to Sanford Berman, 12-14-00, with 5-page "Draft Questions & Answers on Librarian Speech in the Workplace"; letter from Sanford Berman to Charles Harmon, 12-18-00; John Buschman/Mark Rosenzweig, "Intellectual Freedom Within the Library Workplace: an Exploratory Study in the U.S.," *Journal of Information Ethics,* v. 8, no. 2 (Fall 1999), p. 36–45.

4. BIBLIOPHILES AND LIBRARY LOVERS OPPOSE SFPL BOND ISSUE.

Synopsis: A committed band of citizen activists and watchdogs, led by James Chaffee and Peter Warfield, unsuccessfully — albeit energetically — tried to sink the San Francisco Public Library's Fall 2000 quest for over $105,000,000 to ostensibly "improve" library branches. Save Our Libraries— No On Prop. A argued, in effect, that the SFPL management and Foundation had badly mismanaged earlier bond issues, made fraudulent claims regarding such matters as earthquake risks, seemed to be promoting the privatization and corporatization of library service, and just couldn't be trusted to responsively and efficiently handle the wanted funds.

Sources: Gray Brechin, "SF Hoodwinked on Library" (letter), *Bay Area Reporter,* v. 30, no. 42 (19 October 2000); James Chaffee, "Library Privatization Concerns" (letter), *Independent,* October 21, 2000; various press releases and manifestoes, some reprinted as "San Francisco Public Library: the Fight Against the Bond Issue in the 2000 Election," *Librarians at Liberty,* v. 8, nos. 1/2 (December 2000), p. 1, 3–7.

5. LC DOES COKE

Synopsis: As another troubling instance of a now "normal" trend — the commercialization of libraries— the Library of Congress in late December 2000 not merely accepted a gift of some 20,000 Coca-Cola TV commercials (which would have been unexceptional), but shamelessly conducted a PR extravaganza for the pop-maker within LC's hallowed halls. Police ejected protesters who questioned the propriety of a public institution shilling for a "junk food pusher" which incidentally had just agreed to pay millions to settle a suit contending it had discriminated against Black employees. While

Not in *My* Library!

AL noted the donation, neither major library periodical reported on the protest or editorialized on the menace of commercialism and the cascading erosion of library "neutrality."

Source: Russell Mokhiber/Robert Weissman, "The Real Thing: Democracy as a Contact Sport," reprinted from the Focus on the Corporation Internet Column (http://www.corporatepredators.org) in *Library Juice,* 4:1 (January 3, 2001), p. 6–8.

Updates and Additions
(U*L 119, 2001)

Here are two addenda to "The Top Censored Library Stories of 1998/2000" (U*L 118):

6. SELF-CENSORSHIP: LIBRARIANSHIP'S "DIRTY LITTLE SECRET"
Synopsis: The mainstream library press and Intellectual Freedom Establishment seldom acknowledge the rampant failure to select whole categories or genres of material, despite public interest and demand on the one hand or the mandate to reflect a broad spectrum of human belief and activity on the other. Instead, ALA officialdom proclaims an annual "Banned Books Week," largely based on individual "challenges" reported by mainly school and small-town libraries, that effectively masks the far more pervasive self-censorship practiced by librarians themselves. For example, most libraries don't collect comics or many graphic novels. Few get any zines whatever, even though that's arguably the hottest current publishing scene. Recent surveys—resolutely ignored by *American Libraries* and *Library Journal*—demonstrate that small press fiction and poetry, as well as numerous other well-reviewed freethought, labor, and alternative press titles, are woefully underrepresented in public and academic libraries alike. And then there's sex, particularly if it's in the form of photos or film or deals with beyond-the-pale topics like anal intercourse or S&M. Such books and videos—like the excellent products from Down There Press (San Francisco) and Factor Press (Mobile, Alabama)—top most lists of virtually banned material. By contrast, the ongoing trend, particularly in public libraries, is to buy large quantities of circulation-boosting "popular materials," especially conglomerate-produced, heavily-hyped "blockbusters" that typically end up being sold for 25 cents apiece within 6 to 8 months.

Sources: Rory Litwin, "Issues of Inside Censorship and the ALA," *Counterpoise,* January 1998, p. 11–13, reprinted in *Alternative Literature, 1998/1999* (Jefferson, NC: McFarland, 2000), p. 78–80; Charles Willett, "The Almost Banned Book Awards," *Counterpoise,* January 1999, p. 20, reprinted in *ALL, 1998/1999* p. 111; Earl Lee, "Really Banned Books," *Counterpoise,* April 1998, p. 7–10, reprinted in *ALL, 1998/1999,* p. 112–115; "Almost Banned Book Awards of 1998," *Counterpoise,* January 1999, p. 21, reprinted in *ALL, 1998/1999,* p. 116; Scott Walter, "RLIN Holdings of Books Reviewed in *Counterpoise,* Volume 2 (1998)," *Counterpoise,* April 1999, p. 15–19, reprinted in *ALL, 1998/1999,* p. 117–123; Rita A. Marinko/Kristin H. Gerhard, "Representations of the Alternative Press in Academic Library Collections," *College & Research Libraries,* July

1998, p. 363–376, reprinted in *ALL, 1998/1999,* p. 219–229; Sanford Berman, "Foreword," in Toni Samek, *Intellectual Freedom and Social Responsibility in American Librarianship, 1967–1974* (McFarland, 2000), p. xi–xviii; Charles Willett, "Alternative Libraries and Infoshops: the Struggle Against Corporate and Government Indoctrination in American Schools and Universities," *Librarians at Liberty,* December 2000, p. 11–25; Earl Lee, "Almost Banned Books, 1998 and 1999," *Counterpoise,* January/April 2000, p. 32–37; Daniel C. Tsang, "The Alternative Media: Open Sources On What's Real," *International Journal on Grey Literature,* v. 1, n0.2 (2000), p. 61–63; Stephen Harris, "Discourse and Censorship: Librarians and the Ideology of Freedom," *Counterpoise,* July/October 1999, p. 14–18; Nancy Kranich, "A Question of Balance: The Role of Libraries in Providing Alternatives to the Mainstream Media," *Counterpoise,* July/October 1999, p. 7–10; Jason Kucsma, "Preserving Zines in the Library: Countering Marginalization & Extinction," *Zine Guide,* no. 3, p. 11–19.

7. BIBLIO-STALINISM AT HENNEPIN COUNTY LIBRARY

Synopsis: In a scenario uncannily reminiscent of the kind of Soviet (and other totalitarian) excess that George Orwell fictionalized as the "memory hole"—that is, removing inconvenient or undesirable people, events, and ideas from public awareness or consciousness by destroying all references to them and, in the case of persons and groups, also wholly erasing their words and images—all five works in the Hennepin County Library collection *by* me, together with another *about* me, in late January 2000 no longer appeared in the HCL online catalog and likewise seemed to have vanished from the shelves. A December 6, 1999, *Library Journal Digital* article ("Hennepin County Drops Cataloging Bulletin") speculated that the late–1999 termination of the 26-year-old, award-winning *HCL Cataloging Bulletin* "may be an attempt by HCL to purge itself completely of former Head Cataloger Sandy Berman, founder of the *Bulletin,* who resigned earlier this year after a clash with the library's director." In a February 1, 2000, press release, I wondered aloud: Is that also why the books have disappeared? Am I being morphed into a non-person, flushed down an Orwellian "memory hole"?

Library Journal Digital (2-21-00), *American Libraries* (April 2000), *Library Hotline* (2-21-00), and *American Libraries Online* (2-14-00) reported the initial discovery, most noting my charge of "bibliocide" and quoting HCL's Spinmeisterin, who declared that no formal recall had been issued, that a few physical volumes had since been found, and that the wipeout may have been "inadvertent." That concluded coverage of this genuinely unique and extraordinary episode by the orthodox library press. Except that the "episode" was far from over. Developments during the next 8 months included brazen stonewalling by HCL management and the Library Board, failure to notify law enforcement agencies about the indisputable database-tampering and book thefts, rigid denial that any "censorship" had taken place, refusal to share essential details of the event with system staff, no indication of what (if any) measures had been instituted to prevent recurrence of such an intellectual freedom travesty, and—finally—engagement of an outside investigator, who in October produced a lengthy study confirming "that it is unlikely that the deletions ... were anything other than deliberate," but that no "smoking gun" could be identified. No *American Libraries* or *Library Journal* readers knew anything about the post–February saga, even though both publications had been fully informed through press releases, clippings, and documents, among them the 27-page "redacted" investigative report.

Sources: "Books by Sanford Berman Removed from Hennepin County Library Catalog," *LG Communicator* (LAPL Librarians' Guild), January/April 2000, p. 20–21; Robert Franklin, "Publisher's Comments," *Journal of Information Ethics,* Spring 2000; Robert Halfhill, "Forced Resignation Sparks Protest" (letter), *Lavender: Biweekly Magazine for the Midwest Gay-Lesbian-Bisexual-Transgender Community,* June 2, 2000; R. Halfhill, "Shelving Sandy Berman" (letter), *Siren,* June 1, 2000, p. 3; S. Berman, "Where Have All the 'Berman Books' Gone? A Series of Memoranda and Letters," *Librarians at Liberty,"* December 2000, p. 29–32; "Biblio-Stalinism," *City Pages,* January 24, 2001, p. 6; "Sanford Berman Censorship/Intellectual Freedom Issue," *LG Communicator,* November/December 2000, p. 7; "Where Have All the 'Berman Books' Gone?" (press releases): 21-00, 2-23-00 (reprinted in *Library Juice,* March 8, 2000, p. 3–4); 4-27-00, 5-23-00; 6 "Request for reconsideration of materials" forms, submitted 2-8-00 by S. Berman; Charles Brown letter (in response to reconsideration requests), 3-2-00; S. Berman letter to Charles Brown, 3-4-00; Thomas O'Neill (HCL Sr. Human Resources Representative) letters to S. Berman: 7-28-00, 10-13-00, 11-9-00 (with "redacted" report), 12-12-00; S. Berman letters to T. O'Neill: 8-1-00, 10-2-00, 10-25-00, 11-23-00, 11-30-00, 1-16-01.

The Mokhiber/Weissman expose of LC's abject pandering to Coca-Cola, cited as an online document in U*L 118, has since appeared at least twice in hardcopy: "The Real Thing: Democracy as a Contact Sport," *Kids Can Make a Difference Newsletter,* v. 6, no. 1 (Winter 2001), p. 8–9; "Democracy as Contact Sport," *Adbusters,* no. 34 (March/April 2001), p. 37.

This is a worthy addition to the roster of antipoverty and related periodicals appearing in "Must 'The Poor' Always Be Among Us?" (U*L 117, p. 7–9):

Too Much: A Quarterly Commentary on Capping Excessive Income and Wealth. United for a Fair Economy, 37 Temple Place, 2nd Floor, Boston, MA 02111. $15/Year. (America's only newsletter dedicated to the proposition that the United States would be a considerably more democratic, prosperous, and caring nation if we narrowed the vast gap between the very wealthy and everybody else." Also available from UFE: Chuck Collins and Felice Yeskel's "action-oriented, movement building guide," *Economic Apartheid in America,* priced at $16.95; Tamara Sober Giecek's $15 *Teaching Economics As If People Mattered,* "21 lesson plans designed to stimulate active student participation"; and Responsible Wealth's pro-living wage report, *Choosing the High Road,* @ $6.50. Telephone orders: 1-877-564-6833.)

"Why Catalog? (U*L 116, p. 11–12), advocated in-house, local cataloging as a bulwark against the often error-laden, access-limiting, and alienating records produced by "giant, distant, and essentially unaccountable networks and vendors." In "Library of Congress Service Erosion," Maureen Moore details the precipitously declining quality and worth of LC cataloging during the Billington years," exemplified, for instance, by the introduction of next-to-useless "core level cataloging" and the devolution of "copy cataloging" review from professionals to technicians. (See *LG Communicator,* September/October 2000, p. 16–18. Moore's original, more extensive remarks appeared in the Library of Congress Professional Guild's 7-24-00 *Bulletin Board.*) The direct connection between outsourcing, catalog department downsizing, and dramatically reduced access

Not in *My* Library!

to library resources is manifest in this paragraph from the minutes of the Librarians' Guild Professional Concerns Committee meeting held October 1, 2000 at the LAPL union's office:

> At Central Library, Catalog Department has notified the Subject Departments that music CDs will no longer be cataloged because that task was contracted out and it was determined that the cost per unit is too high. Also draft environmental impact reports and rare books will no longer be cataloged because of a lack of catalogers. Two catalog positions have been cut in the 2000–2001 budget.... The cataloging of the new collection for the rebuilt Studio City branch is being contracted out.... There also seems to be a trend to reduce the LAPL collection of government documents because of their need to be specially cataloged.
> (Source: *LG Communicator*, v. 34, no. 6 [November/December 2002], p. 38.)

Updates and Additions
(U*L 120, 2001)

"Why Catalog?" (U*L 116, p. 11) cited a number of bizarre, unfamiliar Library of Congress subject headings that would surely frustrate searching in the all-too-many catalogs that lack adequate cross-references, and in any event reflect poorly on libraries as up-to-date, user-sensitive places. Here are a few more such "news of the weird" examples, the last two courtesy of AACR2, as interpreted by LC:

+LC form	+Instead of
METHYLPHENIDATE HYDROCHLORIDE	RITALIN
SILDENAFIL	VIAGRA
PHENTOLAMINE	VASOMAX
TRASTUZUMAB	HERCEPTIN
KIDNEYS—CALCULI	KIDNEY STONES
DECLARATION OF PRINCIPLES ON INTERIM SELF-GOVERNMENT ARRANGEMENTS, 1993	OSLO ACCORDS, 1993
JABHAH AL-ISLAMIYAL LIL-INQUADH (ALGERIA)	ISLAMIC SALVATION FRONT (ALGERIA)

The lemming-like weeding frenzy—earlier cited as a "Top Censored Library Story" (U*L 118, p. 17)—continues nationwide, erupting most recently in West Virginia and Minnesota, where collections are in danger of being decimated and dumbed-down. Here are three documents related to that ongoing madness, the *first* a 4-28-01 letter from Fred Whitehead (P.O. Box 5224, Kansas City, KS 66119) to Abby Smith at the Council on Library Resources (Suite 500, 1755 Massachusetts Avenue, NW, Washington, DC 20036):

Dear Ms. Smith:

I am writing to comment on the draft report of the Task Force on the Artifact in Library Collections. My credentials: Co-Editor, *Freethought on the American Frontier* (Prometheus, 1992), Contributing Editor, *Encyclopedia of the American Left* (several editions), Editor and Publisher, *People's Culture* and *Freethought History* (newsletters since 1992). The full list of my publications includes more than 80 entries, among them oral histories, philosophical essays, medical history, book reviews, journal issues edited, etc. Therefore, I am writing you in my capacity as an independent scholar.

For more than 20 years, I have had a strong and abiding interest in this very issue of preservation of our historical record. I enclose some items I have written and edited that bear on this topic. In particular, I call your attention to my essay, "Whatever Happened to the Rare Books?" which protested the privatization and sale of the rare book collection of the Kansas City Missouri Public Library. While that essay was subsequently reprinted by various library-related journals and anthologies, I have to say that my effort to save this collection was a failure. The books were sold at auction by Swann Galleries of New York City.

In the wake of that disaster, I contacted the Spencer Library of the University of Kansas, with the aim of arranging to deposit with them (eventually) my extensive archives. In the discussion with them on this matter, I attempted to stipulate that they could not "sell, exchange or discard" anything that they accepted. The Library refused to agree to this, and hence I presently retain these materials.

Among these materials are some 50 audiotaped oral histories with political radicals on the Left, which I began making circa 1980. These constitute a project I have called "Radicals in the Heartland." I also have extensive correspondence with Midwestern writers such as Jack Conroy, Meridel LeSueur, Thomas McGrath, etc.

Your report should address materials such as this that perforce remain in private hands, because libraries will not guarantee their safety and preservation. In the 1930s, various federally-supported programs ensured that many local records were put in order and saved from discard or decay. For example, many counties in this nation had records that were chaotic. WPA-type workers organized these and saved them for the future. Similar projects produced the remarkable State Guides, many of which have now been reprinted.

Nicholson Baker is referenced in your report, but his new book *Double Fold* should be included and assessed for its overview of issues around this topic. In his original *New Yorker* article on newspaper collections and in *Double Fold*, Baker mentions in passing the sale of the newspapers of the Kansas State Historical Society. I enclose for your reference the issue of my newsletter *Freethought History,* which reviews my fruitless attempt to protest this sale, especially their holdings of the *Boston Investigator* newspaper.

Subsequently, I devoted an entire issue of my newsletter *People's Culture* to the issue of "Defending Library Collections." However, I can count on one hand the librarians who offered to assist with the Task Force I proposed. Scholars around the world, however, were interested, but isolated and frustrated. So the Task Force never came to fruition. I did publish some further updates on this in the newsletter; see, for instance, issue #42, which includes a bitter and powerful protest poem by William Witherup, along with more horror stories.

The record on any response from the Library profession to my efforts is one of apathy, confusion, and indifference. Indeed, until I received word of your draft report, there was literally no organized response to these serious problems. People like Baker and myself were voices in the wilderness.

Concerning the Library of Congress, see my note about them in my "Defense of Library Collections" issue. Other "national libraries" are somehow able to take a more pro-active approach to the saving and preservation of their cultural record. Yet, as Baker records, the British Library has a terrible record of discarding newspapers. So some kind of effective approach, such as you propose in your report, should be taken in the United States. I have NO confidence in the present leadership at the Library of Congress to undertake this responsibly. If Congress itself can be persuaded to affirm and support the role of its Library (OUR LIBRARY, in my view, since it is a tax-supported institution almost entirely), it would be welcome. But such a mission must be clearly outlined, assessed by scholars, and carried out conscientiously.

With reference to the passage in your report (p. 22) dealing with those who get

Updates and Additions (U*L 120, 2001)

"hooked" on digital sources, I can tell you this story. About five years ago, I taught a community college course in American history. I asked students to write short papers, not full-fledged research papers, but supplying a few references. Almost all students used Internet sites; in their papers, some listed only the site's address, with no indication of its name. I then explained proper documentation to them. I asked: "Is there a 'down side' to using only Internet sources?" No one could answer, i.e. they could not see any problem in such dependence. I went on to explain that there are many resources that a historian would draw on that have not been digitalized — such as manuscript collections, newspaper files, and so on. They were amazed. The point of this story is that unless our young students understand the nature of the historical record, we will truly go into the world of *1984*, memory holes and all. There needs to be a vision for developing respect and knowledge and support for documentation, by the general public. I think this should be brought more into focus in your report. Depending only on librarians (a doubtful prospect, in my experience) and even scholars will not attain the goal. We need to bring these objectives before our fellow citizens and taxpayers.

Several times in your report, you refer to the National Endowment for the Humanities. Yet in my own experience, they have been completely indifferent to the preservation of such records as I have described. This has been so much the case that I concluded early on that applying to them for any kind of support was futile. Other scholars working in similar fields to mine have had the same experience. Unless some sort of "political test" was met, generally of the "mainstream" type, we were "on our own." Professor Sheldon Hackney of your Task Force can probably supply some insights on the process of politically "vetting" projects for funding.

To summarize, while I welcome your report, I remain skeptical that anything decisive or even helpful will be accomplished unless the problems Baker and I have brought out are squarely addressed.

I would like to ask that you share my letter with all members of your Task Force.

Second, this is the press release issued 5-1-01 by a library watchdog group in suburban Minneapolis:

HENNEPIN COUNTY LIBRARY "DUMBS DOWN"/ABANDONS COMMITMENT TO SUPPORT "LIFELONG LEARNING," DIVERSITY, AND THE LIBRARY BILL OF RIGHTS

Although Hennepin County Library (HCL) has often touted itself as the "people's university" and a partner in "lifelong learning" for its relatively affluent and well-educated users, it now appears that the most intellectually and spiritually challenging materials available to suburban readers may soon be artificially-hyped "blockbusters" and the collected works of Martha Stewart.

Without first consulting frontline staff or library users, HCL's top management has decided to cancel some 1,120 current periodical subscriptions, the "savings" presumably to be expended on DVDs, "popular" materials, and ever-more electronic resources. About 500 titles are to be dropped from the hitherto-flagship Southdale collection alone. And overall, about 340 of the axed magazines are *not* available online, while approximately 170 are not even received by the neighboring Minneapolis Public Library system.

Among the journals and newspapers to be wrenched from HCL shelves are dozens of business, labor, technical, medical, cultural, consumer, and political titles whose absence will markedly shrink the breadth, depth, and vitality of the library's resources, seriously eroding its adherence to the Library Bill of Rights' strictures to provide materials "for the interest, information, and enlightenment of all the people of the community" and present "all points of view on current and historical issues."

Unfortunately, HCL's impending mag-extermination coincides with a nationwide trend to dumb-down library collections, a development spawned partly by the profession's mindless embrace of purely digital resources on the one hand, and a desire to impress funders with big circulation numbers on the other. What gets lost, of course, is the public library's traditional commitment to unfettered access to a wide variety of ideas, activities, and information — to being a genuine, noncommercial alternative to profit-driven bookstore chains, dot-com vendors, and conglomerate-owned mass media. Also increasingly lost is the importance of the library as *place,* a physical space for browsing, reading, and socializing. Current managers don't seem to grasp that turning the pages of *Advertising Age* in comfortable, mouseless surroundings is not the same as "accessing" the full-text version online.

Citizens irate about HCL's coming magazine massacre and its growing emphasis on fluff should contact Charles Brown, Library Director (12601 Ridgedale Drive, Minnetonka, MN 55305-1909; 952-847-8580) and Mike Opat, Chair of the Hennepin County Board of Commissioners (A-2400 Government Center, 300 S. Sixth Street, Minneapolis, MN 55487; 612-348-7881).

SELECT LISTS — BY CATEGORY — OF PERIODICALS SLATED FOR REMOVAL

Business/technology/consumers
AccountingReview
Adbusters
American Economic Review
Amusement Business
Appraisal Journal
Business and Health
Business History Review
Chemical & Engineering News
Chemical Week
Computer Graphics World
Computer Reseller News
Computer Shopper
Constructor
Convenience Store News
Design News

Dollars & Sense
Farm Journal
Finance & Commerce
Finance & Development
Food Technology
Journal of Accountancy
Journal of Broadcasting
Journal of Business
Journal of Communication
Journal of Consumer Affairs
Journal of Consumer Research
Journal of Finance
Journal of Marketing
Journal of World Business
Land Economics
Logistics Management
Mergers and Acquisitions

Metalsmith
Monthly Review
Multinational Monitor
Music Trades
National Tax Journal
New Internationalist
Pensions & Investments
Progressive Grocer
Public Relations Quarterly
Pulp & Paper
Real Estate Review
Realtor Magazine
Risk Management
Successful Farming
Supervision
Taxes
Technology and Learning
Textile World

Updates and Additions (U*L 120, 2001)

Trusts & Estates
U.S. Banker
Vending Times
Windpower Monthly

Culture/arts/literature
African Arts
American Art Journal
American Cinematographer
American Music Teacher
American Theatre
Amusement Business
Aperture
Arts of Asia
Ballet Review
Design News
Film Quarterly
Index on Censorship
Journal of American Culture
Journal of American Folklore
Journal of Negro History
Journal of Popular Film & Television
Journal of the West
Landscape Architecture
Modern Drama
Modern Language Quarterly
Musical Quarterly
Partisan Review
Poetry
Public Art Review
Rain Taxi
Rock & Rap Confidential
Sculpture Review
Sewanee Review
Sing Out
Small Press Review
Symphony Magazine
Women's Review of Books
Yale Review

Health/medicine
American Journal of Psychiatry
American Journal of Public Health
American Journal on Mental Retardation
Business & Health
Journal of Learning Disabilities
Journal of Studies on Alcohol
Lancet
Mental Retardation
Nursing Outlook
Nutrition Today

Politics/world affairs
Adbusters
Asian Survey
Covert Action Quarterly
Dissent
Dollars & Sense
Extra!
Human Events
Index on Censorship
International Affairs
Journal of Modern African Studies
Journal of World Business
Manchester Guardian Weekly
Middle East Journal
Militant
Monthly Review
Multinational Monitor
New Internationalist
Phyllis Schlafly Report
Radical America
Socialist Review
Spotlight
Z Magazine

Science/environment
American Forests
American Journal of Botany
American Naturalist
Bioscience
Canadian Geographic
Journal of Soil and Water Conservation
Journal of Wildlife Management
New Scientist
Physics Today
Recycling Today
Science
Science and Children
Windpower Monthly

Men's
Men Talk
Playboy

Social science/human services/education
American Anthropologist
American Journal of Education
American Music Teacher
American Psychologist
Child Development
Child Welfare
Childhood Education
Chronicle of Higher Education
Contemporary Education
Early Childhood Education Journal
Journal of American Indian Education
Journal of Counseling and

NOT IN *MY* LIBRARY!

Developmental Psychology
Journal of Educational Research
Journal of Family Issues
Journal of Family Psychology
Journal of Marriage & the Family
Journal of Psychology
MEA Advocate
NEA Today
Prison Mirror

Labor/work
Business & Health
Dollars & Sense
Labor's Heritage
MEA Advocate
Militant
Monthly Review
NEA Today
Pensions & Investments
Public Employee
Radical America

Socialist Review
Z Magazine

Women/feminism
BBW (Big Beautiful Woman)
National NOW Times
Off Our Backs
Women's Review of Books

Communication/Journalism
Adbusters
Communication Arts
Extra!
Index on Censorship
Journal of Broadcasting
Journal of Communication
Language Arts

Newspapers
Dallas Morning News
Des Moines Register
Fargo Forum
Miami Herald
Milwaukee Sentinel

New York Times Large Type Weekly
San Francisco Chronicle

History
American Antiquity
American Historical Review
Business History Review
Historic Preservation History
History Today
Journal of American History
Journal of Negro History
Journal of the West
Labor's Heritage

Law
American Lawyer
Bench & Bar of Minnesota
Government Information Quarterly
Judicature
Minnesota Lawyer
National Law Journal

Third, this letter — by Robert F. Gates, President of the West Virginia Filmmakers Guild (1117 Virginia St E., Charleston, WV 25301) — was directed on 5-30-01 to Governor Bob Wise (Capitol, Charleston, WV 25305):

Dear Governor Wise:
It has come to our attention that important films have been disposed of from the collection of the West Virginia Library Commission, films of great significance to the State of West Virginia and especially films by West Virginia filmmakers.
At one time the film and video collection of the West Virginia Library Commission had about 5,000 titles; it was one of the best collections in the country. You can verify that with Bill Sloan, Curator of film at the Museum of Modem Art. For whatever reason, film librarian Steve Fesenmaier was reassigned to doing statistics and as a result there has been absolutely no knowledgeable oversight of the collection nor an informed acquisitions policy that we are aware of. The loss of utilization of Mr. Fesenmaier's talents in this field is a tragedy.
In my recent inquiry about 27 titles nine were no longer available. Missing were the works of five West Virginia filmmakers: Pare Lorenz, Bill Hogan, Jacob Young, David Claypool and myself. There may be others missing as well. That two copies of *The River* are missing is just amazing. This film by West Virginia native son Pare Lorenz is considered

one of the most significant documentaries of the first half of this century. Pare Lorenz personally made a copy of this film for us (West Virginia) after receiving a tribute at one of the West Virginia International Film Festivals. Two of my well-noted films, *Building a Cello with Harold* and *Communication from Weber,* are gone. In the case of the *Cello* film they disposed of the 16mm print worth $2,000 and kept a VHS video copy. It should have been the other way around. For technical reasons Weber cannot be converted to a video. Both of these films were funded in part by the West Virginia Commission on the Arts and have won many awards.

The collection of 16mm films is a valuable asset as they can be shown to audiences with a high quality presentation. For example, this past weekend I was asked to present *Morris Family Old Time Music Festival* as part of the Vandalia Gathering. It was great to see the sharp image of the black and white 16mm print, and the showing was met by a standing room only crowd. Film is also an archival medium; nobody knows about video and the formats change with the decades. I shot the Ivydale film 29 years ago.

The fact that the West Virginia Library Commission has acquired a copy of all of my films has always been very important to me. A marketing manager would never ruin his best market by selling a single copy of a film. However, as an artist I have wanted to have every West Virginian be able to go to their local public library and have access to my work. Also, since the Department of Culture and History does not collect such works I have always viewed the Library Commission's collection as a legacy of my work, even though it is a circulating collection. That two of my films have been trashed is a true disappointment, and the fact that it occurred shows that nobody knowledgeable is running the store.

We also understand that a sizable collection of film posters has been disposed of. Morgantown videomaker John Nakashima said his wife is knowledgeable about such items and that it was probably worth in excess of $10,000. Does this suggest competent and respectful librarianship? I am afraid that there is a growing attitude that if information is not on a computer that it is not of value. Thus we replace newspapers with microfilm, films with video, and movie posters with the choice of a computer image or the trash can.

We call on you to find out what has happened to the film and video collection, its oversight, and its lack of competent acquisitions policy. The West Virginia Library Commission in conjunction with the Department of Culture and History should develop a comprehensive permanent collection of film and video works devoted to West Virginia subjects and West Virginia media artists. A trip to Surplus Property should be made to see if some of the films can still be saved. This issue is not trivial, it is important for the preservation of our intellectual and cultural heritage, and it is an affront to West Virginia media artists.

No More Shushing: Library Staff and Users Speak (Part 1)
(U*L 121, 2001)

It may not always produce immediate results, but traditionally silent library workers and users are now boldly voicing their concerns and ideas about resources and services. For instance, independent scholars and unionized professionals at the Library of Congress successfully opposed a harebrained plan to shelve LC's Capitol Hill collections by height (for details, see the citations in U*L 118, p. 16–17). James Chaffee, Peter Warfield, and other citizen-activists, in concert with the San Francisco Public Library SEIU local, mounted a serious, principled campaign against SFPL's Fall 2000 bid for a 105 million dollar bond issue (see U*L 118, p. 18–19), and later effectively blocked a management scheme to outsource fine collection, instead proposing a more rational, less draconian, approach to retrieving overdue materials and a two-week amnesty that netted almost 5,500 returns (see *American Libraries,* August 2001, p. 25, and May 2001, p. 29). Similarly, a growing corps of readers, filmmakers, and writers—among them Nicholson Baker, Fred Whitehead, Robert F. Gates, and Fred Woodworth—have publicly decried what they perceive as an epidemic of mindless weeding and dumbing-down of library collections (see U*L 118, p. 17, and 120, p, 25–31). This and future columns will document further examples of refreshingly outspoken and heartfelt library populism.

In her own zine, *Spunk* (no. 7), Violet Jones—both a library employee and aficionado—talks candidly and passionately of the need "to fight ... the horrendous historical and cultural vandalism taking place in libraries everywhere ... a nightmare of 'weeded' books, the casting out of irreplaceable old texts, records, microfilms and periodicals, and a deluge of THOUSANDS of ridiculously expensive 'Harry Potter' books, Disney movies on DVD, and computers" (P.O. Box 55336, Hayward, CA 94545). And Bette Sack, writing in the July 2001 *Mpls./St. Paul* (p. 52–3), pointedly echoes and elaborates on Jones' remarks:

> I guess I'm a traditionalist. I want libraries to look like magnificent monuments to the written word—like the main library on Rice Park in St. Paul, for instance. Its white-

No More Shushing (Part 1)

marbled Italian Renaissance exterior looks like a library should, and work is now being done to restore maple woodwork and hand-painted ceilings throughout the building and return the place to its former glory. The handsome 1917 building also houses the James J. Hill Reference Library, a small jewel that always seems to have had a wonderful hush about it. With its long tables, green-shaded lamps, and metal balcony that surrounds the room, it looks like something out of a Masterpiece Theatre production. Unfortunately, this vintage BBC scene is somewhat spoiled by useful but unattractive computers.

I like computers. I use computers. I believe computers belong in libraries for research. But I don't believe computers will replace books. The trend by libraries to "preserve" old books by microfilming and digitizing them saddens me. Apparently, once filmed, the original is usually lost forever, discarded rather than rebound. People (younger people, that is) say that soon everybody will be downloading books into little handheld devices, and the need for traditional books will end. I say that virtual books can't replace the real thing. People who love to read love the feel of books, the smell of them, the weight of them. It all adds to the pleasure of reading.

Imagine not being able to browse among the books in a library or bookstore, picking up one because the cover attracts, another because a new offering by a favorite author catches the eye, still another because a glowing photograph of Ireland or Africa or India draws you in. I can't believe that ordering electronic books from a menu on a computer will be anywhere near as satisfying. Nor can I imagine children curling up on a rainy day with a Palm Pilot, reading *Jane Eyre* or *Wuthering Heights* as I did as a girl.

By 2003, the old and overcrowded main library in Kansas City, Missouri, will move into a new home, the First National Bank Building. A KCPL official noted that the relocation site features "a pretty grand lobby" and that "there's lots of brass and marble." However, C. J. Janovy, in the June 14, 2001 *Pitch Weekly,* adds that "there won't be as many books. A good chunk of the library's collection will be gone by moving day." That "chunk" includes 80 percent of the bound periodicals (1.3 *miles'* worth) plus many nonfiction and government document holdings. Frontline librarians told Janovy that "the weeding process reflects a changing philosophy at the library (and at libraries nationwide), suggesting that it's becoming less of a research institution and more like a bookstore, emphasizing what's new and popular."

Having shared news about SFPL's intended fine policy with Fred Woodworth, who edits *The Match!* and *Mystery and Adventure Series Review* (P.O. Box 3012, Tucson, AZ 85702), he replied with this chilling tale of how easily an inflexible system can alienate an otherwise eager and cooperative user.

> As for that plan to charge draconian fines on overdue materials—one thing no one seems to mention is the possibility of error. Everyone has gotten bills from companies that have neglected to take notice that payment was already made; everyone has had the experience of receiving computer-generated dunning notices on bogus "amounts due," etc. So why isn't it a distinct possibility that this library policy might result in a lot of completely unoffending folks getting hit with collection-agency terrorism for books they did in fact hand back in? Or never even checked out?
>
> This happened to me. In 1981 the Tucson Public Library sent me a notice saying I owed—as I recall—about $12 for some book which I had, in reality, returned some months before. I remembered the circumstances: I'd checked the book out at one branch while on my lunch break from a temp job I was working at, and as the job ended a few days later

and it was inconvenient to drive clear across town to return the book at the same branch—and since I was assured that any book could be returned at any branch—I handed it back in at the downtown (main) library. This resulted in the system thinking I still had the volume.

I refused to pay the $12, was told I could check out no more books, and handed over my library card. About a year later I decided to see whether the ban was still in effect, and applied for another card. It was, and I was denied.

As a result of this, I haven't used the local library system, at all, for 20 years now.

I'm sure cases like mine are "statistically insignificant"—but they sure leave a lasting impression when you're the one involved.

In "Support Christ and Your Local Library" (*Freethought Today*, June/July 2001, p. 8–9), a Redmond (Washington) resident, Matthew J. Barry, describes a "plague of Jesus bricks" adorning the entrance to a publicly-funded institution:

> Imagine my surprise when I saw the following inscription on a walkway outside the brand new public library: "Christ Died for Our Sins. He Rose Again. 1 Cor 15:3–4." I rubbed my eyes in hopes that I was hallucinating, but the message was still there when I stopped.
>
> King County's new Redmond Regional Library is right next door to the old one. The new building is an attractive addition to the city of Redmond, Washington, and it's located on a busy street about a block from city hall. The walkways along three sides of the library contain 3,000 square red bricks.
>
> I learned that the Friends of the Redmond Library (FRL) were selling engraved messages on these bricks as a fundraising effort for the new building. The tiles were 6" by 6" and cost $40, $45, or $50, depending on the length of the caption. There were no—repeat, no—restrictions on the content of the messages...
>
> When I first saw the "Christ" brick on that fateful day in early 2000, only about one-third of the bricks had inscriptions. Those that had messages were closest to the library's two entrances. The FRL told me that there would be another engraving during the summer or fall. Future engravings would apparently spread outward from the entrances to the side streets. So the "Christ" brick, being part of the first engraving, was very close to one of the entrances, only about 20 feet away. A very prominent location.
>
> But that wasn't the only brick with religious wording. Located near the opposite entrance, also only about 20 feet from the door, was this brick: "Christ Is Risen. He Is Risen, Indeed." Another brick encouraged patrons to "Read About Jesus." Another: "Read Your Bible; Prevent Truth Decay." Another tile read, "Thy Word Is a Lamp to My Feet and Light for My Path." Still another: "Psalms 119:160. All Your Words Are True." And, of course, there was a "John 3:16" brick.
>
> It was like a plague! And there were about 2,000 blank bricks remaining, all waiting to be infected with more of this religious proselytizing! I began to have visions of Redmond pastors telling their congregations all about the new library and suggesting that everyone buy a brick for Jesus. Can you imagine a public library surrounded by thousands of 'Jesus Loves You" tiles?

Well, Barry, fearlessly committed to church-state separation and the often-mouthed-but-frequently-neglected idea of library "neutrality," launched a breathtakingly energetic and ultimately fruitful campaign that resulted in a posted disclaimer, forthrightly announcing that

No More Shushing (Part 1)

The inscribed tiles you see on the walkway were purchased by individual library supporters, who chose the messages. The views expressed on the tiles are those of the sponsors, not the King County Library System.

and the ongoing sponsorship of nonreligious, cohabiting bricks with inscriptions like "First Amendment: Keep Church & State Separate," "Evolution Is a Fact. Read About It," and "Jehovah, Allah, Zeus, Thor & Brahma. They're All Myths."

Harry Potter Imperiled, Keyword Searching as Panacea, Robin Hood's Noble Liege, and Other Foolishness
(U*L 124, 2002)

As a kid, I devoured the Robin Hood canon, developing a righteous fury against the evil Sheriff of Nottingham and conniving Prince John, but absolutely revering Robin's liege lord, the toweringly brave and majestic, if often absent, English monarch, Richard-the-Lion-Hearted. Lately, however, I stumbled upon a paragraph in James A. Haught's *Holy Horrors: An Illustrated History of Religious Murder and Madness* (Prometheus Books, 1990) that has completely and forever changed my youthful awe toward Richard I into pure disgust. Says Haught, on page 26:

> In the Third Crusade, after Richard ... captured Acre in 1191, he ordered 3,000 captives— many of them women and children—taken outside the city and massacred. The corpses were cut open in a search for swallowed gems.

This is exactly the sort of nugget that someone may later want to retrieve, but short of painstakingly thumbing through the whole tome, there's no way to identify references to Richard, Acre, massacres, or Crusades. Symptomatic of an alarming, access-limiting trend in book publishing, this volume contained no index. Nor do indexes appear in the thematically-and detail-rich *Nickel and Dimed: On (Not) Getting By in America*, by Barbara Ehrenreich (Holt, 2001), Michael Moore's *Stupid White Men* (ReganBooks, 2001), and *Reclaiming San Francisco: History, Politics, Culture* (City Lights Books, 1998), which incidentally includes Nicholson Baker's "Weeds: A Talk at the Library," the speech that blew the whistle on SFPL's massive bibliocide. So now my righteous fury is directed against writers, editors, and especially publishers who collude in this dumbing-down epidemic, effectively reducing access to potentially significant information and ideas by librarians and general readers alike.

I invite reviewers and reference staff to join me in admonishing publishers not to stint on indexes. They're not luxuries. They're necessities.

After bewailing the sorry state of subject cataloging to a "Banned Books Week" audience, using LC's "Canada. Treaties, etc. 1992 Oct. 7" (the descriptor for what everyone else calls NAFTA or the North American Free Trade Agreement) as a particularly awful example and observing that many libraries don't make the requisite cross-references to the obtuse primary form, a local librarian approached me and somewhat smugly announced: "Oh, that doesn't matter. We get around bad LC cataloging by keyword searching." That colleague undoubtedly echoed a widely-believed myth. Unfortunately, the increasingly heavy reliance upon and devotion to keyword searching reflects not so much the utility of new technology as the demise of truly rigorous, sensible, and consistent subject cataloging. Keyword searching WILL NOT retrieve material unless the searched-for terms actually appear in bibliographic records. For instance, a "NAFTA" or "North American Free Trade Agreement" search will not produce hits for *Amerique Sans Frontiere: les Etats-Unis Dans L'espace NordAmericain* (1995), *Arthur Andersen North American Business Sourcebook: The Most Comprehensive Authoritative Reference Guide to Expanding Trade in the North American Market* (1994), and Bill Moyers' PBS documentary on NAFTA's Chapter 11 and its impact on local governance, *Trading Democracy* (2002), since the titles don't contain those magic words. Indeed, solely a "NAFTA" search will miss works like Ambler H. Moss, Jr.'s *Assessments of the North American Free Trade Agreement* (1993), and *Budgetary and Economic Analysis of the North American Free Trade Agreement* (1993), while a strictly "North American Free Trade Agreement" search won't trap such items as *Anticipating the Impact of NAFTA on Health and Health Policy* (1995), *Assessing NAFTA: A Trinational Analysis* (1993), and *Banking in North America: NAFTA and Beyond* (1999). All of these materials can only be retrieved successfully if they have been assigned the same, consistent subject heading. Further, that single heading should ideally be equipped with "see," "see also," and "see also from" references that will lead searchers to both the primary form and related topics. Keyword searching WILL NOT permit such comprehensive access. It also WILL NOT furnish public or scope notes under specific subjects that helpfully explain what those descriptors mean. To painfully belabor the mythic character of keyword searching:

- Barbara Ehrenreich's volume deals importantly with matters like working poor people, labor exploitation, and service industry workers. As it happens, the Library of Congress assigned none of those terms as subject tracings, although they should have. But keyword searches under those three concepts or categories won't unearth the Ehrenreich report because that language just isn't in the title or even (had there been a contents note) the chapter captions. Only creative and intelligent subject cataloging would "save" the book from bibliographic oblivion.
- It has lately been recommended to LC that headings be promptly established for both INTELLIGENT DESIGN and MOUNTAINTOP REMOVAL MINING, two currently "hot" issues. As long as there are no precise headings available for these topics, forms that could then routinely be applied to the growing body

of film and literature addressing them, keyword searching becomes the sole alternative, an imperfect fallback approach. "Mountaintop removal" will not identify films like Sasha Waters' *Razing Appalachia* and books like Jedediah Purdy's *For Common Things: Irony, Trust, and Commitment in America Today* (1999), which includes extensive data on the subject. And even a "Mountaintop removal" keyword hit will not furnish a possibly useful note, e.g.,

> Here are entered materials on a strip mining method in which the top of a mountain is removed by blasting and drag lines to extract low-sulfur coal. In a process called "valley fill," the "overburden" or excess spoil is deposited into valleys and streams in piles that may be two miles long and over 100 feet high.

Nor would that search mode allow access to relevant records by means of topical variants (e.g., "Mining, Mountaintop" or "Mountaintop mining"). And of course no "see also" references would direct searchers *to* that information from broader subjects like "Coal mines and mining," "Environmental degradation," and "Strip mining."

On June 20, 2002, I wrote the Hennepin County Bibliographic Services Librarian, copying Tom Yee at LC's Cataloging Policy and Support Office:

> Having lately read John Mangels and Scott Stephens' "Intelligent Design Crusader Keeps Campaigning" in the *Star Tribune* (attached) and watched several TV segments on the current campaign to promote "Intelligent Design" as an alternative to evolution, I made a subject search in HCL's online catalog and found nothing (the closest subject heading was INTELLIGENT MACHINES). I then performed a key-word search and did turn up three relevant titles, together with four false drops (i.e., unrelated garbage). While all three works deal explicitly with "Intelligent Design," none were assigned a subject heading for that topic. I've since discovered that the Library of Congress itself has thus far failed to recognize the concept and controversy—despite abundant "literary warrant"—with the pathetic result that ID material is unreachable by subject-searching library catalogs, nor can a user find any catalog-based explanation of what it means or be directed to ID and cognate information through appropriate cross-references.

These are the cross-references and note I proposed, none of which would "kick in" through the keyword approach:

pn	Here are entered materials on the theory that the complexity of life arose by the design of an unnamed, intelligent being		Neocreationism Theistic design
		xx	Biology — Philosophy Cosmology
sa	Creationism Naturalism Religion and science		Creationism Earth — Origin God — Proof
sf	ID IDC Intelligent design creationism Intelligent design theory		Life — Origin Naturalism Religion and science Science — Philosophy

- For another, pithy statement on the hazards of keyword searching and the need for timely creation and application of subject headings, replete with notes and references, see my "Sing a Song of Green Cards," in *Alternative Library Literature, 1996–1997* (McFarland, 1998), pages 151–52.

The nearly religious embrace of keyword searching almost certainly may be linked to a mistaken belief that electronic manipulation of data somehow compensates for the absence or inaccuracy or unhelpfulness of the data itself. And the content, the substance, of centrally-concocted catalog records IS declining, worsening. Most such records supplied to vendors or networks derive from the Library of Congress. Yet professional LC staff themselves recently testified before Congress that

> While cataloging was once one of the Library's crown jewels, a world-renowned operation, now we can no longer afford to perform quality cataloging because of insufficient professional staff. Acquisitions of materials continues to surge, while staff to catalog those acquisitions has plummeted. Just since the end of fiscal 1997 there has been a 16 percent drop in professional book cataloger staffing levels. Faced with these difficult circumstances, Library management has implemented various schemes to catalog more with less, all resulting in a deleterious effect on the quality of our cataloging product and our once pristine data base. This is a grave error because good cataloging is the foundation of good librarianship. Acquisitions and reference staff cannot adequately perform their duties when they cannot rely on the accuracy of our cataloging records. Moreover, this lack of quality has an obvious adverse impact on our patrons, including Congress. Cataloging errors can make any work, including those about weapons development in Iraq, or the political history of Afghanistan, disappear just as completely as a thief's raid on the stacks.

Harry Potter in trouble? Uh-uh. At that Banned Books Week event — hosted by the Red Balloon Bookshop in St. Paul — people proudly wore "Muggles for Harry Potter" buttons. Ordinarily, I'm big on solidarity and supporting underdogs and hapless victims, ever ready to oppose censorship and repression. But, honestly, folks, Harry's not in any serious danger. And the nearly hysteric defense of Rowling, Angelou, Steinbeck, Twain, and other "imperiled" authors actually deflects attention from the truly endangered products, largely from small, alternative, and ethnic presses, that seldom even get into libraries at all. Here are two complementary views on the sham of Banned Books Week, the first by librarian/novelist/dramatist Earl Lee, from his "Almost Banned Books: A Brief History," *Counterpoise,* April 2001, page 16:

> The irony of Banned Books Week is that it celebrates books, like the Harry Potter books, that are not really "banned" in any real sense. Every library and every bookstore in the country has multiple copies of these books. For example, here in my hometown of Pittsburg, Kansas, (population 18,000) every library has copies of the Harry Potter books and every bookstore, even Wal-Mart and several local supermarkets, sell copies. Meanwhile, the new Harry Potter movie appears to be doing a brisk business, and our local Cinema Eight has 3 of 8 screens devoted to showing the Harry Potter movie. If this is what it means to be "banned" I would gladly volunteer. In fact Banned Books Week is a kind of bait-and-switch game. Most of the books on the list are not banned, but only "challenged" — meaning that some parents somewhere in the USA have objected to their children reading these books in school, in the case of Harry Potter for religious reasons.
>
> ALA's Banned Books Week is actually a "celebration" of books that parents and others

have recently objected to (but not "banned") along with some classic books, like *Ulysses*, which was banned sixty years ago in the U.S., or the Bible, some versions of which were banned 500 years ago in Europe. Today the Bible is not "banned" in any country within a thousand miles of the USA, but owning a copy can get you into serious trouble if you live in Afghanistan. Like the Harry Potter books, every library and bookstore in America seems to have multiple copies and several editions and formats are easily available. Unlike Harry Potter, most of the Almost Banned Books [exclusively small and alternative press titles previously reviewed in *Counterpoise*] are hard to find in bookstores or libraries. The ABB list for 2000 has seven titles that are not available in any of the … OCLC libraries worldwide. Another seven titles can be found in four libraries or less, and another seven titles can be found in nine libraries or less. For a multinational database like OCLC to show such low numbers means that these books are truly unavailable, and they are truly "banned" in the sense of being controlled by market and institutional forces and thus effectively excluded from the marketplace of ideas."

The second screed emanates from Fred Woodworth, editor/publisher of *The Match*. These comments appeared in the Winter 2001-2002 issue, under the caption "Crap-Detection Department" (page 21):

> Considering some of the items that have received notice in this column over the past years, it may seem hard to believe that we have now whiffed out probably the most incredible one yet, but surely it's true. See what you think after reading this notice from the September 14, 2001 edition of the *Arizona Daily Star* (sec. B, page 3):
>
>> LIBRARIES TO MARK BANNED BOOKS WEEK. The Downtown Tucson Public Library will join library branches across town in marking Banned Books Week, Sept. 22 through Sept. 29. The library hopes to call attention to hundreds of worthwhile books that would-be censors have tried to ban.
>> Libraries and bookstores across the country want to really help remind people of some of our freedoms that we need to safeguard, library spokeswoman Elizabeth Burden said.
>> We want to say what a great loss it would be if these books were banned… It's important to make them available.
>
> And what books are in this horrible danger of being subjected to censorship? What ones are direly threatened with being unavailable, relegated to dark corners and kept off the library shelves if not for heroic, enlightened efforts like this one?
>
>> … Maya Angelou's *I Know Why the Caged Bird Sings* (and) J. K. Rowling's popular Harry Potter books…
>
> HARRY POTTER! The recipient of uncounted millions of dollars of publicity, much of it donated by newspapers and other willing accomplices of the billion-dollar promotion machine dedicated to thrusting a copy of this chunk of printing into the hands of every man, woman and child—possibly every infant—in the English-speaking world! HARRY POTTER—the lurid covers in carefully painted likenesses of a young Bill Gates, no doubt to cross-reference propaganda for his own giant corporation at the same time!
>
> Harry Potter—millions sold! Libraries buying as many as 80 copies APIECE to meet the artificially pumped demand created by incredible "bestseller" lists published before a single copy is sold! Inflated by newspapers with as many as five separate articles in one single edition, examining, hyping, promoting, and bludgeoning parents and schools to lay down their cash lest young Johnny and Sally feel deprived as EVERYONE ELSE reads HARRY!
>
> Censorship? You want to hear about CENSORSHIP?! In the city where I've been writing and publishing for 32 years, NOT ONE S I N G L E WORD of mine resides in any branch of the public library system.

> Each library branch will mark the week differently. Some branches will wrap targeted books in plain brown wrappers, and those who check them out will receive bookmarks and other commemorative items. The Downtown branch will cater to area workers with "brown bag banned book lunch specials" displayed on carts decorated like food vendors' wagons...

> As for Maya Angelou: How somebody who was feted by the Clinton administration, published slavishly by major outfits no matter what feeble swill she produced, and anthologized in one-half of the high school textbooks of this country, can be regarded in any way as having even the most distant resemblance to a censorship victim, is a topic on which I will offer no further remarks.

Since I'm the columnist, I get the last word. Here's the blurb I contributed to the 5th edition of *Alternative Publishers of Books in North America,* edited by Byron Anderson (CRISES Press, 2002):

> The most effectively "banned books" in America are not the "challenged," invariably mainstream titles widely publicized by the American Library Association. Instead, they're the works produced by the diverse, independent and unorthodox presses listed in APBNA. No book-burning zealot has the chance to "challenge" the presence of alternative press materials on library shelves, simply because too many such volumes aren't there in the first place. They're not selected, not bought, not cataloged, not loaned, not displayed. But it doesn't need to be that way. The profession can stop murdering its own noble Library Bill of Rights by actively identifying and collecting the varied, enlightening and sometimes unsettling stuff issued by non-corporate publishers. APBNA is a splendid, essential guide to that universe of exciting and even empowering ideas, opinions and information.

"Not in MY Library!"
(U*L 125, 2002)

Says Michael Moore on page 115 of *Stupid White Men* (ReganBooks, 2001):

> For most of us, the only time we enter an American high school is to vote at our local precinct. (There's an irony if there ever was one — going to participate in democracy's sacred ritual while two thousand students in the same building live under some sort of totalitarian dictatorship.)

Well, Michael, an even greater irony thrives inside libraries, invariably hailed as "bulwarks of democracy" and "exceptionally democratic institutions," which are commonly operated much like medieval fiefdoms, replete with hierarchy, secretiveness, and arbitrary decision-making. This is from the minutes of LAPL's Librarians Guild Professional Concerns Committee (5-3-01):

> Regimentation and deprofessionalization of LAPL librarian work: Those present discussed the ominous trend within our Department to standardize every aspect of our work environments and even the ways in which we organize our desks, the tone of our voices, and our facial expressions. This leads to an inflexibility in responding to public needs, actually lowers efficiency in the workplace, and results in an unpleasant work atmosphere. Paperwork has been greatly increased, with unnecessary justifications required for every professional decision.

That is not the stuff of democracy. Indeed, the D-word, while often enough bandied about in self-promoting PR, is actually regarded with contempt by most library managers in real-time administration. During nearly three decades as a supervisor at Hennepin County Library, I attended many Management Team meetings. Almost always, suggestions to expand and diversify that policy-making group by adding the Children's Services Coordinator or a senior clerical supervisor elicited anguished wails from hierarchs who jealously sought to maintain their monopoly on power and status. Likewise, proposals to survey the whole staff on critical policy matters evoked angry reactions from the managerial elite, typically expressed in nonsensical, not to mention hysterical, declarations such as "You can't expect us to consult with 500 employees on every little thing! (No, not on "every little thing," but why not on "every big thing"?)

I've cataloged a few of my own unfree-speech tribulations at HCL in "'Inside' Censorship" (http://web.library.uiuc.edu/ahx/ead/ala/9701040a/berman/intro.html) Here's an excerpt which incidentally illuminates the frequent charade of "team-based decision-making":

"Not in My Library!"

In the summer of 1996, I was accused in the Director's office, with only my immediate boss present, of being disruptive and undermining. It was manifest that I would be disciplined in some way. And what terrible act had I committed? I publicly opposed the first proposal to emerge from a Revenue Generation Team assembled by the director: a plan to raise $100,000 a year by doubling the juvenile fine rate. The purpose was not to get books back on time or to instill greater responsibility in youthful borrowers. It was single-mindedly to impress the Board of Commissioners downtown with how tough and effective the Library could be in reducing reliance on property taxes, on public money. It happens that neither the Board nor County Administrator had ever made a formal, written request or demand to raise non-tax funds.

It was just something that our administration thought they should do. And realizing that much of the staff, not to mention public, might question such a kid- and also poor-bashing policy, the Team deliberately did not consult with the system's two dozen children's librarians or anyone else who might have objected. Instead, the plan was railroaded through the Management Team and Library Board with great haste and minimum opportunity to criticize or debate. I and the Children's Services Coordinator testified at a board meeting, where we were rudely received. The day before, there had been a brief discussion among the Management Team, concluding with a 10–10 split vote on the proposal—a vote that was never even intended (I had to ask for it). Half the senior managers opposed it, but the Administrative Committee that afternoon approved it anyway and the appointed Library Board did likewise the next day, with only one member dissenting.

Given the appalling lack of staff and public input, I talked to someone at the alternative news weekly who ran a short story on the issue, captioned "Library Pinches Nickels, Kids" and I initiated a simple petition, finally signed by nearly 140 staff, which asked that the fine policy be withdrawn. As it happens, the policy did get revoked, but probably because of a call from one county commissioner, who had been alerted to the library's plan and surely recognized it to be both unfair and a probable PR disaster. I wasn't the person who contacted the commissioner, but I know who was: someone I had merely spoken to, a citizen and library activist who realized that this was bad news for kids and poor people. Anyway, for testifying publicly, talking to the press, and starting a petition, I was about to be reprimanded. And I would have been—except that I could afford $500 to hire labor lawyers who phoned, faxed, and mailed the administration, advising that free speech rights might be involved and that they intended to represent me at any hearing or trial. That did it. They backed off. But how many librarians can afford the $500 to buy their First Amendment rights? How many have their mortgages paid off already? I did, but I was lucky.

As a footnote, during that dressing-down, the HCL director became particularly livid concerning the petition then circulating among staff. I earlier called it "simple." In fact, it went something like this: Based on reasons already articulated by HCL's children's librarians, we, the undersigned HCL staff, request that the new juvenile fine increase be withdrawn.

It garnered about 140 signatures without any special effort. Anyway, that morning I mumbled a few words about the "right of petition" and "First Amendment." The Director's very deliberate reply, from just two feet away, eyes bloodshot, was: "NOT IN MY LIBRARY!"

Later, in the course of that same encounter, I was asked to swear that in the future I would uphold all management decisions. I refused, observing that no one could any longer do that in good conscience since the Nuremberg Trials. You can imagine how that went down.

The problem of workplace repression and biblio-fascism is hardly limited to Los Angeles Public Library and Me. Colleagues in recent years have been rebuked or dismissed for:

- Conducting a program on Israeli censorship.
- Writing pro-labor freelance newspaper columns and — as City Librarian — scheduling a series of labor films, which offended local business interests. (This person was summarily dismissed from her job and escorted with her belongings to the sidewalk by a security guard.)
- Questioning why a system closed on Easter but not on Rosh Hashanah or Yom Kippur. (The library's "Diversity Coordinator," she was admonished for raising the "Jewish Question" and being "controversial." The Deputy Director banned her from attending any further systemwide committee meetings.)
- Criticizing library management at a City Council meeting.
- Supporting a Black coworker who charged the administration with job discrimination.
- Opposing a new main building with inadequate space for books.
- Asking for improved security after a violent sexual assault.

(Several of these cases are documented in a June 2001 University of Alberta course paper by Stephen Carney, soon to appear in the *Journal of Information Ethics*.)

So what recourse is there within the profession to bolster and protect workplace speech and democracy? These are three approaches:

One, where the library staff is organized, is to bargain for a contract clause guaranteeing members the right to express themselves freely on library policy and other professional matters. In the aftermath of my experience at Hennepin, the nonsupervisory librarians union there — 100 strong — got such language included in their contract. (That's AFSCME Local 2864. So far the clause hasn't been invoked, but it COULD be and in the meantime perhaps contributes to a slightly more open workplace.)

Second, the national profession itself could be much more forthright and vigorous in supporting staff free speech. In June 1999, while still a member of ALA Council, I submitted a resolution to amend the holy Library Bill of Rights by adding

> 7) Libraries should permit and encourage a full and free expression of views by staff on professional and policy matters.

What happened to that effort to secure the same protection for library staff as for library materials and meeting rooms is summarized in a letter I sent in August 2001 to Bill Gordon, ALA Executive Director:

> In March 1999, I proposed an amendment to the Library Bill of Rights that would have extended free speech rights to library staff. On June 29th, in New Orleans, Council referred the proposal to its Committee on Professional Ethics. In an "Open Letter to ALA Members" I warned that this "vital issue" of workplace speech might ultimately be buried or muted. I believe, two years later, that what I feared has indeed happened.

"Not in My Library!"

The Ethics Committee unilaterally decided that "the existing tenets of the ALA Code of Ethics address this issue" although they palpably do ***not***, and then undertook preparation of a question-and-answer document to clarify the matter. The Q&A draft I examined in late 2000 I subsequently characterized as "a manifesto supporting 'managerial prerogatives,' not free speech."

Apparently not even the craven, diluted Ethics Committee "explication" has yet reached Council. When (and if) it ever does, that manager-friendly body will doubtless approve it, effectively consigning librarians' workplace rights to oblivion. Believing that our OWN free speech deserves at least as much attention as anyone else's, I ask that my proposed LBR amendment be presented to the entire ALA membership as a referendum. To date, it has not been voted upon within ALA, Council in 1999 merely having "referred" it to a committee.

If there is a better way than a referendum to get action on workplace speech and librarians' rights, I'd welcome it. What's essential is not to let the issue evaporate or vanish down a bureaucratic "memory hole."

As you can perhaps guess, I'm still awaiting an answer. And nowhere in the august library press, that bastion of First Amendment advocacy, has there ever been an editorial endorsement of free speech in the workplace — or of that Library Bill of Rights amendment in particular.

Third, in Stephen Carney's words, "in order to ensure that library employee intellectual freedom is protected and to foster a 'free speech situation,' libraries and librarians should consider adopting organizational structures or practices that allow the worker to take an active, participatory, responsible, and equal role in the operation of the library workplace." As one actual model, he cites Dickinson College Library in Carlisle, Pennsylvania, which in 1975 scrapped "the hierarchical underpinnings of traditional management" in favor of a "collegial pattern ... with a rotating chair." Still another precedent is reported by Tom Eland in the July 2000 *Counterpoise* at the Minneapolis Community & Technical College library, a "peer-based collegial department." According to Eland:

> We have no library director and all decisions are made by consensus. Sometimes our staff meetings get a bit long, and on occasion we enter into spirited debates, but the entire staff is invested in the process and we keep each other honest.

Jeff Schmidt, in *Disciplined Mind: A Critical Look at Salaried Professionals and the Soul-Battering System That Shapes Their Lives* (Rowman & Littlefield, 2000), offers a whole panoply of ways that individuals within institutions can contribute "to more equality and democracy, to less hierarchy and authoritarianism." Here are examples from his final chapter, "Now or Never":

> ... encourage coworkers to connect themselves with radical organizations and to read and subscribe to radical publications. You circulate antiestablishment periodicals, or selected articles from them, to professional and nonprofessional coworkers who might be interested.
>
> ... air your institution's dirty laundry in public. When you make public an internal fight over the nature or quality of the institution's products or services, you expose your bosses to pressures that make an outcome in the public interest more likely and the usual outcome

that serves elites less likely. This pressure can be strong, because even members of the public who seem to be apathetic perk up when let in on what is going on behind the scenes; they can see where the decision is being made and can, for a change, imagine themselves influencing it.

... debunk the myth of neutrality of the profession and its working principles. You challenge the social role of the profession.

... help lay bare the intimate details of management's decision-making about the content of the work. Because workplace secrecy increases the power of the bosses by ensuring that they are the only ones with a comprehensive knowledge of what is going on, you work to spread around as much information as possible. When you know the details of how the bosses made a particular decision, you inform people inside and outside of the organization, and you encourage coworkers to do the same. This helps reveal management's politics and enables people to predict its decisions in the future.

... encourage openness in personnel matters, specifically, in individual disputes with management. When you have a dispute with management, the bosses insist on discussing it with you behind closed doors not because they want to protect your privacy, but because they want to deny you the support of coworkers. Behind closed doors you stand alone against the institution. Hence, you try to handle conflicts with the boss in front of coworkers to whatever extent possible. In any case, you recount the details of your disputes to coworkers, and you encourage coworkers to do the same when they have disputes with management.

... help organize a union. After all, management is organized and sticks together to defend its interests.

(An extremely concise and persuasive critique of "hierarchical power structures" appears on pages 271 and 273.)

The wrap-up goes to Stephen Carney who eloquently summarizes the D-word dilemma:

> The protection of intellectual freedom and freedom of expression for all people is essential to the proper functioning of modern liberal democracy. It must be recognized, however, that these tenets cannot be fully exercised or protected unless they exist alongside a commitment to the substantive social and economic equality of all citizens. In other words, the civil right to freedom of expression requires a recognition that not all citizens in western society are equal, and that social and economic status may have a direct impact upon a person's ability to exercise his or her own right to freedom of expression... The public library is often conceptualized as an arena in which freedom of expression and intellectual freedom can be achieved and thoroughly defended. The library, as a site in which the public sphere can be realized, is in this context thoroughly democratic. Often the defense of intellectual freedom requires the library employee to take a specific stance or position on an issue and to recognize that not all people are automatically afforded the same civil rights. Just as certain societal factors inhibit the protection and defense of these principles, certain institutional practices and structures that are common to the library as a place of work inhibit the library worker from openly recognizing that these societal factors and limitations do actually exist. When the library worker is unable to challenge these practices, factors, and limitations, the defense of universal intellectual freedom and freedom of expression is inhibited as the voices that wield more power are allowed to dominate the dialogue of human communication. Challenging the hierarchical organizational structure that is common to the library as a place of work may then be looked upon as a first step towards the development of an egalitarian free speech situation, where intellectual freedom actually exists alongside real social and economic equality.

Updates and Additions
(U*L 127, 2003)

Recently I invited reviewers and reference staff to admonish publishers not to stint on indexes (U*L 124). Robert Hauptman, editor of the *Journal of Information Ethics*, reminds me that he had made a similar appeal four years ago, inveighing in the *Chronicle of Higher Education* (2-12-99, p. B10) against the growing and alarming absence of both indexes and bibliographies, especially in scholarly tomes. Said Hauptman, in part:

> I vividly recall stumbling across the first book that I thought should have contained a bibliography but did not. That incident, I admit, occurred some 30 years ago, and the book—Joseph Wood Krutch's *The Modern Temper*—was published in 1929. I was particularly annoyed because I had profited greatly from the book, and I thought Krutch's sources might also be helpful. But either Krutch had relied entirely on totally assimilated material and his own genius or, more likely, his publisher wanted to attract a broader, popular audience and had suggested that a bibliography would put off readers who might otherwise be interested in the book.
>
> In Krutch's day, though, most monographs did include bibliographies. Even 20 years ago, few scholarly publishers would have considered publishing a monograph without one. Now, many academic volumes—including those from the best university presses—contain no systematic, alphabetical listing of source materials...
>
> The index is another part of the traditional scholarly book that is becoming scarcer. Although one of my early books didn't include an index, I now realize how important indexes are in helping the reader retrace his or her path through a book, or in locating a specific piece of information. Yet publishers are increasingly willing—if not eager—to eliminate indexes. Often the publisher asks the author to compile the index, which some authors then subcontract to professional indexers. In other cases, the publisher pays for the compilation, but deducts the cost from the author's royalties. Whatever the option offered, authors should do their utmost to include indexes in their scholarly works.
>
> We owe the decline of the index and the bibliography to economic pressures—and to scholars' failure to resist them. Scientists in particular now consider knowledge a commodity; in growing numbers, they choose to delay publication of their work in the hope of selling or patenting their results, rather than sharing data freely with their colleagues. Publishers—especially university presses, which have small print runs and narrow profit margins—try to save money producing books. If no one complains when a scholarly book arrives without a bibliography or an index, why bother including the scholarly apparatus in forthcoming volumes?

Not in *My* Library!

The stat-driven, business-modeled weeding frenzy continues nationwide (U*L 118, p. 18; 120, p. 25–31; 121, p. 21–22). Observes Matte in his *Resist* zine (no. 44; Bicycle Lane Industries, P.O. Box 582345, Minneapolis, MN 55458):

> I've written about the library before. Back when I was this solitary jobless and depressed kid, it used to be one of my favorite places to hang out. The library is kind of a neutral spot that takes on whatever mood you need it to. If you're depressed, it can be a nice depressing place to mope around looking for depressing books to read. If you're excited, and enthusiastic about something, it's a great place to go to fuel that. If you're just there to get some business or research done, it's good for that too. I've talked with a few people about the pros and cons of the public library lately. I know that libraries throw out a number of books, and that a number of them are very good books that just aren't read as often as the popular trash. I think it's pretty tragic when libraries throwaway books. I mean, they're supposed to be the resource you check when you can't find a book that's not that popular, and sort of hard to find. If they don't hold on to them, who will? They'll just end up in a landfill.

From the Southwest, another library user ruefully notes, that "to make room on its shelves for Harry Potter books, "the Tucson-Pima County Library system recently sold off ... compact discs at one of its discard sales. I bought two Rossini operas, *Semiramide* and

> *Il Turco in Italia*, and three wonderful Deutsche Grammophon pressings or recordings made by soprano Kathleen Battle. On some songs she is accompanied by violinist Itzhak Perlman; on others, by pianist James Levine.
>
> The odd find, however, and the one I'm perhaps most glad to have now in my collection, is *Watkins Ale: Music of the English Renaissance,* performed by The Baltimore Consort. (Iris J. Arnesen, *The Opera Glass,* no. 16, reprinted in *Free Press Death Ship,* no. 1, mid. 2002, p. 1718).

On the East Coast, a Baltimore area public library staffer disgustedly writes (in *The Match!* no. 99, Winter 2002-03):

> I'm tempted to suggest having a "Discarded Books Week." We could set up an empty cart with a sign saying: "This represents all the books we've thrown out that you can't check out anymore." The Nazi-style book burning (I mean WEEDING, sorry) continues — if anything, the pace has been stepped up — with foreign-language fiction remaining an especially tempting target. And though we claim to support the "freedom to read," employees' freedom to talk is another matter — we're not supposed to tell outsiders about these policies. So while I know people who could use the discards, if they came in asking about them they'd only be rebuffed. Of course, this isn't New York or San Francisco. It's a city with an illiteracy rate of one-third, where perhaps few would care, even if they knew, how many books are being trashed. The situation IS hopeless, at least in this lifetime, which is the only one we have...
>
> As for the "weeding" (a putrid term I use with derision) of the foreign-language books, we're particularly devoted to tossing them out by the boxful. Meanwhile there's been an influx into the city of people whose native tongue is Spanish, Serbo-Croatian, and many others. It may make sense to discard, say, a 1998 guide to passing the G.E.D. that's been superseded by the 2002 edition, or a totally ruined book when other copies are available, but that's not what's happening here. I'm talking about stacks of boxes of books carted away to the landfill, week after week.

Updates and Additions (U*L 127, 2003)

This is supposed to be perfectly okay because periodic "surveys" have ostensibly established what people like to check out and what they don't.

(Editor's note: Such a policy overlooks, of course, the many volumes people read AT the library and [people] do not check out because, perhaps like me, they have been refused library cards.)

Is this any way to run a library? Is a library worth anything if it doesn't include the obscure, the unpopular, the esoteric, the downright weird? (Yes, Fred, I'm including poetry, even if it doesn't get the point across like "good old prose," as you stated in an earlier *Match*.)

Readers may be saying, "At least he probably gets to snag all kinds of cool discarded stuff." Not exactly: discarded books retain their barcodes, which means they'll set off the library's security system on the way out. The result is that employees accumulate piles of discards they can't take home, and this stuff stays in their lockers or in a closet, doing no one any good.

As a flip side to the otherwise dismal Baltimore weeding scene, Jim Hightower describes The Book Thing, a basement store operated by Russell Wattenberg that supplies scrounged books at no charge to homeless shelters, schools, "and any other place where people might welcome free reading material." Among the hundreds of thousands of yearly giveaways are "mint-condition coffee-table volumes" and "tattered classics." Hightower writes:

> People are not only eager readers, but eager donors as well. [Wattenberg] particularly relishes the subversiveness of Baltimore's librarians while city regulators officially prohibit them from donating their used books, he says he "gets anonymous calls telling me 50 boxes will be in an alleyway at five o'clock" ("The Free Book Thing," *Street Spirit,* May 2002, p. 11).

One of the most incisive lay indictments of library discard-madness is Iris Lane's "Books and Periodicals Vanish Down Memory-Hole" (*The Match!,* no. 97, Winter 2001–2, p. 29–30). These are a few passages:

> For some thirteen years I have been attending library discard sales in my city: those several-times-a-year events in which the public library sells off, mostly at very low prices, tens of thousands of unwanted books.
> In the beginning I was overjoyed at being able to build a personal library at rock-bottom prices, but I soon became deeply disturbed by the scope of and the purpose behind what the library system refers to as the "weeding" of its collections.
> My particular interest is classical music, and the sheer numbers of really valuable reference books that were being tossed out appalled me. Again, I was glad to get such volumes for my own collection, but the fact that no one else would now be able to consult them, and that most of the books were being sold for a tiny fraction of what they originally cost, angered me, both as a music lover and as a person who had been taxed so that the library could purchase these books in the first place.
> Occasional out-of-town newspaper articles made me aware that in other cities librarians were shipping their unwanted books to landfills, only to be met, to their great surprise, by angry book lovers who were denouncing them as heirs to the Nazi book-burners. I had already begun to consider myself to be a rescuer of books, and these articles made me aware that there were others like me all across the country. All of us were outraged by the deliberate destruction of our cultural heritage by those who had been hired to protect it,

and all of us were buying from the discard sales as many irreplaceable books as we could squeeze into our homes.

Modern librarians don't like books. They like computers, boxes of microfilm, and neatly arranged shelves of brightly-colored copies of today's hottest bestsellers. What matters to them is not the depth and breadth of human knowledge in their collections, but how little space is used and how frequently their materials are "accessed."

Earlier columns decried the increasing commercialization of public libraries. Violet Jones, an outspoken opponent of wanton weeding, tellingly connects discard policy and corporatization in "Harry Potter: A Foot in the Door" (*Xerography Debt*, no. 8, June 2002, p. 26–28). Here's the nub of her remarks:

> About a year ago, I started to notice that the library had many, MANY copies of *Harry Potter* on their shelves. I looked through their catalog, to find out just how many. It took me almost an hour to count them all. These 11 library branches had a total of 837 *Harry Potter* books in their collections. (I didn't even count the books on tape and compact disc, of which there were plenty.) That works out to 76 books per branch on the average. I was beginning to see why there was no room on the shelves for the unfortunate "weed" books, books which, incidentally, DON'T have multimillion dollar publicity machines behind them.
>
> Jump forward to the present. Last week, I walked into the children's department in one of these libraries, and was greeted by a large, 3' by 5' poster, displayed in a prominent spot, advertising the Harry Potter film. I couldn't believe my eyes at first—I stepped closer and saw that, yes, it was indeed an "official" advertising poster. This advertisement would undoubtedly have cost cold, hard cash to put on a bus stop or billboard—a lot of it. So, I asked the librarian about it. She told me she was very excited to have the poster on display, because the promoters of Harry Potter were giving her library ONE FREE COPY of the movie in exchange.
>
> What a shining exemplar of the noble librarian profession this person is! She sold out a public library for a $10 video disc. Of course, now that Harry Potter's advertisement is on display, there will have to be other advertisements on display in the future—a public library must, above all, *be fair,* you see. (Watch other libraries across the nation follow suit in the months to come. Why not? They have always done so in the past, what with their "weeding" out of old books without public review, microfilming of irreplaceable texts and then destroying the originals, tossing out books to make room for more and more budget-wrecking computers, handing over control of book selection to private, for-profit corporations, and so on.) How long will it be until this lucrative, till-now-unavailable advertising space—i.e., the public library—is filled with ads for the films of Stephen King, Michael Crichton, and Tom Clancy, and other big-budget, big-profit book/film products?

Earl Lee and Fred Woodworth addressed—indeed, exposed—the sham of Banned Books Week in U*L 124, p. 28–31. That Baltimore library worker adds a footnote:

> It's Banned Books Week at a Baltimore area public library and yes, that's a hypocritical, self-serving farce. To my knowledge, not one book included in the "Banned Books" display has been banned from any American public library (and if they had, they'd still be available through retail outlets, of course). They've merely drawn attacks, generally from uptight, right-wing parents (who have a right to express their views like anyone else, right?). The display itself is small (a few books thrown into a box, on a table, with a sign reading "BANNED BOOKS" in lettering designed to look like spray-painted graffiti) and embarrassingly ugly, as though the library administrators have lost interest in the whole idea and are

*Updates and Additions (U*L 127, 2003)*

merely going through the motions. Or perhaps there's some subliminal guilt at work here, considering that thanks to the USA Patriot Act, Americans have lost the right to check out what they like without the possibility of government snooping into their reading habits. (And — in a blatantly unconstitutional provision — library personnel are forbidden to tell their patrons, or anyone else, that snooping has taken place. Disgusting!)

Cuba Libre!
(U*L 128, 2003)

It's right there in Article 1 of the Cuban Constitution:

None of the liberties recognized for the citizens can be exercised against what is established by the Constitution and the laws, or against the existence and objectives of the socialist state, or against the decision of the Cuban people to construct socialism and communism.

As Amnesty International has commented: "The Constitution conditions the exercise of fundamental freedoms on support for the system." That Constitutional clause represents a mandate, a prescription, for censorship and repression. (The same would be true were the salient phrase "Christianity and capitalism" instead of "socialism and communism.")

On June 30, 2003, I submitted this letter to *American Libraries*:

In mid-March some 75 dissidents, including at least 10 "independent librarians" or private library owners, were summarily tried by the Cuban government at remote locales with only family members being allowed to observe the proceedings. All were sentenced to jail terms of up to 28 years. Although defenders of the crackdown characterize the defendants as paid U.S. agents who deserved what they got, Amnesty International concluded that the conduct for which the dissidents were prosecuted was "nonviolent and seemed to fall within the parameters of the legitimate exercise of fundamental freedoms as guaranteed under international standards." AI declared the 75 to be "prisoners of conscience." And Human Rights Watch came to a similar conclusion.

Should there be any doubt concerning whether the "librarians," in particular, were imprisoned because of dealing with information and ideas, consider that they were accused, among other things, of "disrespect" and receiving "subversive and counterrevolutionary" books, and that the government raiders confiscated literature, FAX machines, and typewriters.

During its Toronto conference, ALA failed either to sponsor a debate on the topic of "independent librarians" and intellectual freedom in Cuba (despite 5 invited, government-sanctioned librarians being allowed to speak for nearly 3 hours without opposition) or to pass a resolution calling for the immediate release of the self-described librarians and return of all confiscated material. However, even though the American Library Association fumbled this issue, individual ALA members can still take action by writing directly to:

Cuba Libre!

Dr. Fidel Castro Ruz
Presidente de los Consejos de
Estado y de Ministros
La Habana, Cuba

As Rosa Luxemburg, the socialist revolutionary martyr, warned 85 years ago: "Freedom for only the supporters of the government, however many there may be, is not freedom. Real freedom is freedom for those who think differently.... Without general elections, without freedom of the press and unlimited freedom of assembly, without a contest of free opinions, life stagnates and withers in all public institutions, and the bureaucracy becomes the only active element" (quoted by Eduardo Galeano, "Cuba Hurts!," *The Progressive*, June 2003, p. 12).

It appeared in *AL*'s 8-2003 "Reader Forum," minus the last paragraph.

Following my own advice, I mailed this message to Havana, also on 6-30-2003:

Excelencia,

I oppose the American embargo against Cuba and last week, at the American Library Association Conference in Toronto, Canada, publicly declared both the blockade and Helms-Burton Act to be "stupid," stating that they must immediately end.

However, although I respect and defend Cuba's national sovereignty and integrity, I cannot remain silent about the severe human rights abuses represented by the mid–March arrest and conviction of some 75 dissidents, including independent journalists and librarians. Not only were their "trials" suspect—conducted summarily in remote locations—but there appears to be no evidence that these persons truly posed a threat to Cuba's security. (Even Philip Agee doesn't think they did.) They seemed to have essentially expressed or promulgated dissenting opinions in a nonviolent way. They may wish for a "regime change" in Cuba. Well, so do I in the United States. But as long as we're not plotting the violent overthrow of the government, we don't deserve to be suppressed, to be imprisoned.

In order to correct an obvious injustice and also to regain the esteem of friends and supporters worldwide, I urge the immediate release of all the people jailed in March and the return of their confiscated books and other materials.

En solidaridad,
Sanford Berman
Former Head Cataloger
Hennepin County Library
Minnesota

Robert B. Downs Intellectual
Freedom Award Winner
ALA Equality Award Winner

To date, there has been no response.

For a detailed overview of the March arrests and convictions, including many of the specific accusations against individual dissidents (e.g., "visiting prisoners and their families ... and maintaining ties to the international organization ... Doctors Without Borders" and "carrying out activities and meetings, using our national flag and showing posters asking for freedom for political prisoners and prisoners of conscience, in a frank challenge to the judicial, political and social system"), see AI'S 57-page, "Cuba: 'Essential Measures'? Human Rights Crackdown in the Name of Security": http://web.amnesty.org/library/Index/ENGAMR250172003

No More Shushing: Library Staff and Users Speak (Part 2), More on Cuba
(U*L 129, 2003)

Well, that subtitle should now be changed to "library staff, *students* and users speak" because here is the thoughtful, if also blistering, critique of library ed by a recent LIS grad, Donny Smith (dwanzine@hotmail.com):

November 18, 2002

Dean
School of Information Studies
Syracuse University
4-206 Center for Science & Technology
Syracuse NY 13244-4100

Dear Professor von Dran:
 I understand that you are chair of the external review panel for ALA accreditation of Drexel University's College of Information Science and Technology (IST). I was a graduate student in the Master's of Library and Information Science program from January 2001 till August 2002, when I received my degree.
 I'm writing to say that I believe Drexel's program should lose its ALA accreditation.
 I'm not sure what Drexel's plans are regarding library science, but the reality is that IST is becoming a "systems school." Newly hired IST professors are "techies," often with little library experience, and most IST professors lack the humanistic orientation I would expect from library professionals. Course reading assignments are usually narrow statistical studies or technical manuals and tend to avoid broad overviews and philosophical questions.
 I have found most IST professors distant and uninterested in the intellectual development of their students. My first advisor never answered a single one of my e-mails or voice-mails. Even when I was enrolled in one of his courses and would try to speak with him after class, he would walk past me as though he'd never seen me before. (A former adjunct professor at Drexel has told me that the university administration has let it be known that professors are to avoid making themselves too available to students. This means keeping short office hours, not answering e-mails, not getting involved with student groups, and so on.)
 Some IST professors seem to be severely limited, pedagogically. They often seemed confused by the basic tasks of running a classroom and easily rattled by student queries. I remember one professor's look of panic when a student asked, "What is HTML?" He then

spent the next two hours of class time answering the question in excruciating (and unnecessarily confusing) detail.

IST seems to rely excessively on adjuncts. Four of the eleven regular courses I took were taught by adjuncts. One adjunct instructor seemed barely conscious during her lectures. She never once took roll, rarely looked at any of us students, let alone addressed us by name. Her lectures were incoherent and rambling. Her handouts were jumbled and often illegible.

The poor faculty would be less of a handicap if the student body were of high caliber. However, IST seems to admit any applicant who can pay the tuition. Most of my classmates seemed interested only in getting through with the minimum amount of work. On those rare occasions when professors attempted to engage students in discussion, participation was listless.

The facilities provided to library science students demonstrate the poor standing of the discipline at Drexel. The classrooms and labs in the Rush Building leave much to be desired, and the collections at Hagerty Library were inadequate for my research needs. (Fortunately I was able to use the library where I worked.) I feel cheated by my Drexel education. The only reason I have any pride in it at all is that I spent so much time studying independently. Drexel should not be allowed to call itself a library school any longer.

John Gehner, currently an LIS student who also works full-time at a Minneapolis homeless shelter, directed this plea to the Minneapolis Public Library Board and Director on March 26, 2003:

I am writing to share my concern about the potential closing of Franklin Library without a clear plan for and formal commitment to its future.

In 2002, Our Saviour's Housing provided shelter and support services to nearly 1,000 people experiencing homelessness. This has been our mission for over twenty years. Our Chicago Avenue facilities are located six blocks away from Franklin Library, which allows the people we serve to reach the building and its important resources easily on foot.

It has been my common experience to see Franklin Library books (marked as such) in use throughout the shelter. Shelter residents also rely on Franklin's computer services in seeking employment and housing opportunities. Although we provide four computer terminals with Internet access, our operating license requires that we close our shelter during the day. As a result, residents must turn elsewhere for their information needs at that time.

Right now, a resident in our transitional housing is taking college classes. She uses Franklin Library's resources at least two hours a day to do schoolwork. If the Franklin Library were to close, she would have to travel out of her neighborhood on multiple buses and would compete with other dislocated library users for more limited time on a computer and for access to other important learning tools.

Having visited the Franklin Library on many occasions, I know that the materials, services, and assistance provided there are invaluable to other low-income residents of the Phillips community. Judging from the number of youth I see obtaining homework help, the presence of recent immigrants, and the constant foot traffic to Sally Munger's reference desk, the library is vital to so very many people.

Librarian John Buschman writes in *Poor People and Library Services,* "I believe there is serious cause for worry in librarianship about our commitment and ability to serve the poor. It is clear that the historical and economic basis of professional values which has guided an increasing commitment to equality of access is being eroded [today]... What is most disturbing is the steady erosion of principle which drives our commitment to service."

No More Shushing (Part 2)

I believe Franklin Library is an anchoring point, a place of stability and promise, for the people of Phillips. And I believe that the budgetary decisions that the Library Board makes with regard to Franklin Library will reflect its principle(s) and commitment to Minneapolis' poor.

Please work to ensure that the library retains its vitality and is encouraged to grow.

Please keep Franklin Library open. Thank you for your consideration.

John Gehner
Our Saviour's Housing
2219 Chicago Ave. South
Minneapolis, MN 55404

Dave Evad, an assertive, 20ish library user, offered right-on, empowering advice to his cohorts in a letter to the March/April 2003 *Punk Planet*:

Your article on library reform was admirable, but I feel that you left out one of the most important parts of a library revolution: filling out order forms. This method of change can come about more easily than breaking up the bureaucracy and hierarchical system.

Most libraries are funded greatly by local or municipal tax dollars. Because of this, members of the community are permitted to make requests for desired items. It is a rare case that the library does not put in a decent effort to fill the order. People need to take advantage of this!

For seven years now (I am 23), I have been filling up my library's CD rack with records from Matador and Kill Rock Stars, not to mention all the books and movies they have added to their collection. This gives the 13-year-old kid stuck in suburbia a shot to try something new while they glance past the rest of the status quo titles.

I come from a regular, lower-middle-class community and have not yet been shut off by the local librarians. In some cases they fail in their search, but this is a rare event. Once, I was even called up by a librarian to ask me where they could find a Blonde Redhead CD and I pointed them towards Southern Distribution. The 70-something year old librarian couldn't have been happier.

So it doesn't take a radical movement of librarians to make a change (though it helps). It's the millions of kids armed with library cards that are able to carry the flag. March on!

Moral (for all ages): It's YOUR library. So tell them what YOU want in it.

Finally, veteran SF activist James Chaffee (63 Stoneybrook Avenue, San Francisco, CA 94112) addressed issues of shrinking book stock and growing corporatization in a 4-4-03 communication to the San Francisco Board of Supervisors:

I have enclosed two articles in the local media regarding the de-emphasis of books in our library that appeared earlier this year. These articles portray this controversy as an expression of the divergence between the old fashioned media of books and the new media of technology. This casts the debate along an axis that favors the destruction of our intellectual heritage on the premise that it is an arcane debate and a matter of emphasis.

The truth is entirely otherwise. The media issue is a smokescreen the primary effect of which is to prevent the real debate from taking place.

In most corners of our society the techno-hype that inflated the *dot.com* bubble has been exposed as a fraud. Enron was a now-you-see-it-now-you-don't shell game. Most of the get-rich-quick schemes have crawled back under a rock. But the library still operates on the premise that the book is a dying technology and there is a pot of gold at the end of the Internet rainbow.

New forms of communication and electronic media will come and they should be welcomed. The interesting question is whether in the midst of this wave of new forms there is a place to preserve the past, treasure our intellectual heritage, and our traditions of free and equal access to information. There are gathering forces that will attempt to persuade us that there is no room for such things in the modern library. It is not books but the connection to the past that we are losing.

The apologists for the new library will tell you that the library will never survive without product placement, commercialism, entrepreneurial spirit, and their cherished philanthropy. The contention is that the library must become software help desks, homework centers, and social venues. There is no contention that this is really the library that people want. The contention is that it serves the "public-private partnership" of corporate sponsorship and political influence peddling that all of our institutions seem to be slaves to.

The San Francisco Public Library has been in the forefront in the adaptation to the "public-private partnership" in the building of the New Main Library and even [Mayor] Willie Brown admitted that was a disaster.

Now we are told that we have to get rid of the books to make way for technology. That is not true. We have to get rid of the books because the space is for sale to the "public-private partnership" so that they can spin their web of philanthropy and corporate sponsorship.

In every area of our public life there has been awareness that "money talks" and that as a society we need to minimize or eliminate the destructive influence of greed. The various ways that this is done include conflict of interest laws, financial disclosure laws, open meeting "sunshine" laws, lobbyist registration, political contribution reform, term limits, district elections, and the list could go on. None of it seems to have much effect and the abuse of the public sector by private monied interests continues apace. Nowhere is that abuse more apparent where we have a corporate controlled private non-profit corporation called the Friends and Foundation of the San Francisco Public Library that lives like a parasite off the majestic tree of our San Francisco Public Library. The "Friends and Foundation" took in over $2 million last year and gave the library $278,000. This "non-profit" reaps the benefits of selling the "naming opportunities" in our branches that are being remodeled with public bond funds passed in 2000 totaling $106 million. The Foundation claims to be raising $15 million for those branches, but it still has $19 million in its own bank account after "raising $30 million" for the new main library. The current library consultant, selected by the Friends and Foundation because the first payment was a grant, claims that "a better library has fewer books" and now she is paid with public funds.

And so it goes. Will San Francisco come to its senses and decide to keep libraries that are libraries? If it does, it will have to happen soon.

Editor's Note: Two letters were received by U*L in response to Sanford Berman's article in U*L 128. The first of those letters follows, along with Mr. Berman's response. The other letter from Ann Sparanese, because of its length, will appear in issue 130, along with Mr. Berman's response. Mjf.

Letter to the Editor
re: Cuban Librarians, *U*L 128, Berman's Bag*

I would like to comment on Sandy Berman's column in Issue 128 (number 3 of 2003) ("Berman's Bag: CUBA LIBRE!"). With all due respect to my friend and colleague, we need to make some further distinctions to better understand a complicated situation. Although Sandy clearly states his opposition to the U.S. embargo and the Helms-Burton Act, he doesn't seem to fully understand the consequences of these U.S. policies in evaluating the current situation and what we should do about it.

For those who haven't followed this debate, a small group called Friends of Cuban Libraries led by Robert Kent has forcefully brought the issue of the "independent librarians" to ALA and IFLA. I have carefully read the recent Amnesty International report on Cuba cited in Sandy's column and compared it with Robert Kent's reports. The result is quite eye opening.

Mr. Kent calls those arrested "independent librarians" but Amnesty calls them "private librarians." The terminology here is important. There is much evidence, including in the Amnesty report, that these "private librarians" are not independent, but rather they get much of their support directly from the U.S. Government's representatives in Havana, the Cuban Interests Section. This aid is authorized by the Helms-Burton Act. Moreover, the Friends of Cuban Libraries have also finally acknowledged that they receive support from U.S. Government sources. Probably more importantly, it is very hard to see why we should call these people "librarians." The Amnesty report clearly shows that most of them are journalists and politicians (and a few poets, medical doctors, etc.) who also have private libraries in their homes. As far as we know, none of them were ever educated as librarians or practiced librarianship before their recent endeavors, and they have no connections with the two Cuban library associations. Their primary activities are entirely political and they do a bit of book lending on the side. Visits to these home libraries have shown that most of them are really just small unorganized book collections which are rarely used as "libraries." The point is that these journalists and politicians are not "independent" or "librarians." It is clear that they are using the term "librarian" to get our attention for political reasons.

Just as with the Iraq war, we have to evaluate what the Bush Administration is doing in Cuba and how they are portraying their activities. We know President Bush has lied on just about everything concerning Iraq, including the evidence of weapons of mass destruction, ties to Bin Laden, and how the situation is improving every day.

The current Bush Administration has installed a new head of the U.S. Interests Section in Havana who has vigorously and openly interfered in the Cuban domestic political situation. The U.S. Government would not let the reverse happen here, so why should we expect the Cuban Government to act any differently? It is very convenient to portray these opponents of the Cuban Government as librarians in order to get our attention and worldwide sympathy, but the problem is that it is just not true.

According to Amnesty International, it seems clear that those arrested in the recent crackdown are indeed political prisoners. So instead of addressing a false issue, let's address the real issue. How best can we influence shortening their sentences or getting them out of prison? The answer is really quite simple. We need to improve relations between the Cuban and U.S. Governments by ending sanctions, repealing the Helms-Burton Act, and providing mutually beneficial contacts such as the recent agreement between ALA and ASCUBI, the main Cuban library organization. If the U.S. repeals Helms-Burton perhaps the Cubans might repeal the laws they passed in retaliation. What a novel idea! Let's combat the lies with a call for a rational foreign policy.

Al Kagan, African Studies Bibliographer and Professor of Library Administration, Africana Unit, Room 328, University of Illinois Library, 1408 W. Gregory Drive, Urbana, IL 61081. akagan@uiuc.edu

Sanford Berman replies:

The jailed "independent librarians" are independent of the Cuban government and Communist Party apparatus. They are librarians because they operate libraries. Most do not hold the equivalent of an MLS. Neither does the director of the Cuban National

Not in *My* Library!

Library. Neither does the Librarian of Congress. Nor do scores of persons running both state-supported and private libraries, including infoshops, in the United States.

Al mentions Robert Kent. I did not. The central issue is about intellectual freedom and repression in Cuba, not Robert Kent. In March, individuals were summarily arrested, convicted, and sentenced to long prison terms essentially for harboring or expressing ideas not approved by the one-party regime. Some collected books and other literature for borrowing by anyone interested. Some held meetings and talked. Some mounted human rights posters. Some committed the heinous act of visiting prisoners and their families. None advocated the violent overthrow of the Cuban government. None stockpiled munitions. Not only were some 10 voluntary, private, or independent librarians among the 70 or 80 detained dissidents, but their books and other materials were also confiscated and have since reportedly been burned as "worthless."

Al and other regime-apologists are curiously coy about the very language of the Cuban Constitution that explicitly limits basic liberties to only citizens who support the existing system. Criticism and dissent are in effect unconstitutional.

Yes, Helms-Burton is a bad law. But so is the copycat Cuban retaliatory legislation, which circumscribes freedom of speech and association. It is childish and repressive.

Cuba has achieved many fine things in education, agriculture, and medicine. They deserve credit for that. But when they conduct kangaroo courts and wantonly punish people for nonviolently circulating books, writing, and organizing, they deserve rebuke. George W. Bush is no more responsible for their accomplishments than for their delinquencies. And what further merits demolition is the omnipresent, if often unstated premise that a society simply can't pursue social justice *and* maintain human rights at the same time. These are not mutually exclusive projects.

King County Responds, "Banned Books Week" Deconstructed, Cataloging Blues at LAPL, Loompanics' Mike Hoy on Censorship, Deep-Sixed Afghan Atrocity Film, Cuba Again

(U*L 130, 2004)

As reported in the October 2003 *Freethought Today* (page 16), published by the Freedom From Religion Foundation, member Sergin Codreanu of Bellevue, Washington, asked his local library "why it doesn't carry such classics as *The Future of Illusion* and other freethought titles, while carrying thousands ... of Christian ideological and apologetical titles." Says Codreanu, "Now, the library has ordered a dozen new freethought titles. Many are quite popular with patrons." Here, in part, is the response sent by the library's collection management services, (960 Newport Way NW, Issaquah, WA 98027, 425-462-9600, http://www.kcls.org):

Dear Mr. Codreaunu:
   Thank you for taking the time to comment on the services of the King County Library System. We value feedback from our patrons. You indicated that you "suspect some bias against atheism in KCLS," and point out that when you searched our catalog using the keyword approach for the term "Atheism" you get 60 results, while for "Christianity" you get 4,500 results. In addition, you note that, since around 10 percent of the population of the U.S. is nonreligious, "it is unclear why 10 percent of the KCLS books dealing with faith are not atheistic."
   First, I can assure you that the King County Library System is not biased against any particular point of view. We do attempt to provide access to information on all points of view. We rely on many factors when making purchase decisions, including reviews, demand, and publishing trends. A quick search of our vendor databases (which represent what is available for purchase) for books on Atheism and Christianity gave similar results to those produced by searching our catalog. One vendor had 34,420 items listed under

NOT IN *MY* LIBRARY!

Christianity and only 192 for Atheism. Our other vendor had 8,585 books listed under Christianity and 54 books for Atheism.

Since books on Atheism are often not reviewed in the library journals, we checked for recently published titles we may have overlooked. This search resulted in several titles, 12 of which will be ordered. We particularly appreciate the suggestion for Freud's *Future of an Illusion*. We could only find one title written for adults in print by Dan Barker, *Losing Faith in Faith,* and will order this. In addition, we will be ordering:

2000 Years of Disbelief, by James A. Haught.
Atheism as a Positive Social Force, by Raymond W. Converse.
Atheism, Morality and Meaning, by Michael Martin.
Beach Blanket Atheism: The Beginner's Guide for the Non-Believer, by Edward P. Tolley.
Celebrities in Hell, by Warren Allen Smith.
Has Science Found God? by Victor J. Stenger.
Life Without God, by Nicolaos S. Tzannes.
Naturalism and Religion, by Kai Nielsen.
Religion Without God, by Ray Billington.
Western Atheism: A Short History, by James Thrower.

Lesson for library users everywhere: TELL 'EM WHAT YOU WANT!

In late October, 2000, Russ Kick (russ@mindpollen.com) contributed to the ongoing critique of Banned Books Week with this right-on rant:

From September 23rd–30th, 2000, retailers and libraries have blown off the dust and moved the usual suspects, such as *Huckleberry Finn* and *Catcher in the Rye,* from their Literature sections to displays in the front of their buildings to show that they're in the vanguard on the fight against censorship. They're feeling righteous.

Only thing is, Banned Books Week is ... well, weak. I like the general principle, but there are several problems with it in practice.

The book-stores, libraries, web sites, and other parties involved in the festivities always choose the books that are easiest to defend. There are still a few people who have a burr up their ass about *Tom Sawyer* and *I Know Why the Caged Bird Sings,* but these books are laughably easy to find and they're recognized as classics, which are easy to defend. Sure, a bookstore will trot out *Fanny Hill* (originally published in 1748), but what about *Macho Sluts* by Pat Califia?

Some libraries may display *Mein Kampf,* which is still controversial in a way, but it's attained the level of cultural artifact and is therefore so safe that its current publisher is the mainstream Houghton Mifflin corporation.

These libraries may pat themselves on the back for being so daring, but then why not also display *The Protocols of the Elders of Zion, White Power* by George Lincoln Rockwell (American Nazi Party founder), and Holocaust-revisionist publications? If you want to show a censored book of Mark Twain's, how about *Letters from the Earth?* His estate blocked its publication until the 1950s, and its mocking of the Christian concepts of Heaven and Hell is still controversial.

Libraries and book-stores also use odd definitions of censorship. Maybe a South Dakota high-school principal threw a hissy fit over *Of Mice and Men,* but does that hold a candle to the multi-pronged governmental attacks on the photography books of Jock Sturges, Sally Mann, David Hamilton, and other artists whose subjects are often nude young people? Several city/county governments charged bookstores such as Barnes & Noble with felonies for carrying these books. Think we'll see those books displayed this year? How about a display of drug books, which came under major attack by Congress over the past year? What about the very few books on explosives that are still in print after the 1998 federal law threatening publishers with 20 years in jail? Don't hold your breath.

In this age of litigation, a lawsuit will more likely take a book out of print than a governmental edict. A few bookstores might display *In the Spirit of Crazy Horse,* which was the subject of the longest lawsuit in the history of American publishing, but what about the books that are currently being attacked, such as *Running Scared* (an exposé of casino kingpin Steve Wynn), *The Downing of TWA Flight 800,* and (heaven forbid) the publications of the group that everyone loves to hate, NAMBLA? Let's not forget about the books that have been attacked but survived: *Fortunate Son* (the Shrub bio), *Lo's Diary, A Piece of Blue Sky* (Scientology exposé), and *L. Ron Hubbard: Messiah or Madman?* among others. It would also be nice to see a roll call for the books that were burned because of recent litigation: *Hit Man, The Senator Must Die,* and *The Oklahoma City Bombing and the Politics of Terror.*

There are also inexplicable gaps in the canon of banned books. Yes, Salman Rushdie's life is still in danger though the fatwa was technically lifted, but Taslima Nasrin still has an Islamic death warrant on her head because of her novel *Shame.* I'm sure a few bookstores and libraries will trot out *The Satanic Verses,* but I'll eat my hat if more than five in the whole country show Nasrin's novel.

Between the oversimplified, uneven definitions of censorship, the tendency to display the same old easily defensible warhorses, and many other problems, Banned Books Week has a very long way to go before it lives up to its promise, or even its name.

Does new technology invariably expand access to library materials? Not when administrative policy gets in the way, as illustrated in this excerpt from the October 6, 2002, meeting minutes of the LAPL (Los Angeles Public Library) Librarians' Guild Professional Concerns Committee: "LAPL has stopped cataloging recorded music except by genre designation (such as 'Jazz,' 'Popular,' etc.) This makes finding a particular work which a patron needs very difficult. All recorded music which the Art, Music, and Recreation Department bought is now shelved in the Popular Library, where no one is able to do any shelf checks, thus essentially making it unavailable to anyone but the browser who personally visits the Popular Library."

The Fall Supplement to Loompanics Unlimited's 2003 catalog features a candid and challenging interview with Mike Hoy, Founder and President of the "publishing and bookselling company specializing in odd unusual controversial, and wild-ass books, with an emphasis on questioning authority." These two queries relate directly to intellectual freedom:

> Q: Many of your books deal with violence and criminal activity. Aren't you harming society by making available information on how to manufacture illegal drugs, or offering how-to-do-it violence manuals?
>
> A: Of course not. Nothing harms "society" more than censorship and dogmatism. I believe that people are mature enough to be allowed to find out anything they want to know about anything they want to know about, and that any attempt to suppress the free transmission of ideas and information will cause much more harm than freedom ever could. Mostly, the "harm" of freedom is to institutions and ideologies that don't want us to be able to find stuff out. The "harm" from publishing, say, *Secrets of Methamphetamine Manufacture* (now in its 6th edition) is nothing compared to the harm of having the DEA

be our only source of information about drugs, or the harm of throwing people in prison for talking about drugs in a way that they don't like.

Q: So you think it would be harmless for a fourth grader to get hold of a copy of *Secrets of Meth...?* How can you say that?

A: In the first place, I do not sell to fourth graders, but for the sake of argument, let's say that I did sell a copy of *Secrets of Meth* to a 9-year-old — what could the "harm" possibly be? Here is a brief excerpt from that book: "Another way of doing the electric cell method of turning the propenylbenzene into phenylacetone is given in the *Journal of Organic Chemistry* article, Volume 49. If, at the conclusion of passing current through the reaction mixture, a little 1 percent solution of sulfuric acid is added and stirred for an hour, the product of the cell is 98 percent yield of the same glycol by the formic acid and peroxide method." That is from page 72.

Now, I submit that if we had a fourth grader who could actually *understand* that passage, what we ought to do is give that kid a state-of-the-art laboratory and get the hell out of his way. A guy like that might discover a cure for cancer, or something. A phenom like that ought to be encouraged to study chemistry. And furthermore, the passage demonstrates that a goodly part of any illegal drug manufacture book is going to rely heavily on mainstream chemistry — because life itself is chemistry.

Contact Loompanics at P.O. Box 1197, Port Townsend, WA 98368; 360-385-2230; email: operations@loompanics.com; web: http://www.loompanics.com.

On Friday, May 23, 2003, Democracy Now!, the acclaimed Pacifica program hosted by Amy Goodman, premiered a documentary film, *Afghan Massacre: The Convoy of Death*. According to a press release:

The film provides eyewitness testimony that U.S. troops were complicit in the massacre of thousands of Taliban prisoners during the Afghan War.

It tells the story ... of prisoners who surrendered to the U.S. military's Afghan allies after the siege of Kunduz. According to eyewitnesses, some three thousand ... were forced into sealed containers and loaded onto trucks for transport to Sheberghan prison. Eyewitnesses say when the prisoners began shouting for air, U.S.-allied Afghan soldiers fired directly into the truck, killing many of them. The rest suffered through an appalling road trip lasting up to four days, so thirsty they clawed at the skin of their fellow prisoners as they licked perspiration and even drank blood from open wounds.

Witnesses say that when the trucks arrived and soldiers opened the containers, most of the people inside were dead. They also say U.S. Special Forces re-directed the containers carrying the living and dead into the desert and stood by as survivors were shot and buried. Now, up to three thousand bodies lie buried in a mass grave.

The film has sent shockwaves around the world. It has been broadcast on national television in Britain, Germany, Italy, and Australia. It has been screened by the European parliament. It has outraged human rights groups and international human rights lawyers. They are calling for investigation into whether U.S. Special Forces are guilty of war crimes.

But most Americans have never heard of the film. That's because not one corporate media outlet in the U.S. will touch it. It has never before been broadcast in this country.

Afghan Massacre is produced and directed by award-winning Irish filmmaker, Jamie Doran. Doran has worked at the highest levels of television film production for more than two decades. His films have been broadcast on virtually every major channel throughout the world. On average, each of his films is seen in around 35 countries. Before establishing his independent television company, Doran spent over seven years at BBC Television.

The film was researched by award-winning journalist Najibullah Quraishi, who was beaten almost to death when he tried to obtain video evidence of U.S. Special Forces' complicity in the massacre. Two of the witnesses who testified in the film are now dead.

I heard the broadcast on a Twin Cities' community radio station. This is exactly the kind of thing that public and academic libraries should get in order to genuinely implement the Library Bill of Rights and provide alternatives to the "safe," bland news and reportage typical of corporate-dominated, mainstream media. To order an audio or video copy of the broadcast [not the film,] call 1-800-881-2359.

Letter to the Editor from Ann Sparanese,
re: "Sandy's Bag: Cuba Libre" (U*L Issue 128, pp. 8–10) and "Sanford Berman replies" (U*L, Issue 129, p. 22) to Al Kagan "Letter to the Editor" (U*L Issue 129, p. 20–22)

Sandy Berman is entirely incorrect about why his "independent librarian" heroes are in prison in the first place. They were charged and convicted not "essentially for harboring or expressing ideas" as Sandy maintains, but for violating Article 91 of the Cuban Penal Code and Law #88 (1998), *The Law of Protection of the Independence of the National Independence and Economy of Cuba.* They were CHARGED with and convicted of—with ample evidence presented—taking money and materials in complicity with the Helms-Burton Act of the United States.

Both of these statutes, as well as Law 80 (1996), *The Reaffirmation of Cuban Dignity and Sovereignty Act,* criminalize collaboration with, or aid to, a foreign power seeking to overthrow the Cuban government. This is as serious a crime in Cuba as it is in the United States. Is Sandy totally ignorant of U.S. laws that forbid foreign intervention in and funding of the U.S. political process? Is he completely unaware that there are people in prison and about to go to prison in the USA for violating these laws?

The Helms-Burton Act (1996) is a huge piece of interventionist legislation which mandates the *funding* of subversion in Cuba to the tune of millions of U.S. taxpayer dollars each year. It instructs the Cuban people about who may run in their elections and who may not; and it tightens trade restriction on other nations which have the temerity to trade with Cuba, among its many other onerous provisions. Cuba was not the only nation to pass legislation outlawing collaboration with Helms-Burton—so did the Canadian government, which saw it as a threat to their right to establish their own trade relations. Amnesty International reports that Helms-Burton "has been explicitly condemned by members of the international community but has not been repealed."

Sandy Berman insists that "Criticism and dissent are in effect unconstitutional" in Cuba. Really? Then *why* is the most prominent member of the dissident opposition, Osvaldo Paya, not in prison? Why did Paya himself, as reported in *The New York Times* (May 20, 2003), warn his fellow dissidents *not* to accept U.S. funding for their activities? It is not "criticism and dissent" that is illegal in Cuba; it is criticism and dissent bought and paid for by the United States government that is illegal.

Elizardo Sanchez, often described as Cuba's "leading human rights activist," is reported by Wayne Smith (former head of the U.S. Interests Section in Havana) to have said, "Because we value our nationalist credentials and are determined to work strictly within the law in our efforts to bring about reforms, our organization [Commission for Human rights and National Reconciliation] would not even consider accepting support under Section 109 [of the Helms-Burton Act.] That section, and in fact the whole Helms-Burton Act, is harmful to the cause of a more open society in Cuba." (*The Nation,* July 3, 2000.) Sanchez is *also not* in prison.

The Rev. Oden Marichal, the president of the Cuban Council of Churches, also told Smith: "We want to see expanding freedom of religion and various other adjustments in our society. But we will work with the government and within our own laws to bring that about. Your government's references to supporting independent organizations in Cuba in efforts against the existing system here seem almost designed to suggest that those independent organizations represent a potential fifth column. As such they are misleading, unhelpful and irresponsible. None of us, I assure you, would ever accept any of those Section 109 funds." Guess what? The Rev. Marichal is a free man and free to work for change in Cuba. And Wayne Smith is no "coy" "apologist" for any regime.

Sandy's "independent librarians" may be independent of the Cuban government, but they have never been "independent" of the U.S. government. That is the root of their problem. They even have a mailing address in Miami, Florida!

Sandy Berman calls the Helms-Burton law "stupid," when it is really a cunning and total assault on Cuban sovereignty. Sandy calls the Cuban legislation "copycat," but do the Cuban laws call for the overthrow of ANY other government? In his chauvinistic arrogance, Sandy Berman calls Cuban laws "childish." These are all simplistic characterizations unworthy of an intelligent observer. More importantly, they deny over forty years of aggression by the United States towards Cuba that continues to this very moment. The Bush administration has continued to implement the strategy summarized by Marc Thiessen, Senator Jesse Helms' assistant, when he said, in a 1998 discussion about assistance for groups within Cuba, "...the debate on Cuba has to be about ways to subvert the Cuban government."

If Sandy Berman is genuinely interested in seeing those convicted get out of prison before their terms are served, he might consider the following: Rather than writing letters to the president of Cuba, why not address himself to the President of the U.S. and the U.S. Congress to demand the (1) repeal of the Helms-Burton Law; (2) the repeal of the Torricelli Law; (3) an end to the embargo; (3) the end of the travel ban; and the normalization of relations with Cuba. In the meantime, I think it is unrealistic for Sandy Berman to expect the Cuban people or their government to commit suicide for **his** misplaced beliefs.

Ann Sparanese, ALA Councilor-At-Large, and Head of Adult and Young Adult Services, Englewood Public Library, 31 Engle Street, Englewood NJ 07631.

Sanford Berman replies:

The quoted clause from the Cuban Constitution says nothing about denying basic rights to persons "who intend to overthrow the Constitutional order." It does, however, deny civil liberties—like freedom of speech and association—to anyone who disagrees with the stated, dogmatic objective "to construct socialism and communism." In short, beliefs and opinions—including anarchism, liberalism, and democratic socialism—are regarded as anathema, and impermissible.

Many dissidents over the past 40 years—as tellingly documented in the film, *Nobody Listened*—have been exiled, abused, jailed, or executed. This is not a new phenomenon related purely to the Helms-Burton Act. I discussed that law and Cuba's infantile response to it in U*L 129 (p. 22). No one seriously claims that the imprisoned dissenters posed a real threat to Cuban sovereignty and independence. Helms-Burton did not jail them. The Cuban government did (incidentally using "snitches" or infiltrators in the same way as our own, ugly COINTELPRO operation during the 1960s and 1970s).

Yes, U.S. foreign policy is "clearly unjust." And I have publicly said so, condemning the embargo and Helms-Burton, as well as calling on my Congressional representatives to secure the fair and speedy trials or release of the hundreds detained at Guantanamo. My "professional and personal values" mandate opposition to injustice and repression anywhere. Unfortunately, that currently applies to both the United States and Cuba.

Access Denied
(U*L 133, 2004)

In U*L 130 appeared a report on "Cataloging Blues" at Los Angeles Public Library, noting that recorded music is no longer being fully classified. Now the situation has grown infinitely worse. According to the Jan./Feb. 2004 *LG Communicator,* "there is the constant diminishing of the Catalog Department. Since they are 'not a public service agency, we can't fill their vacancies.' Yet if these are not filled, the public has to rely on very general cataloging that is often inconsistent with the variations of our system. It seems that this department is being slowly eliminated by attrition."

In the course of exposing the hypocrisy of Banned Books Week and many libraries' selection practices, Russ Kick (in U*L 130) asked: "How about a display of the very few books on explosives that are still in print after the 1998 federal law threatening publishers with 20 years in jail?" In the meantime, Tony Doyle has addressed the fundamental issue, albeit with an Internet focus, in the Spring 2004 *Journal of Information Ethics.* His "Should web sites for bomb-making be illegal?" examines the arguments for banning or filtering online data concerning homemade explosives, concluding that prohibition isn't worth it: too tough to enforce, likely to damage searchers' privacy rights, and, facilitating prosecutorial witch-hunts. He further observes that there is no suitable evidence of "a causal connection between an uncensored Internet and homespun bombings."

Is keyword searching truly an effective substitute for rigorous, ample, and consistent subject analysis? I resoundingly argued "No!" in U*L 124. That view has since been reinforced by Tina Gross and Arlene Taylor, who made a presentation at ALA's annual conference in Orlando on June 27, 2004, provocatively titled "What Have We Got to Lose? The Effect of Controlled Vocabulary on Keyword Searching Results." Speaking under auspices of the LITA/ALCTS Authority Control in the Online Environment Interest Group, Gross and Taylor shared these study results:

- If subject headings were to be removed from catalog records (or no longer added to them), users performing keyword searches would lose more than one-third of the hits they currently retrieve (35.9 percent on average).
- The loss of hits would be in addition to the loss of other functions and advantages provided by controlled vocabulary in general.
- Without subject headings, a keyword user whose search retrieves an overwhelming

number of hits with a high proportion of "false drops" would have few options in trying to find a smaller, more relevant set of hits.
- And a large proportion of the lost one-third of hits would be likely to be relevant to the user because the lost records would actually have at least one keyword in subject headings, and not just in any random place.

Writing four years ago, in U*L 117, I implored libraries to look "at policies, practices, and attitudes that either keep poor people out altogether or treat them as though they don't deserve equal, first-class service." How widely has that advice, coupled with the 15 mandates of ALA's Policy on Library Service to Poor People, been observed? It's hard to know, short of a proper survey, but several recent press reports hardly inspire much glee or hope. This, for starters, is the summary of an article by Nancy Mitchell in the May 22, 2004, *Rocky Mountain News* ("Group says facilities in poorest areas are open fewer hours"):

- On Friday, an advocacy group for low-income communities released a report indicating that libraries in Denver's poorest areas are open fewer hours than those elsewhere.
- Seven libraries in low-income communities are open, on average, 29.5 hours per week.
- Fifteen libraries in more affluent communities are open, on average, 43.3 hours per week.
- Fewer library hours contribute to learning gaps between low-income and more affluent students, the report contends. Schools in southeast Denver tend to have higher state test scores than those in the other three quadrants of the city.
- Southeast Denver also is home to more libraries — eight — than the other three quadrants, and those libraries are open more hours each week — 364 total.
- The next closest total, in northeast Denver's six libraries, is a total of 214.5 hours open per week.

The library: Denver Public. The advocacy group: Metro Organizations for People (MOP). Mitchell indicated that MOP and the DPL Director expected to shortly discuss the report and what to do about it. In the interim, however, access has surely been denied.

The same holds for Kansas City, Missouri, which lately unveiled a new downtown library. Noted *Kansas City Star* columnist Lewis W. Diuguid ("Doors Open to All; Libraries, As Public Treasures, Should Not Exclude Homeless," March 10, 2004): "The $50 million renovation of the 98-year-old former First National Bank building will turn it into a beautiful library and make it an attractive hub for downtown workers and people throughout the metropolitan area." Then he added:

> But it should be just as open and inviting to homeless people as the old downtown library was. People on the street had always sought shelter, read books and periodicals, used computers and napped at the old Kansas City Public Library until it closed in January for the opening of the new place.

Access Denied

The Main Branch was a midway stop for people walking from shelters east of downtown to the Grace and Holy Trinity Cathedral for a free midday meal. Now the city's neediest people may be "poverty profiled" and kept from the new library. Officials also are proposing a "compassion campus" near shelters to keep homeless people away from downtown's new library and upscale condominiums and loft apartments.

The compassion campus could include a homeless day center and soup kitchen. But people I talked with in January at a free blues concert by King Alex and the Untouchables for the homeless at the Grand Avenue Temple were outraged by plans to limit their freedom.

One homeless man said the irony is people like him would be excluded from the area they've helped rebuild. Homeless people often are picked up as day laborers rehabbing old buildings for new occupants. Here's another thing: The Temple calls its homeless parishioners "sojourners" because they rarely stay in one place.

Reflecting on an annual trek to some 20 libraries in both Missouri and Kansas, where he spent at least 30 minutes in each facility, attired in an old army coat, black knit cap, faded jeans, and a frayed shirt, Diuguid exults that the "people I encountered in the libraries were great." He continues:

> I found on my sojourn this year that the libraries also reflect the character of the communities they serve. Mostly black and Hispanic patrons frequented libraries in the urban core while mostly whites were in libraries in the suburbs. The library in Belton has a Hispanic section to keep up with that community's changing demographics.
>
> But many libraries aren't keeping up. Other branches could use some of the wealth sunk into the new library. There were never enough computers. Libraries help bridge the digital divide between rich and poor.
>
> I also found that the downtown passers-by should be the occupants of a "compassion campus." For yet another year, they treated me badly because of how I was dressed. They need to see everyone regardless of appearance as a human being. What's happening now adds to the misery of the homeless.
>
> "Anybody can become homeless," said Cindy Butler at the Grand Avenue Temple. "Everybody falls down sometimes."
>
> She's right. Everyone needs kindness and warmth, especially at libraries.

The next month, Hearne Christopher, Jr. commented wryly on KCPL's 33 "Customer Behavior Expectations," brochures "handed out by library security at the entrance" and intended to thin "the new library's down-and-out ranks." Said Hearne: "Moses needed only ten. Downtown KC's trendy new library has 33" ("33 Commandments," *Kansas City Star,* April 26, 2004). An unsolicited suggestion to the KCPL honchos: Why not also hand out copies of ALA's Poor People's Policy at the same time?

My U*L 124 column inveighed against an "access-limiting trend in book publishing": the absence of indexes. Among the cited culprits: Michael Moore's *Stupid White Men* (ReganBooks, 2001). Regrettably, Moore's next opus, *Dude, Where's My Country* (Warner Books, 2003), likewise lacks an index, making it inordinately hard to quickly locate information and opinions, for example, on church and state separation, creationism, corporate greed, Kenneth Lay, Enron, Paul O'Neill, the Republican National Committee, Donald Rumsfeld, Coalition of the Willing, Unocal, Halliburton, and WMDs. In retrospect, I realize my rant didn't go far enough. Yes, *no* index qualifies as a major delict. But not far behind come *inadequate* indexes. Let one example illustrate the problem, which should deeply concern librarians and readers alike: Nan Levinson's *Outspoken: free speech stories* (University of California Press, 2003). This tome *does* conclude with a 7-page index that *seems* comprehensive and useful. But it isn't. To begin, there's an entry for "conscientious objectors," but no duplicate entry under (or cross-reference from) the equivalent or variant "COs." In like manner, "culture, popular," "Gulf War," and "prayer: in schools" appear, but no analogs for "popular culture," "Persian Gulf War," and "school prayer." Next, some entries required additional page citations, e.g.,

Clinton, Bill, 132
Democracy, 21–22
Gulf War, 10–11

moral panics, 138, 253
Whitman, Walt, 158

And finally, dozens of mentioned names and topics just don't show at all, among them:

Alyson Books, 177
anarchism, 252
Anderson, Larry, 118
antiporn feminists, 144, 153–55, 246, 249
Church Rock radioactive waste spill, 119
coverups, 29–50
culture wars, 8, 137–41, 156, 159, 208, 216
Damiano, Gerard, 145
dildos, 180–82
Dirty Secrets (film), 34
documentary film censorship, 115–34
Douglas, William, 147
erotic dancing, 323
flock worker's lung, 297
Goodman, Amy, 112
government coverups, 29–50
Graham, Billy, 195, 197
Grenada invasion (1983), 10
homoerotic (word), 131
Hughes, Langston, 184
hydrogen bomb, 10

"information mosaic" theory, 10
insubordination, 229–30
masturbation, 152, 159–60, 162, 258
Navajo Reservation radioactive contamination, 119
Panama invasion (1989), 10
Presley, Elvis, 266
Progressive, 10
Protocols of the Elders of Zion, 197
Rainey, Ma, 184
Satanism, 225–26, 242, 262
School of the Americas, 35
Searching for Everardo (Harbury), 34
sex panics, 143
Sixty Minutes (TV show), 37–39
Smith, Bessie, 184
Sunshine Act, 10
swearing, 225–26
United Nuclear Co., 119
United States Public Health Service, 119
vibrators, 180, 182

The U. of C. Press could, and should, have done better.

Squelched Letters, More Access Denied
(U*L 134, 2005)

City Pages, a Minneapolis "alternative newsweekly," failed to print this "letter to the editor," dated July 21, 1999:

Dear Friends,
Abolishing JEWISH QUESTION and YELLOW PERIL from the Library of Congress subject heading list did not, as a letter-writer assumes (7/21), diminish access to library materials. In fact, JEWISH QUESTION was routinely assigned to works dealing with either government policy toward Jews or Jewish-Gentile relations, topics more precisely denoted by standard, non-"loaded" descriptors like JEWS—GOVERNMENT POLICY and JEWS—RELATIONS WITH GENTILES. Similarly, YELLOW PERIL typically had been applied to material on projected Asian population growth and immigration, subjects easily and non-judgmentally represented by such headings as ASIA—POPULATION—FORECASTS and ASIA—IMMIGRATION AND EMIGRATION (perhaps further subdivided by—MORAL AND ETHICAL ASPECTS or—POLITICAL ASPECTS). Any titles addressing the history or significance of "Yellow Peril" and "Jewish Question" as terms or concepts *should,* of course, be subject cataloged with a glossed heading, e.g., YELLOW PERIL (TERM) or JEWISH QUESTION (CONCEPT). Comparing ANAL FISTING to YELLOW PERIL and JEWISH QUESTION splendidly illustrates the apples-and-oranges fallacy. The "fisting" form simply describes an activity and is not intrinsically pejorative. It's the best, most familiar way to express the subject. The other two headings, by contrast, qualify as inherently biased terms for which there are unbiased and far more accurate substitutes.
This is not an issue of hypocrisy or stark-raving liberalism," or "hypnotic p.c. denial," but rather of accuracy and fairness.

Sent to *Library Journal* on May 21, 2004, this missive was never published:

Dear Colleagues,
John N. Berry ("Don't be muzzled by fears about your job or your career," 5-15-04)" has been lucky. Despite being "controversial," he survived. Even prospered. However, as documented by Stephen Carney in the Fall 2003 *Journal of Information Ethics* ("Democratic communication and the library as workplace," pages 43–59) and by me in U*N*A*B*A*S*H*E*D *Librarian,* no. 125 ("Not in my library!" pages 17–23) and "*Inside Censorship*" ("Workplace repression," sanfordberman.org), many of our colleagues are not so lucky.

Not in *My* Library!

A firm ALA commitment to free speech in the workplace would surely help to unmuzzle otherwise fearful library staff. In 1999, such a formal commitment was proposed as an amendment to the Library Bill of Rights, but was referred by ALA Council to the oblivion of the Ethics Committee. Perhaps now, in 2004, it's time to resurrect that affirmation of free speech not just for writers, artists, and performers, but also for us. So here's a draft "Resolution on Workplace Speech" that hopefully circumvents the qualms concerning changes to LBR:

WHEREAS the American Library Association is firmly committed to fostering human rights and freedom of expression (Policies 53 and 58.4.1); and

WHEREAS candid, robust debate is essential to the making of sound policy; and

WHEREAS library staff do not universally enjoy the right to openly discuss library and professional issues without fear of reprisal;

THEREFORE BE IT RESOLVED that ALA Council amends Policy 54 (Library Personnel Practices) by adding:

54.21 Workplace speech

Libraries should permit and encourage the full and free expression of views by staff on professional and policy matters.

An *LJ* editorial endorsement would be most welcome.

Perhaps needless to add, there hasn't been any "editorial endorsement," either. In the meantime, the resolution was discussed at ALA's 2005 Midwinter Meeting, ultimately being deferred by the ALA Council, which sought "legal advice" before voting on the measure. Apparently, many squeamish administrator-Councilors worried that the new standard might affect **them!**

An 11-30-04 "Feedback" submission to *LJ* similarly went unpublished:

Dear Colleagues,

In about 1960, at the Catholic University of America Library School, our book selection instructor admonished us not to buy anything by or about Paul Robeson because that would be directly "contributing to the international Communist conspiracy." Of course, that was foolish, censorious advice.

Equally foolish and censorious is Karen Favreau's declaration (11-15-04, p. 10) that by "purchasing [Jenna] Jameson's book *[How to make love like a porn star]* librarians actively contribute to the mainstreaming and glorification of pornography." Not wishing to "participate in the legitimization of the adult entertainment industry," she advocates that we "gatekeepers ... can at least try to keep it off library shelves." What about reader interest, if not demand? What about the work's merit? What about making collections more diverse?

I personally find Jenkins and LaHaye's "Left Behind" books divisive, bigoted, and, repulsive. Selecting them almost certainly contributes to a perverse species of Christian fundamentalism. So what? They represent a distinct and influential viewpoint that should be accessible to both believers and critics. They belong in libraries. And so do Robeson and Jameson.

Here's another example to complement the cases of serious undercataloging noted in U*L 132: Franklin Rosemont and Charles Radcliffe's *Dancin' in the streets! Anarchists, IWWs, surrealists, situationists & provos in the 1960s as recorded in the pages of "The Rebel worker" & "Heat wave"* (Chicago: Charles H. Kerr, 2005). The Library of Congress helpfully and accurately assigned subject headings for "Revolutionary literature" and "Anarchism," the latter subdivided by both "United States" and "Great Britain." LC further mandated access points for the series ("The sixties"), for editors Rosemont and Radcliffe, and for the two anthologized publications. Hey, no problem! But what's so starkly missing? Well, for starters, topical descriptors denoting the Industrial Workers of the World (IWWs), surrealists, and situationists. Why not Provos, too? And how about an alternative press tracing for "Charles H. Kerr Publishing Company," as well as title added entries for "Dancing in the streets!" and such permutations as "Anarchists, IWWs, Surrealists, Situationists & Provos in the 1960s"? A subject heading like "The Sixties (20th Century)" would be useful. So would a tracing for "Counterculture," subheaded by "United States" and "Great Britain." Lastly, the volume deserves a note capturing its graphic dimension, possibly: Illustrated with photos, cartoons, and facsimile pages and covers.

Chris Dodge, *Utne* librarian, demonstrates actual, access-denying aspects of Hennepin County Library's decision to demolish its previous, widely-applauded bibliographic database and authority file, replacing both with strictly "standard" LC and OCLC records and forms:

January 21, 2005
Judith Friedrich
Collection and Bibliographic Services
Hennepin County Library
12601 Ridgedale Drive
Minnetonka, MN 55305-1909

Dear Judith, I write today as a colleague, Hennepin County Library catalog user, and former HCL cataloger, trying to answer questions for myself—and for a library intern cataloger at *Utne* magazine.

Once, I told my intern, users of the HCL catalog could search for "Mystery stories" and immediately be presented with links to many "see also" headings—showing that the library collection included, for example, gay mystery stories and lesbian mystery stories, among others ("Culinary mystery stories" comes to mind). These links provided not only more specific access—but hit lists that weren't unmanageably large. Now—as I showed my intern—a search for "Mystery stories" results in "See 'Detective and mystery stories,'" from which one goes—dysfunctionally—to a hit list of nearly 11,000 titles. Not only is it a problem that a step is bypassed showing "see also" references, but there's now, it seems, only one "see also" heading left (to "Noir fiction").

Ah, I said. Let's look up author Michael Nava—a gay author whose first books were published by a gay press, whose characters are typically gay detectives. A look at the MARC record for the oldest of his books held by HCL *(The Little Death)* shows seven headings tagged 695:

695: 0 $a Lawyer-detectives $z California $v Fiction.
695: 0 $a Gay mystery stories.
695: 0 $a Chicano lawyers $z California $z Los Angeles $v Fiction.
695: 0 $a Chicano detectives $z California $z Los Angeles $v Fiction.
695: 0 $a Mystery stories, Chicano.
695: 0 $a Gay detectives $z California $z Los Angeles $v Fiction.
695: 0 $a Gay Chicanos $z California $z Los Angeles $v Fiction.

Not in *My* Library!

My question is: Why aren't these indexed? Why were these access points removed? And do you have a count of how many such headings exist in the HCL bibliographic database?

I'll never forget the day I tried to find a citation for a book I'd cataloged, and couldn't find it because access to a subject heading had been removed. Frankly I was horrified.

Gone now is access to materials on such topics as "New baby in family" and "Moving to a new neighborhood." Gone is access to books assigned such generic headings as "Minnesota poetry"—for poetic works by Minnesota authors—and "Minnesota fiction." Gone is access to works representing countless genres, from "Restaurant cookbooks" to "Ecofiction." My mind boggles.

Hoping for answers,
/s/ Chris Dodge

While bibliocide-by-cataloging most commonly results from imprecise, inadequate, or simply mistaken treatment of a given work, there's another variant stemming from something even more basic: *not* cataloging certain library resources at all. As a case-in-point, consider this 1-19-05 press release from the Library Users Association (P.O. Box 170544, San Francisco, CA 94117-0544):

> Thirteen years after author and former *San Francisco Chronicle* reporter Randy Shilts gave archival materials to San Francisco Public Library (SFPL), the material remains "unprocessed" and "not open for research," and there is no mention of its existence in the Library's online catalog.
>
> At a press conference at the Main Library October 10, 1991, Mayor Art Agnos called the donation an "invaluable collection." Shilts also worked for KQED and authored *And the Band Played On*, *The Mayor of Castro Street: The Life and Times of Harvey Milk,* and *Conduct Unbecoming.*
>
> Additional archives donated at the same time by film maker Rob Epstein, who won two Oscars for *The Times of Harvey Milk* and *Common Threads,* and film maker Peter Adair (*Word Is Out* and *Absolutely Positive*) are in the same "unprocessed, unavailable, and uncataloged" condition. Incomplete cataloging causes a search for Peter Adair's work to omit *Word Is Out* from a list of three of his films, although the film can be found by searching for it in the catalog by title.
>
> At the 1991 press conference, many of the participants spoke of the importance of making the material available to the public. But Library records *show* that the gifts—150 cubic feet of Shilts papers, including research notes and book drafts, 54 cubic feet of Peter Adair papers and videotapes, and 150 cubic feet of Rob Epstein papers—"are not processed and therefore not open for research." For those who know where to look, an uncataloged list of "Unprocessed Collections" containing short, one paragraph, 45-word or less printed descriptions of the gifts is available in the Library's San Francisco History Center. After noting the unavailability of materials, the list says "inquiries regarding access to these materials should be directed to" one of two librarians in the Center, and library sources say that limited access may be available in some cases.
>
> Arthur Lazere, who attended the 1991 press conference and at the time expressed concerns about potential lack of access, said this week, "A collection that's not processed has no value to anyone. The promise of making the materials available to the public has been broken." Lazere was a member of the Gay and Lesbian Historical Society in 1991 and subsequently became a member of the Board of Directors and Treasurer.
>
> More than thirty additional collections are "unprocessed," including papers of Harry Hay, "often called the founder of the modern gay rights movement" (22 cubic feet), and a

list of authors, activists, and organizations that includes former Supervisor Harry Britt, aide to Harvey Milk, Dick Pabich, Jim Foster, Jessea Greenman, writers Thorn McBean, Larry Bush, Daniel Curzon, Paul Mariah, and Jean Swallow, and Atlas Savings & Loan.

Shilts spoke at the 1991 press conference of the value of a place where the material would be "accessible to everyone," and said that, with many people dying of AIDS, it is "important we don't lose our history as well." Bill Walker of the Gay and Lesbian Historical Society said establishment of a Gay and Lesbian Center at a public library was important in "making accessible the diverse histories" to everyone, not just those affiliated with universities at which some gay and lesbian archives had already been established.

"My goal is creating access," said then–City Librarian Ken Dowlin, adding, "The mission of this library is focussed on access."

When SFPL completes processing for an archive, the result is a "finding aid" that should be included in the online catalog, an SFPL librarian explained. For example, the finding aid for the Barbara Grier collection can be found in the online catalog by searching for Grier as subject or author, and the material is listed in the category of "Archives and Manuscripts."

Peter Warfield, Executive Director of Library Users Association, who found the "unprocessed" condition of the materials and reviewed a videotape of the 1991 press conference, said "The material's omission from the online catalog and its inaccessibility are very unfortunate, especially given the promises that were made at the time. It is inexcusable given that the Library's budget has more than tripled from under $20 million per year prior to 1994 to more than $58 million this year, thanks to 1994 Prop. E." Warfield added, "It's a matter of priorities, and the Library should be focusing on basics like making all materials accessible and cataloging them."

Fighting the USA PATRIOT Act, Updates and Additions
(U*L 135, 2005)

On May 16, 2005, Regional Research Associates, the Minnesota Library Association, and the College of St. Catherine's GSILS co-sponsored a morning-long conference at the University of Minnesota's Continuing Education Center in St. Paul. The title: "Libraries and the Patriot Act: Your Loss of Privacy?" The organizer asked me to contribute a short essay to include in the registration packet. This is it (slightly revised and corrected from the edited original):

LIBRARIES AND THE PATRIOT ACT: TOO MUCH TALK, NOT ENOUGH ACTION
Several years of speeches, columns, editorials, panel discussions, books and press releases, and hundreds of municipal, state and county resolutions declare unmistakably that Section 215 of the Patriot Act (if not the entire law) is Bad News. Bad for the First Amendment. Bad for privacy. Bad for libraries and bookstores dedicated to the Freedom to Read, whose users expect their reading and viewing to remain confidential.

National and state library associations have forthrightly condemned the Patriot Act. Minnesota's resolution typically went to the whole Congressional delegation, President Bush and then–Attorney-General Ashcroft. Most associations have mounted conference programs or special seminars. And the American Library Association's Office for Intellectual Freedom and Washington Office have prepared critical materials, issued news releases, and created at least three websites, one titled "Take Action," another permitting persons to sign an online petition in favor of protecting privacy, and a third collating data on the Act.

But apart from scattered and often repetitive evidence—largely anecdotal—it really doesn't seem that much has happened at the absolutely crucial level of specific libraries and library systems to inform the public (and staff) of the Act's privacy and free speech implications, to reexamine record retention policies in order to best circumvent or frustrate government snooping, and to actively oppose the Act, or at least agitate for the repeal or amendment of Section 215. The most significant impact—and action—are local.

What COULD be done?

INFORM: Stock and display Nat Hentoff's *War on the Bill of Rights and the Gathering Resistance* (2003) and Herbert Foerstel's *Refuge of a Scoundrel: The Patriot Act in Libraries* (2004).

Submit op-eds or letters-to-the editor of community newspapers explaining the Act's threat to privacy and free libraries and suggesting what concerned citizens can do about it. Post similar information on the library home page and make available explanatory fliers and brochures, like the three-fold "What You Should Know About the USA PATRIOT Act" (attached) produced by the Colorado Association of Libraries (http://www.cal-webs.org/if_patriot.html) filling in the empty panel with contact information for the American Library Association (http://www.ala.org/), Minnesota Library Association (http://www.mnlibraryassociation.org/), American Civil Liberties Union–Minnesota (http://wwwaclu-mn.org/), Minnesota Bill of Rights Defense Committee (http://www.mnbillofrights.org/) and other groups opposing the Act. Mount "Warning" signs in the library itself (e.g., the "Big Brother" color poster available from Northland Poster Collective (http://www.northlandposter.com/) and the downloadable messages created by Vermont Librarian Jessamyn West (http://www.librarian.net/technicality.html).

RESIST: Reconsider what user records are currently kept, and for how long, with the objective of shredding or deleting such records (like computer signup sheets and borrowing data) as quickly as possible to render them unavailable to snoops.

ACTIVATE: Get library management, unions, Friends groups, and boards to actively support the sunsetting of Section 215 in December 2005, or — should that fail — to endorse pending legislation, like the Freedom to Read Protection Act (H.R. 1157) and Safety and Freedom Enhancement Act (S. 737), that seek to amend Section 215, communicating such endorsements to local members of Congress, Senators, President Bush, Attorney General Gonzalez, and the neighborhood press.

In "Not in My Library!" (U*L 125), I listed several known cases of library staff who experienced workplace repression, being disciplined or rebuked for speaking out on professional issues. James Chaffee, in a 3-22-05 letter to the San Francisco Board of Supervisors, cites two more derived from recent SFPL history:

> One librarian who was a history specialist in the main library was given a punitive reassignment for going to a Library Commission meeting to speak about a problem in the Main. The Librarian's Guild put in a grievance and she got her job back three years later. Another librarian circulated a petition to communicate issues about planning for the New Main. The library administration approached him with charges of sexual harassment. He looked at the administrator rather quizzically and said, "You do know I'm gay." You know the rest. Three days after that he was fired for child molestation. The Librarian's Guild supported him and five years later an arbitrator threw the charges out as unsubstantiated and gave him his job back. He still works in the library and I suspect that the administration is happy to have him around as a warning to others.

The ALA Conference presentation by Tina Gross and Arlene G. Taylor, reported in U*L 133 (p. 17–18), has since morphed into a full-length study, replete with ample notes and tables: "What Have We Got to Lose? The Effect of Controlled Vocabulary on Keyword Searching Results," *College & Research Libraries* v. 66, no. 3 (May 2005), p. 212–30. A primary conclusion: "More than one-third of records retrieved by successful keyword searches would be lost if subject headings were not present, and many individual cases exist in which 80, 90, and even 100 percent of the retrieved records would not be retrieved in the absence of subject headings."

In a "squelched letter" (U*L 134, p. 25), I declared that Jenna Jameson's *How to Make Love Like a Porn Star: A Cautionary Tale* (ReganBooks, 2004) should not be excluded from library collections because of content or the possibility that it might legitimate the "adult entertainment industry." That argument still stands. However, Jenna's memoir also demands a few more observations:

Not in *My* Library!

- The LC cataloging sucks. "Motion picture actors and actresses—United States—Biography" and "Erotic films" just don't cut it as subject access points. More accurate and specific would be: "Erotic film actors and actresses—Personal narratives" and "Erotic film industry." Two more candidates: "Women's autobiographies" (a onetime Hennepin County Library form) and "Striptease dancers—Personal narratives." Further, the tome deserves at least two composed notes:
Includes interviews and facsimile diary entries.
Heavily illustrated with cartoons and photos, some unpaged and in color.
- Notably missing: both a bibliography and filmography.
- Also absent: an index that would have permitted direct reference to a host of names and topics (e.g., Chasey Lain, film contracts, antibiotic allergies, Wicked Pictures, Free Speech Coalition, penis size, Ray Liotta, anal sex, *Penthouse, Hustler,* Lyle Danger, Steve Orenstein, Rodney Hopkins, Randy West, "Air Tight" bonus, Nikki Tyler).
- "UNCUT! UNCENSORED!" appears prominently on the front jacket. But inside a red or black X deliberately—and censoriously—sanitizes many photographs.

UCLA Cross-Refs, AACR3, Library Openness
(U*L 136, 2005)

I've often argued that name and subject headings be constructed in their most familiar, likely-to-be-sought-after form, in part because many library catalogs don't contain cross-references (for example, "NAFTA. *see* CANADA. TREATIES, ETC. 1992. OCT. 7"). Here's further confirmation, as reported in the June 2004 *Africana Libraries Newsletter* under the caption, "Searching subject headings in OPACs" (p. 4):

> UCLA non-catalogers are upset with a new system that will not allow keyword searches of subject headings. The current absence of cross-references in their OPAC makes it critical that the most common form be used in headings.

On February 1, 2005, I sent this letter to the ALA/SRRT Liaison to CC:DA (Committee on Cataloging: Description and Access):

Dear Cynthia M. Whitacre,
    Heartfelt thanks for your 1-21-05 invitation to comment on the draft AACR3.
    Together with colleagues like Joan Marshall, Marv Scilken, and Mitch Freedman, I agitated years ago for AACR2 to be at once user-friendly (i.e., readily comprehensible) and likely to promote maximum access to library resources. In short, the aim was to produce catalog records that ordinary people could easily understand and that would significantly aid users in deciding whether to actually examine a given work. We also sought to formulate names—individual and corporate alike—that as either authors or subjects could be painlessly and swiftly identified.
    While admittedly not having scanned the full draft, my guess is that those original goals still have not been met. I believe that a socially responsible approach to descriptive cataloging requires that bibliographic records not be intimidating or confusing, that they contain sufficient data to helpfully clarify the substance and even tone of the cataloged work, and that adequate access points be mandated to facilitate effective searching.
    The several enclosed documents elaborate the elements that a genuinely useful code should embrace. Perhaps AACR3 does, in fact, incorporate some of these elements. Perhaps not. Among them:
- Content-related notes should not only be permitted but encouraged as a means to clarify what's actually in a work and to facilitate keyword searching.
- It should be explicitly recommended, particularly in the interest of supporting diversity, that small, alternative, ethnic, and regional presses or media producers be traced, together with NGOs and public agencies that either produced the material or contributed to it.

Not in *My* Library!

- Unfamiliar and unnecessary information—like spine length, dashes, slashes, equal signs, and brackets—should be eliminated.
- To be understood, abbreviations ought to be spelled out and Latinisms either dropped altogether or converted into comprehensible English. (If the publisher or place of publication is not known, for example, why say anything, much less such Latin abbreviations as "s.l." or "s.n."? Why not simply leave that data-area blank?)
- Revert to collection main-entry under editor or compiler, which enhances effective shelving (e.g., collocating all Isaac Asimov sci-fi anthologies) and doubtless makes more sense (in terms, of editorial responsibility) to most users.
- Reformulate name-making rules that produce such embarrassing and frustrating monstrosities as "Canada. Treaties, etc. 1992 Oct. 7" (instead of "NAFTA," or "North American Free Trade Agreement"), "Declaration of Principles on Interim Self-Government Arrangements, 1993" (for "Oslo Accords, 1993"), and "Jabhah alIslimiyal lil-Inquadh" (rather than "Islamic Salvation Front [Algeria]").
- When including an author statement following a title and no "by" appears in the work itself, the statement should be prefaced with "by" for clarity.
- Honorifics like "Sir," "Lord," and "Lady" should not be included in personal name forms unless there's no other way to distinguish two or more identically-named persons. (The twin motives: to eliminate unnecessary clutter and snobbery.)
- Not only should all prime titles be traced, without exception: so should subtitles and title permutations or variations that might be remembered and sought.

As I recall, "general material designations" were devised at the outset as essentially "early warning indicators": that is, to alert the catalog-user that a given item appeared in a particular format perhaps requiring special equipment or skills to use. If that remains the purpose or objective, why not mandate that GMDs express exactly what the material is in direct, familiar language (e.g., film, video, DVD, compact disc, computer software)? This was the practice at Hennepin County Library for about two decades. And it worked well.

With best wishes to you, CC:DA, and JSC,
/s/ Sanford Berman
P.S. More possible GMDs: art print, slide, photograph, puppet, microfiche, microfilm, poster.

There are many ways that libraries may commit acts of what I've sometimes deemed "'inside' censorship." Kate Barsotti itemizes a few based on her experience at Kansas City's newly-opened downtown building (*Kansas City Star*, 7-22-04):

- Parking is a dollar per 20 minutes, up to $8 a day. One hour is free with library validation. The library would be more attractive to students, researchers and parents if parking were less expensive, perhaps with reduced weekend rates.
- Third-floor study rooms may be reserved for 50 minutes. If the occupants leave during that interval, the door locks behind them. They must locate an attendant to be readmitted into the room.
- These rooms could be accessed by pass cards. A library patron would put down a refundable deposit to replace the card if it was lost or the room was vandalized in some way. I would be able to reserve the room for a longer period of time, and I could leave to do some research, too.
- The DVD cases used to be on easy-to-scan open shelves, increasing the likelihood of finding a title of interest. Browsing is no longer possible as the DVDs are now housed in a secure location—the former bank's vault.

- The new library has numerous security guards. No doubt, library patrons can be a nuisance, even destructive. They should be dealt with accordingly. The guards' presence, however, made the atmosphere tense. They watched me as I browsed the shelves.

I wondered if obvious security were a new trend in library management or if downtown patrons had been singled out as untrustworthy. Will all the branches have so many guards? I did not appreciate their scrutiny. I left the library early that day.

In an address called "Libraries as Acts of Civic Renewal" at the Kansas City Club in 2002, Vartan Gregorian said:

> The Kansas City library, after all, is the most natural, capable and democratic institution for centering and connecting these diverse communities through the free and open provision of information, entertainment, culture and knowledge.

Storing materials out of sight and creating restrictive policies is the antithesis of what a library is about—openness, curiosity and the exchange of ideas. We need a better balance between protecting resources and providing access to them.

Cataloging Zines and Widgets
(U*L 137, 2005)

I made these remarks at a panel on October 16, 2005, during the Second Annual Madison (WI) Zine Fest:

Although I'm expected to talk about cataloging zines, the Terrible Truth is that I never cataloged a zine. So it's with some chutzpah that I approach the topic. However, in self-defense: I have either myself cataloged or supervised the cataloging of library materials *about* zines.

Let's address three issues or possibilities:

1. How did ZINES finally get established as a bona fide Library of Congress subject heading? And how can it be used in library catalogs to identify zines themselves and material about them?

2. Would it be useful—for catalog users and librarians—to be able to reveal, through the assignment of specific sub-genre headings, particular categories or kinds of zines?

3. Why not make ZINES available as a subheading, like—PERIODICALS? Thus, instead of assigning BOOKS AND READING—PERIODICALS to Jenna Freedman's annual *Lower East Side Winter Solstice Librarian Shout Out*, it would get BOOKS AND READING—ZINES.

First: Once upon a time (well, actually in early 1993, or 12 years ago), Hennepin County Library in Minnesota established a new subject heading for ZINES, announced it—together with a scope note and cross-references—in *HCL Cataloging Bulletin*, no.123, and formally recommended to the Library of Congress that they do likewise. We first assigned the ZINES rubric to Gunderloy and Janice's *World of Zines: A Guide to the Independent Magazine Revolution*, a 1992 title. That assignment was made with a subhead for—HISTORY AND CRITICISM.

Until that time, the closest available LC form was FANZINES, which of course could legitimately apply to pop culture and sci-fi fan magazines, but no longer truly categorized or denoted what in our public note we described as

"Underground," counterculture magazines that typically are printed, cheap, often given away, and rarely profitable, self-published as "voices of individuality and dissent" by people committed to self-expression.

Cataloging Zines and Widgets

We retained FANZINES as a subcategory, making a "see also" reference to it *from* ZINES. Subsequently, the *Bulletin* printed many further usage-examples and definitions for "zines," always sharing them with LC in the ever-optimistic hope that they, too, would enlarge access to the growing zine phenomenon by recognizing it with a discrete subject heading.

I left Hennepin County Library in 1999. Perhaps a year ago, I renewed the campaign to create a ZINES heading by directly sending articles, fliers, and brochures, as well as bibliographic citations, to the Chief of LC's Cataloging Policy and Support Office. All these forwarded items clearly demonstrated the reality, vitality, and uniqueness of zine publishing. (Incidentally, HCL had also innovated a descriptor for ZINE PUBLISHING in 1993.) As of about March this year, the response — to me, at least — had been decidedly tepid. Certainly not exuberant or welcoming. And then, by the end of June — maybe due to divine intervention or more likely additional requests and pestering from people like Andrea Grimes at San Francisco Public's zine collection and Steve Fesenmaier at the West Virginia Library Commission — LC did it, finally establishing a ZINES heading. They have not yet, however, also innovated headings for ZINE DISTRIBUTORS or ZINE LIBRARIES, nor have they mandated a "see also" from SELF-PUBLISHING to the new ZINES — PUBLISHING. They *have*, unfortunately, introduced a potentially "blind" see-also reference *from* ZINES *to* UNDERGROUND PERIODICALS (which itself deserves replacing by the more commonly-employed and inclusive ALTERNATIVE PRESS).

Okay. Now that we belatedly have the heading, what's to be done with it? I suggest two things, following HCL practice:
- Assign ZINES alone as a genre heading only to actual zines in the collection. Thus, a ZINES search will retrieve all zine holdings in presumably an alphabetical, main-entry order.
- Assign ZINES to material dealing *with* the genre only with subheads: for example: ZINES — BIBLIOGRAPHY, ZINES — HISTORY AND CRITICISM, ZINES — POLITICAL ASPECTS, or ZINES — REVIEWS.

Second: Given the proliferation of zines, it might enhance searching and produce fewer indigestibly long sequences if a series of sub-category headings were developed and then assigned, when appropriate, instead of the simple ZINES rubric. (Naturally, these forms would enjoy a *see also* reference from the broader, umbrella term, ZINES.) My sense is that many zine sub-genres have emerged — and so should be identified and made retrievable — just as we already do with the larger concept or genre, PERIODICALS (for instance, GAY PERIODICALS, POLITICAL PERIODICALS, and RELIGIOUS PERIODICALS). Laura Griffin, way back in 1993, already observed such categories as "literary zines, sports zines, computer zines, and science fiction zines." In the meantime, I've noticed or heard references to girl (or grrrl) zines, queer zines, graffiti zines, Goth zines, perzines, travel zines, music zines, Third Wave feminist zines, food zines, and sex zines. My hope is that somewhere — perhaps at Ohio State or Salt Lake City Public or Minneapolis Community and Technical College — someone is confecting a mini-thesaurus of zine categories that might be proposed to L.C, but in any event could be employed in-house by sizeable zine collections to permit more specific and helpful access to the zine cosmos. (Parenthetically, Mike Diana's infamous and ultimately censored *Boiled Angel* might have merited a heading like COMIC ZINES or MINI-COMICS. LC now recognizes two sub-genres: E-ZINES and FANZINES. And HCL in the late '90s innovated a rubric for QUEER ZINES.)

Third: Understanding that zines, like any other periodicals, should be assigned relevant topical headings, why not subdivide those topical headings by—ZINES itself rather than by—PERIODICALS? The result, for instance, would be that Jenna's product would appear under BOOKS AND READING — ZINES and LIBRARIANS — ZINES, instead of being subsumed (and possibly less retrievable) within the larger standard categories: BOOKS AND READING—PERIODICALS and LIBRARIANS—PERIODICALS. (Again, *see also* refs should be made from the "Periodicals" form to the "Zines" sub-category.)

As exemplified by the 12-year (or longer) delay in establishing a ZINES heading, I've repeatedly lamented LC's failure to create needed subject descriptors and also Dewey numbers in a timely, responsive, and even proactive fashion. Invariably, the question arises in talks and conversations: Why? How come the laggardliness? Surely, some of the several plausible reasons include underfunding, insufficient staff, and unending backlogs. But there's another reason, too: Attitudes or management priorities, which currently seem to regard digitization as a panacea for space problems, preservation, and searching. (An older and probably continuing mindset is basically conservative and bureaucratic, hesitant to innovate until somehow shamed or otherwise pressured to do so.) These are not merely the speculations of a jaundiced and frustrated outsider. Lately, when a high-ranking member of the LC cataloging establishment was asked how LC creates new subject headings and whether individual catalogers propose them, she replied:

> Yes, catalogers are responsible for setting up new subject headings when needed for a work they're cataloging. However, our catalogers are under a lot of pressure to produce widgets. Since they don't get any credit for setting up new subject headings or classification numbers, this work takes a definite back seat to cranking out cataloging.

For more on "the value and future of LC cataloging practices," see these three statements assembled by LC's Professional Guild, AFSCME Local 2910, at its website http://www.guild2910.0rg/future.htm:
- *The future of cataloging,* by Deanna B. Marcum, Associate Librarian of Congress
- *Will Google's keyword searching eliminate the need for LC cataloging and classification?"* by Thomas Mann, Reference Librarian, Main Reading Room, LC
- *Survey of library user studies,* by Mann.

Questions
(U*L 138, 2006)

Andrew Joffe (New York) submitted this letter to the June/July 2005 *Freethought Today* (p. 20):

Last week I looked in at my local library's semiannual used book sale, to show my support and see if I could pick up something interesting

I hit the jackpot! I walked away with a 12-volume set of the works of Col. Robert G. Ingersoll, published in 1900, for $10.00! I had already owned a single volume of his writing, but this was a real find: his lectures, correspondence, debates, dinner speeches, and unpublished fragments. His advocacy of freethought is as fresh and timely today as it was in his day, perhaps more so, His prose is lucid and forceful, his sarcasm gentle and easy, and his passion and indignation burning in its sincerity and intelligence. We need him today.

Question: The buyer got a good deal. But if Joffe's assessment of Ingersoll's significance and relevance is correct, why did the library discard such a valuable collection?

Writing in the July 28, 2005 *Star Tribune* (Minneapolis), columnist Nicholas D. Kristof expressed a heartfelt outrage that not only policymakers, but also the American media, have been shamefully and unhelpfully silent regarding "the first genocide of the 21st century" ("Media Share Blame for Passivity on Darfur," p. A23). He observes, in part:

... If we journalists are to demand a legal privilege to protect our sources, we need to show that we serve the public good — which means covering genocide as seriously as we cover, say, Tom Cruise. In some ways, we've gone downhill: The American news media aren't even covering the Darfur genocide as well as we covered the Armenian genocide in 1915.

... If only Michael Jackson's trial had been held in Darfur. Last month CNN, Fox News, NBC, MSNBC, ABC and CBS collectively ran 55 times as many stories about Michael Jackson as they ran about genocide in Darfur.

The BBC has shown that outstanding television coverage of Darfur is possible. And, incredibly, mtvU (the MTV channel aimed at universities) has covered Darfur more seriously than any network or cable station. When MTV dispatches a crew to cover genocide and NBC doesn't, then we in journalism need to hang our heads.

Question: Have library media — like *Choice, LJ, American Libraries, Booklist, College & Research Libraries, Multicultural Review,* and *Reference & User Services Quar-*

terly—performed any better than the mass-market publications and networks that Kristof excoriates? Have any highlighted Internet, print, and AV resources on the continuing genocide, perhaps including contact data for relevant human rights and student activist groups? Have any individual institutions or consortia produced pathfinders or study guides? I haven't seen such lists or directories. However, I'd be delighted to cite examples in future columns. It's not too late. (See my mailing address below.)

On December 20, 2005, I sent this missive to LC's Cataloging Policy and Support Office (Washington, DC 20540-4035):

> Enclosed is a copy of Wendy McElroy's *Sexual correctness: the gender-feminist attack on women* (McFarland, 1996).
> When originally cataloged, LC assigned three subject headings:
> FEMINISM — UNITED STATES
> FEMINIST THEORY — UNITED STATES
> POLITICAL CORRECTNESS — UNITED STATES
> Since the very first sentence of the "Preface" states that the book "sketches a new ideological paradigm for feminism — individualist feminism," and inasmuch as "Individualist Feminism" is discussed at length on pages 16–18 as well as in "A brief biobibliographical essay" (pages 169–79), handling this work *should* have immediately produced a new rubric, which I now formally recommend:

INDIVIDUALIST FEMINISM

SN	Here are entered materials on the ideology or principle of self-ownership, the conviction that every human being has moral jurisdiction over his or her own body.		Individualism Libertarianism
		UF	Feminism, Individualist Feminism, Libertarian Libertarian feminism
BT	Feminism		

> Additional retrospective assignment-candidates may be gleaned from the bibliographical essay. Because whole chapters deal importantly with topics like abortion, prostitution, pornography, sexual harassment, comparable worth, and affirmative action, these subjects merit discrete analytics. And, of course, a partial contents note would be immensely useful in both revealing the volume's scope and permitting keyword searching.
> P.S. Suggested added-title entry: The gender-feminist attack on women.

Given the LCSH precedent of such phrase-forms as FEMINISM AND ART and FEMINISM AND EDUCATION, these descriptors would fit the pattern, together with affording direct access to relevant material in the McElroy book — plus many other works:
- FEMINISM AND ABORTION
- FEMINISM AND PROSTITUTION
- FEMINISM AND AFFIRMATIVE ACTION
- FEMINISM AND PAY EQUITY
- FEMINISM AND SEXUAL HARASSMENT

Syndetic model:

Questions

Feminism and abortion.		BT	Abortion
UF	Abortion and feminism		Feminism
	Abortion — Feminist views	NT	Pro-choice movement

Question: Why (as of February 1, 2006) has there been no acknowledgment of these suggestions, much less an indication of whether they are being considered or implemented? (The same holds for even earlier recommendations to establish new headings for GI MOVEMENT, SECOND-WAVE FEMINISM, THIRD-WAVE FEMINISM, FEMINIST ZINES, ANARCHA-FEMINISM, ZINE DISTRIBUTORS, ZINE LIBRARIES, SEX TOYS, EROTOPHOBIA, TRANSGENDERED PERSONS, GOD (CHRISTIANITY), QUEER THEORY, CULTURE WARS, BUTCH AND FEMME (LESBIANISM), RECOVERED FACTORY MOVEMENT, SLOW MOVEMENT, and TRANSHUMANISM, as well as replacing ARMENIAN MASSACRE, 1915–1923 with ARMENIAN GENOCIDE, 1915–1923, and BLACK CARIBS with GARIFUNA. If readers have opinions on all or some of these proposals, contact the Cataloging Policy and Support Office, Library of Congress, Washington, D.C. 20540-4305, directly.)

"Genocide" or Merely "Massacres"?—The Politics of Subject Cataloging
(U*L 139, 2006)

My previous column (no. 138, p. 19–20) quoted Nicholas D. Kristof's reference to "the Armenian genocide in 1915." Well, that event, like the ongoing nightmare in Darfur, also has library implications. On September 26, 2005, I sent this letter to the Chief of the Library of Congress Cataloging Policy & Support Office (Washington, DC 20540-4305):

Dear Colleague,

At an EMIERT-sponsored program on resources related to the Armenian Genocide that took place on Saturday, June 25th, during this year's American Library Association Conference in Chicago, I asked whether the present, misleading Library of Congress descriptor, ARMENIAN MASSACRES, 1915–1923, should be converted to the more accurate and scholarly acceptable ARMENIAN GENOCIDE, 1915–1923. The presenter and entire audience emphatically endorsed such a change, especially since "massacres" suggests occasional, limited, and even haphazard actions, failing to adequately denote or express the systematic and deliberate campaign waged by the Turkish regime to exterminate Armenians within the Ottoman Empire.

In April 1990, Hennepin County Library in Minnesota replaced the "massacres" form with a "genocide" rubric, reporting that reform in *HCL Cataloging Bulletin* no. 105, p. 5–6:

Armenian genocide, 1915–1923.**
cn   LC form: ARMENIAN MASSACRES, 1915–1923. Authority: "Bush reaffirms opposition to Armenian bill to visiting Turkish President," *Asbarez*, Jan. 27, 1990., p. 19 ("President George Bush assured Turkish President Turgut Ozal Thursday that he would vigorously oppose the pending Senate resolution to designate April 24 as a day of remembrance for Armenians massacred by Ottoman Turks during the Armenian Genocide, according to an Administration official"). Assignment: Lindy V. Avakian's *Cross and the crescent* (1989).
sf   Armenian Holocaust, 1915–1923
     Armenian massacres, 1915–1923
     Genocide, Armenian, 1915–1923
     Holocaust, Armenian, 1915–1923
xx   Genocide

The HCL treatment was later noted in *The Reference Librarian*, nos. 61/62 (1998), p. 223:
150 Armenian genocide, 1915–1923.

"Genocide" or Merely "Massacres"?—Cataloging Politics

450 Armenian Holocaust, 1915–1923.
450 Armenian massacres, 1915–1923.
450 Genocide, Armenian, 1915–1923.
450 Holocaust, Armenian, 1915–1923.

550 Genocide
681 LC form: ARMENIAN MASSACRES, 1915–1923.

In the meantime, as stated by Gary Bass in the attached 5-3-04 *New Yorker,* both the *Boston Globe* and *New York Times* adopted style guidelines preferring "Armenian Genocide" to "Armenian Massacres."

Please make the substitution as a matter of historical accuracy and fairness.

More than three months passed. No response. So on January 11, 2006, I directed this missive to James H. Billington, Librarian of Congress, with copies to Minnesota's two Senators and my local Congressman:

Dear Colleague,

On September 26, 2005, I formally recommended to the Chief of the Library of Congress Cataloging Policy and Support Office that the LC subject heading, ARMENIAN MASSACRES, 1915–1923, be replaced with ARMENIAN GENOCIDE, 1915–1923. That communication, which cited relevant precedents and scholarly justification, produced no reply. Subsequently, on 10-18-2005, 10-22-05, 10-28-05, 11-7-05, and 11-10-05, I submitted further documentation, from such sources as the U.S. Holocaust Memorial Museum and University of Minnesota Center for Holocaust and Genocide Studies. These, too, elicited no response.

In the meantime, I have heard—albeit indirectly—that this overdue change has been stymied or prevented by the State Department, presumably in order to avoid disturbing or inflaming relations with a NATO ally.

I have two concerns:

1. The failure of the Library of Congress to acknowledge my suggestion and report on its status in a timely fashion.

2. The outrageous interference (or influence), *if true,* by an executive agency in the operation of the Library of *Congress,* in this case possibly damaging the historical accuracy and intellectual integrity of LC's product and undermining both the credibility and autonomy of the institution itself.

I trust you agree that serious communications should be treated with speed and courtesy, and that professional cataloging decisions should be immune to political intervention. The Library of Congress should not be an instrument of foreign or domestic policy.

With best wishes,
Sanford Berman
Former Head Cataloger
Hennepin County Library (Minnesota)
ALA Honorary Member

P.S. In the event there has *not* been any State Dept. tampering, what acceptable reason remains for not making the terminological switch supported by 95 percent of historians and academics (according to the CHGS Director)?

Finally, on February 3, 2006, Deanna B. Marcum, Associate Librarian for Library Services, wrote:

Dear Mr. Berman:

Regarding your suggestion that the Library of Congress change its subject heading "Armenian massacres, 1915–1923" to "Armenian genocide, 1915–1923," you are probably aware there are resolutions on this subject currently pending in both the U.S. Senate and the House of Representatives. It is inappropriate for the Library, as an agency of the Congress, to attempt to anticipate the outcome of the Congressional debate on this subject and to change the heading prematurely. We are carefully following the debate in Congress, and will consider changing our heading should the pending resolutions be adopted. I can reassure you that neither the State Department nor any other executive branch agency has in any way been involved with or "interfered" with the Library in this matter.

A reference has been made from the term "Armenian genocide, 1915–1923" to the established heading, so no library user who looks under that term is denied access to relevant material.

That prompted this reply, which to date (4-6-06) has gone unanswered:

Dear Colleague,

While relieved that "neither the State Department nor any other executive branch agency has in any way been involved with or 'interfered' with the Library" concerning the replacement of the primary subject heading, ARMENIAN MASSACRES, 1915–1923 with ARMENIAN GENOCIDE, 1915–1923, I am nonetheless dismayed that the decision to reform a palpably inaccurate and outdated LCSH descriptor for an historical event should depend on the outcome of pending Congressional resolutions. Forgive my youthful idealism, but I had imagined that determination of subject heading language was a professional and intellectual, not political, process.

Although LC, as I noted in my 1-11-06 letter to James H. Billington, is surely the "Library of *Congress*," since when does that signify that Congress—rather than LC's own subject specialists—should dictate the form of LC subject headings? If executive agency tampering in subject cataloging is unconscionable (and it *is*), so is Congressional tampering. Moreover, the essentially passive approach manifest in your 2-3-06 communication, can—and likely will—result in the perpetuation of an imprecise and unscholarly representation of those 1915–1923 events. (There is, of course, no assurance that Senate or House will *ever* pass those pending resolutions. And I dearly hope that—in any event—Senators and Representatives do not wish to arrogate to themselves the power to dictate the formation of library subject headings. That's the business and responsibility of librarians, not legislators.)

The new "see" reference from "Armenian Genocide" to "Armenian Massacres" does not mitigate the elemental truth that the primary heading is wrong, its correction apparently being held hostage to both passivity and political deference.

Incidentally, background and activist data on Darfur may be found at:
- www.darfurdiaries.orq
- arcsudan@vahoo.com (American Refugee Committee Khartoum)
- huyp@archq.orq (ARC International Headquarters)
- www.ajws.orq (American Jewish World Service)
- http://SaveDarfur.orq
- www.hrw.orq (Human Rights Watch)
- www.amnestv.orq (Amnesty International)

Darfur Revisited, GLBT Access Denied
(U*L 140, 2006)

In an earlier column (no. 138, p. 20) I invited readers and the library press to report what has been done by librarians to highlight the ongoing genocide in Darfur, Sudan. To date (6-23-06) there have been no responses. None. Not even from the major library media. In desperation and disbelief, I sent this draft resolution to eight members of the American Library Association Council, asking them to introduce it at the annual conference in late June:

> WHEREAS over the past three years between 180,000 and 400,000 civilians have been killed in the Darfur region of Sudan, 2,000,000 people have been displaced, 2,000 villages have been burned and their wells poisoned, and women of all ages have been raped by government-supported Janjaweed militias; and
>
> WHEREAS this first genocide of the 21st century could be slowed, if not ended, by an aware and aroused public in the United States and elsewhere; and
>
> WHEREAS the media, including library publications and websites, have—with few exceptions—been derelict in raising awareness and knowledge of this issue; and
>
> WHEREAS it is the oft-proclaimed mission of American libraries to contribute actively to informing and educating citizens on public issues;
>
> THEREFORE BE IT RESOLVED that the American Library Association Council urges all relevant ALA units and the profession-at-large to highlight the Darfur Genocide through programs, displays, resources, guides, and other suitable means.

Whether or not ALA ultimately passed it, the text may serve as a model or template for state and local library associations and unions.

Here are a few more online resources:
- Save Darfur Coalition: http://www.savedarfur.org
- United Nations High Commission for Refugees: http://www.unhcr.org/cgi-bin/texis/vtx/chad
- Yale Law School: http://www.acir.yale.edu/yaleLowensteinSudanReport.pdf
- U.S. State Department's Sudan Country Report on Human Rights Practices: http://www.state.gov/g/drl/rls/hrrpt/2005/61594.htm
- Genocide Intervention Network: http://www.genocideintervention.net

A cataloging program at the May 2006 GLBT Archives, Libraries, Museums, and

Not in *My* Library!

Special Collections (ALMS) Conference, held at the University of Minnesota, underscored the continuing sorry state of access to gay, lesbian, bisexual, and transgender materials. To improve the situation, here's a letter that can — perhaps with additional elaboration and refinement — be sent directly to the Library of Congress by GLBT library and archives boards and staff:

Barbara Tillett, Chief
Cataloging Policy and Support Office
Library of Congress
Washington, DC 20540-4305

Dear Barbara Tillett,

We recognize that simply collecting and preserving materials in GLBT archives and libraries is not sufficient, but rather must be accompanied by user-oriented cataloging that renders these resources accessible to the whole community. Further, we realize that Library of Congress cataloging records and subject headings represent the national standard, importantly influencing the findability of works in local collections.

However, we believe that access to GLBT–related items is presently impeded by the absence of needed descriptors and the presence of some outmoded or biased rubrics. We therefore strongly recommend that the Library of Congress

- establish and retrospectively assign these topical and genre headings:

BUTCH AND FEMME (LESBIANISM)	LESBIAN DRAMA
CULTURE WARS	LESBIAN FICTION
DRAG QUEENS	LESBIAN GRAPHIC NOVELS
EROTOPHOSIA	LESBIAN LOVE STORIES
GAY DRAMA	LESBIAN MYSTERY STORIES
GAY FICTION	LESBIAN POLYAMORY
GAY LOVE STORIES	LESBIAN PULP FICTION
GAY MYSTERY STORIES	LESBIAN SADOMASOCHISM
GAY PULP FICTION	POLYAMORY
GAY SADOMASOCHISM	QUEER ZINES
GENDERQUEERS	REPARATIVE THERAPY (SEXUAL ORIENTATION)
HOMOPHOBIA IN EMPLOYMENT	
HOMOPHOBIA IN THE ARMED FORCES	SEXUAL FREEDOM
INTERSEXUALS	TRANSGENDERED PERSONS
LESBIAN COMIC BOOKS, STRIPS, ETC.	

- replace

HERMAPHRODITISM with INTERSEXUALITY

- cease using GAYS as an umbrella term encompassing both males and females, instead employing the more specific and less confusing GAY MEN and LESBIANS
- expand the scope-note under TWO-SPIRIT PEOPLE to include all GLBT Native Americans

With thanks in advance for your attention to these suggestions,
[Optional complimentary close and your signature]

LC Subject Cataloging (Part 1)
(U*L 143, 2007)

The August 9, 2006 *Library Juice* (http://libraryjuicepress.cotn/blog) featured an extensive "Interview with Barbara Tillett," Chief of the Library of Congress Cataloging Policy and Support Office, conducted by Rory Litwin. The conversation centered on how LC creates and changes subject headings and particularly on the issue of "subject heading reform" and "Sanford Berman's activism."

Since Tillett's remarks seriously mischaracterized my "reform" efforts and sugar-coated LC's own practices, I immediately prepared 5 pages of "random notes" in response. That was on August 12th. Although distributed to *Library Juice,* together with massive documentation, nothing has since appeared [as of January 1, 2007] in Litwin's blog. So here, in the first of two parts, are my "random notes":

- Adding "Culture wars" as a UF (unused form/"see" reference) under CULTURE CONFLICT effectively buries the considerable literature on that topic, which particularly refers to contention in the U.S. over public morality. In a 12-26-04 missive to LC, I wrote: "Hennepin County Library established this form in late 1996, initially applying it to 13 titles in the collection. This is HCL's new-heading report in *Cataloging bulletin* 145:

Culture Wars in HCL form. Assignment: Mark Gerson's *Neoconservative vision: from the Cold War to the culture wars* (1996); Ira Shor's *Culture wars: school and society in the conservative restoration, 1969–1984* (1986); James Davison Hunter's *Culture wars: the struggle to define America* (1991); Gerald Graff's *Beyond the culture wars: how teaching the conflicts can revitalize American education* (1992); Richard Bolton's *Culture wars: documents from the recent controversies in the arts* (1992); Fred Whitehead's *Culture wars: opposing viewpoints* (1994); Russell Jacoby's *Dogmatic wisdom: how the culture wars divert education and distract America* (1994); Tom Sine's *Ceasefire: searching for sanity in America's culture wars* (1995); William J. Bennett's *De-valuing of America: the fight for our culture and our children* (1992), which includes "Culture wars"; Camille Paglia's *Vamps and tramps* (1994), which includes "Culture wars"; Daniel Starer's *Hot topics: everything you wanted to know about the 50 major controversies...* (1995), which includes "Culture wars"; Chip Berlet's *Eyes right: challenging the right-wing backlash* (1995), which includes "Culture wars and freedom of expression."

sf	Cultural wars	Culture conflict
	Wars, Culture	Educational policy
xx	Cultural policy	

This innovation was formally recommended to LC. The original cross-reference structure should be augmented with these additional BTs:

xx	Church and state	Social policy
	Popular culture	United States—Politics and
	Religion and politics	government—1980–

And this is a possible scope note, derived in part from the myriad "Culture wars" entries presently available (even, I suspect, to LC catalogers) on the Web:

pn Here are entered materials on disputes and confrontations in American public policy and culture dating from the early 1980s and typically involving such ideologically- and religiously-based issues as abortion, gun control, censorship, church-state separation (including school prayer, the Pledge of Allegiance, teaching evolution, and faith-based government programs), and homosexuality.

That model scope-note also appeared in a *Library resources & technical services* "Letter to the editor," Jan. 2006, p. 4.

LC Subject Cataloging (Part 2)
(U*L 142, 2007)

- Yes, "Mr. Berman" does occasionally submit "news clippings," strictly to further document term-usage for a recommended heading, not as assignment-candidates. (Occasionally, however, a clipping or journal article explicitly mentions books, periodicals, films, or Websites dealing with the subject, in which case I highlight them for possible application.)
- Finally transforming "Vietnamese Conflict" to "Vietnam War" *in 2006* should be cause for embarrassment, not exultation.
- "Lobbying members of Congress" is something I've rarely done. However, if I hadn't prompted the late Senator Paul Wellstone to ask LC why they hadn't yet created a heading for NATIONAL HEALTH INSURANCE, that rubric wouldn't have entered LCSH. (Nothing else had worked.) Similarly, copying my Minnesota Senators and Congressmen recently when querying Librarian of Congress Billington why ARMENIAN MASSACRES hadn't been converted to ARMENIAN GENOCIDE and how come no one at CPSO would respond to my concern at least produced a reply from Deanna Marcum, Associate Librarian for Library Services (reproduced in *Unabashed librarian,* no. 139, p. 15–18).
- It's too bad that anyone needs to resort to "grandstanding" to prompt obviously desirable changes. I plead "guilty" to the charge. Publicly ridiculing the heading WATER CLOSETS at an ALA program later that day translated into a conversion to TOILETS. And repeatedly displaying a light bulb during talks and asking the audience what that item was termed in their catalogs eventually spawned a discrete rubric for LIGHT BULBS (which had previously been termed "Electric lamps, Incandescent."). Too bad, but that's what it took to do the sensible thing.
- I had recommended replacement or dissolution of JEWISH QUESTION as early as 1971 (*Prejudices and antipathies*, p. 22–26). I (and others) repeated that suggestion for the next many years. Nothing happened. Then, as I reported in *Technical services quarterly,* Fall/Winter 1984, p. 188–189: "Finally, in June 1983, nearly 13 years after that heading had been publicly and thoroughly

denounced, LC agreed to scrap JEWISH QUESTION. Marjorie Greenfield, an irate Jewish-American librarian, persuaded the Anti-Defamation League to intercede. And that did it."
- Introducing "GOD (CHRISTIANITY)" was likewise proposed in *Prejudices* (p. 56–57). And has been often repeated by me in print and public speech. There is no compelling reason for not having established the more accurate and fairer form long ago. (This doesn't involve replacing anything, merely creating a new rubric and assigning it consistently to material that treats with God from a Christian perspective, instead of indigestibly mish-mashing such works with material that deals in general or from a multifaith viewpoint with the idea of God. The longer the wait for the new heading, the greater the bibliographic pollution and irretrievability of desired items.)
- Incidentally, the trouble with the "God"-treatment simply represents a much larger deficiency regarding a host of other religion-related headings (for more examples, see the "Christocentric headings" index entries in the 1993 *Prejudices* reprint).
- "Before we made the change from 'Gypsies' to 'Romanies,' staff members from CPSO ... consulted closely with a renowned expert and advocate in this field." That expert/advocate was doubtless Ian F. Hancock, Linguistics Professor at the University of Texas–Austin and himself an English Romani. Writings and correspondence by Hancock years before had led Hennepin County Library to make the ethnonym-switch. And those Hancock-sources (as well as HCL's treatment-details) had been regularly forwarded to LC. With no positive result.
- No explanation is given for continuing to cling to "Lepers" and "Leprosy," except for a reference to "MeSH" as an authority for such forms. Well, what about the U.S. Public Health Service as a suitable authority? USPHS has favored "Hansen's Disease" and "Hansen's Disease patients" for decades. And they actually *deal* with HD patients and medical personnel. (For more on this terminological dispute, see Fall/Winter 1984 *TSQ*, p. 155–60, and "Hansen's Disease, not Leprosy," *Librarians at liberty,* Dec. 2000, p. 27–28.)
- "Most of our correspondence contains helpful and constructive suggestions." The clear implication: my correspondence is not either helpful or constructive. Yet for 26 years, I duly forwarded to LC copies of HCL's bimonthly *Cataloging bulletin,* replete with full syndetic workups for new & changed headings, assignment-citations, and quoted usage-examples. Lately, in retirement, I have privately recommended dozens of new headings and changes, accompanying each with backup documentation and proposed scope-notes and cross-references. (I'll gladly supply photocopies to anyone. Topics range from EROTOPHOBIA and RECOVERED FACTORY MOVEMENT to MORAL PANICS and GENDERQUEERS. Also available: two installments of "Who did it when?," dating from 1990 and 1992, which compare LC and HCL heading establishment by date and language.)

- One unstated reason for why headings aren't created or corrected in a timely fashion is that catalogers may be discouraged from doing so. This is from my column in *Unabashed librarian,* no. 137, p. 25:

  As exemplified by the 12-year (or longer) delay in establishing a ZINES heading, I've repeatedly lamented LC's failure to create needed subject descriptors and also Dewey numbers in a timely, responsive, and even pro-active fashion. Invariably, the question arises in talks and conversations: Why? How come the laggardliness? Surely, some of the several plausible reasons include underfunding, insufficient staff, and unending backlogs. But there's another reason, too: Attitudes or management priorities, which currently seem to regard digitization as a panacea for space problems, preservation, and searching. (An older and probably continuing mindset is basically conservative and bureaucratic, hesitant to innovate until somehow shamed or otherwise pressured to do so.) These are not merely the speculations of a jaundiced and frustrated outsider. Lately, when a high-ranking member of the LC cataloging establishment was asked how LC creates new subject headings and whether individual catalogers propose them, she replied:

  Yes, catalogers are responsible for setting up new subject headings when needed for a work they're cataloging. However, our catalogers are under a lot of pressure to produce widgets. Since they don't get any credit for setting up new subject headings or classification numbers, this work takes a definite back seat to cranking out cataloging.

LC Subject Cataloging (Postscript), Self-Censorship
(U*L 143, 2007)

Since composing those "random notes" (U*L 142 and 143) in mid–August 2006, I'm extremely pleased to report that LC established MORAL PANICS within 4 or 5 months of my initial suggestion. Ditto for WICCA, recommended in late August. And GOD (CHRISTIANITY) finally entered LCSH, albeit some 35 years after having been first suggested. So there's some hope. However, such rubrics as ANARCHA-FEMINISM, ANARCHO-PRIMITIVISM, ANTI-ARABISM, BUTCH AND FEMME, DRAG QUEENS, GI MOVEMENT, GENDERQUEERS, INTERSEXUALS, FAT STUDIES, RECOVERED FACTORY MOVEMENT, EROTOPHOBIA, SECOND WAVE FEMINISM, SLOW MOVEMENT, and THIRD-WAVE FEMINISM — all proposed between 2003 and 2006 — have yet to be sanctified. Further, necessary corrections — like extending the scope of the new TWO-SPIRIT PEOPLE to include all GLBT Native Americans, replacing ARMENIAN MASSACRES with ARMENIAN GENOCIDE, substituting INTERSEXUALITY for HERMAPHRODITISM, and making TRANSGENDER PEOPLE a primary heading rather than an erroneous see-reference to TRANSSEXUALS — still await attention. Also, while literary works now enjoy much more topical access than they did about 20 years ago, the treatment could be fuller and better. (For instance, John LeCarre's *Mission song* got tracings for INTELLIGENCE OFFICERS — FICTION and WORLD POLITICS — FICTION, but nothing to represent the occupation of the lead character, an interracial Congolese interpreter, nor any thematic access points for Congo, coups d'état, and mineral resources. Similarly missing: a genre heading, perhaps SPY FICTION, ENGLISH.)

The actual postscript goes to David Lesniaski, a Cataloging teacher at the College of St. Catherine in St. Paul, Minnesota. In an unsolicited letter, he wrote:

> I couldn't tell whether Tillett was a witness for the prosecution or the defense. Forty years to come up with "Vietnam war?" Insistence on taking submissions only through their forms and their process (not realizing that making those requirements, along with the others — such as the need for "expert" opinion and the reluctance to establish "ephemeral" terms — effectively torpedoes precisely the sorts of headings LC is most deficient in).
>
> Aside from the problems with actual headings and with the process to submit headings/changes, the interview, along with other evidence, suggested to me that LC is the problem, and until the cataloging community finds a way to create its own list (thesaurus,

etc.) of headings to make up for the ones LC won't do, or does badly, neither we nor our public are going to see any significant positive changes anytime soon. "Cooperative" is hardly the term for the subject heading situation, for cooperation implies some sort of joint give-and-take, and the evidence is overwhelming that LC doesn't think that way. I think of the series authority debacle last spring, or the Calhoun report, commissioned by LC, that (among other things) talked about a business model and the virtue of cutting back on subject and descriptive cataloging in order to get things through faster — these hardly seem like overtures for the betterment of cataloging through cooperation.

I do wish librarians, and catalogers in particular, were less passive, prone to accept authority, and more willing to do what they know is right. While creating/maintaining headings takes some thought, the mechanics are so simple in any decent online system that the old complaint about time just doesn't hold water any longer.

To which I add only a heartfelt AMEN!

In the February 2007 *American libraries,* lesbian cartoonist Alison Bechdel was asked what she thought about her recent graphic novel, *Fun home,* being removed from a Missouri library. She replied that "the issue is not the content of my book but the fact that there are pictures of people having sex. Not just pictures, but comic pictures, which everyone interprets as somehow geared ... to children. And that's true. Kids love funny drawings. So do grownups. But I don't think you can use that as a reason to ban books from libraries." A noble sentiment. However, the longstanding reality is that libraries have consistently and systematically excluded myriad books and films from their collections specifically because of explicit, graphic sexuality. This is the "dirty little secret" never addressed by Banned Books Week and our intellectual freedom cheerleaders. In 1993, Robert P. Holley observed that two of "the most famous X-rated videos," *Behind the green door* and *Deep throat,* "each had two reporting libraries in the OCLC database." He added that "perhaps the best-known X-rated video, *Debbie does Dallas*... is missing from the OCLC database though it has sold an estimated 50,000 copies as the 'most popular sex video.'" As of August 2006, WorldCat showed three libraries holding *Debbie,* all of them academic. As an example of all-too-common hypocrisy, twelve libraries own a 2006 documentary, *Debbie does Dallas uncovered,* "a fascinating peek at the turbulent lives and times surrounding the world's most famous porn film." That group includes eight public libraries, *none* of which own the actual film that the Docurama flick deals with. From the usually-invoked standards of "demand" (or user interest) and production quality, these "classic" erotic movies should qualify for adult collections. So why don't they? It's the selection taboo on visual sex. And if librarians aren't (yet) willing to overcome the taboo, they should at least muster the honesty to admit it.

As of late January 2007, 16 WorldCat libraries reported having acquired the 3-volume, widely-hailed graphic novel, *Lost Girls,* by Alan Moore *(V for Vendetta)* and Melinda Gebble. The work imagines that Dorothy Gale, Wendy Darling, and Alice (Lewis Carroll's creation) meet at an Austrian hotel in 1914, recount their youthful adventures, and engage in a variety of bawdy activities as adults. Only three public libraries figure among the 16. That's not much. Why aren't more institutions buying such a fascinating, inventive, and, yes, hot work? It's the pictures. Maybe selectors are scared of complaints (as in Missouri). Maybe they're erotophobic. Maybe both. Whatever the reasons, it doesn't advance or support "intellectual freedom."

Of course, there's a cataloging dimension to all this. The WorldCat bibliographic record for *Lost Girls*, originally created by the British Museum Library and subsequently modified by Baker & Taylor, Vancouver Public Library, and the University of South Carolina, mandated only one subject heading: EROTIC COMIC BOOKS, STRIPS, ETC. Apparently that was the best access that four institutions could collectively provide. Not impressive. Here's how it might have been done:

> 1. Erotic graphic novels. 2. Darling, Wendy (Fictitious character)—Comic books, strips, etc. 3. Gale, Dorothy (Fictitious character)—Comic books, strips, etc. 4. Alice (Fictitious character: Carroll)—Comic books, strips, etc. 5. Women—Sexuality—Comic books, strips, etc. 6. Girls—Sexuality—Comic books, strips, etc. 7. Hotels—Austria—Comic books, strips, etc. 8. Nineteen fourteen, A.D.—Comic books, strips, etc.

Headings 1 and 3 do not currently appear in the LC subject list, but have been recommended.

Obsessions
(U*L 144, 2007)

These are remarks I made to students and faculty at two library schools: the College of St. Catherine, St. Paul, Minnesota (3-29-07) and UCLA (4-26-07):

I'd like to share some recent obsessions and activities, which just might illustrate the challenges and possibilities of library activism.

About two years ago, I attended an EMIERT-sponsored program during an ALA conference. It dealt with websites and online resources concerning the Armenian Genocide that took place nearly a century ago in Anatolia, during the Ottoman Empire, resulting in the death of up to a million and a half Armenians and a thorough "ethnic cleansing" of that group from Turkey. During the discussion period, I asked whether "Armenian Genocide" wouldn't be preferable and more accurate as a subject heading used in library catalogs than LC's "Armenian Massacres." The presenter and entire audience agreed that the misleading descriptor should be replaced by the more historically correct form. I furnished LC contact data to the speaker, who assured me he'd approach the Library of Congress directly. I don't know if he did or not. But some time afterward, nothing had happened: the "Massacres" heading remained unchanged. So I initiated the correspondence partially reprinted in a recent *Unabashed Librarian* column. Subsequently, I forwarded even more documentation affirming that most scholars and experts, including a number of courageous Turks themselves, unreservedly favored the "Genocide" designation. LC still has not budged. They appear to be waiting for the President or Congress to grant them permission, rather than exercising their own best judgment and intellectual integrity. Of course, it's all about not hurting Turkey's feelings, since the government there — a NATO ally — is in full denial of the genocide. However, subject cataloging should not be about hurting another government's feelings or obeying the palpably political dicta of your own government. It should be about telling the truth and reflecting the consensus of scholarly opinion. This is a sad case of bald political deference in professional practice. And of intellectual cowardice. (Parenthetically, should anyone think that words don't matter: *Frontline* lately reported that 60 Turkish journalists have been prosecuted for "insulting Turkishness," which usually stemmed from talking about the Armenian experience plainly and calling it "genocide." Further, the American ambassador to Armenia last year was dismissed for publicly using the "G" word, a nice irony inasmuch as the same President who fired the diplomat for *not* denying the Armenian Genocide has fiercely rebuked the President of Iran for *denying* the Nazi Holocaust.)

Incidentally, the U.S. Holocaust Memorial Museum in Washington has a website and library catalog. On its website, the language regarding those events in Anatolia is invariably "Armenian Genocide." That terminology appears in documents, curricula, and program announcements. So the staff and historians employ one terminology, the librarians another. This particular disconnect or disparity probably doesn't derive from political considerations. In a way, it's worse: It's because the library uses LCSH and will not depart from it even if it conflicts with the terminology favored by its own scholars and staff. It's another unhappy instance of slavishness, of lack of autonomy, local initiative, and critical thinking. They know better, but they won't do better — because they refuse to deviate from the "national standard" — even when that standard is demonstrably wrong.

Continuing on the admittedly morbid and depressing theme of Holocaust and genocide: Several years ago I *became* aware, as perhaps many of you did, of something terrible and unacceptable happening in Western Sudan. I first heard eyewitness reports on Amy Goodman's radio show and slowly realized that not only was a momentous event unfolding in Darfur, but that it was being severely underreported in mass media. The first genocide of the 21st Century has involved 200,000 to 400,000 deaths, untold rapes, at least 1,200 villages destroyed, wells deliberately poisoned, and 2,000,000 people forced into exile, some migrating to neighboring Chad or the Central African Republic. There is no question that the Sudan government orchestrated the genocide and that Sudanese military forces, using Russian-supplied bombers, participated in the slaughter and displacement.

I've found that most issues and problems have potential library ramifications. And so it struck me that libraries should indeed function as the oft-vaunted "bulwarks of democracy" by highlighting the Darfur Genocide and hopefully raise public consciousness and even foment citizen action. To that end, I submitted a resolution that ALA Council approved last summer, calling upon libraries to spotlight and frame the issue through collection development, displays, programming, and resource guides. Now that might sound like an achievement, like a real source of satisfaction in getting the profession to address a serious matter.

But it's not. Because in the meantime, unless I've missed them, no ALA publication has published resource guides. In fact, none has even reprinted the full resolution. And locally, I three times wrote the directors of the Minneapolis and Hennepin County libraries, asking them to implement the ALA mandate. After the third time, HCL finally announced that my suggestion would be forwarded to "appropriate librarian staff." Minneapolis later said they'd had something on their website last year. That's all. Even though they have brand new auditoriums at their downtown building and a Center for Holocaust & Genocide Studies (to tap for speakers or films) only miles away at the University.

Having become properly fixated on the subject, I next contacted the ALA President, asking her to investigate divesting ALA funds from firms doing business with or in Sudan. I got a brief reply to the effect that ALA had no such investments. I wrote back with details regarding how such investments could be masked. That yielded a formal letter from the ALA investment manager assuring me that no association money was invested, for instance, in Chinese oil companies operating in Sudan.

My fixation also spawned two Darfur-related columns in the *U*N*A*B*A*S*H*E*D Librarian,* one citing a few online resources, another including the draft ALA resolution. I also practically begged readers to tell me about local or other efforts to generate information and interest on Darfur. None did.

Nearly everything has a cataloging dimension. So does Darfur. I discovered that material on the topic was being subject cataloged by LC under SUDAN — HISTORY — DARFUR CONFLICT, 2003 –. LCSH did have a "see"-reference from "Darfur Genocide, 2003 –," but most catalog searchers I believe are far more likely to first seek "Darfur Genocide" itself. (And many libraries, unfortunately, do not input cross-references, so the primary term is important.) Moreover, like the Armenian case, the chosen LC primary form in effect trivializes and misstates what's actually taking place. I recommended to LC that they switch or flip the terms. No answer yet.

Since I'm a member of the *MultiCultural Review* Education Advisory Board, I duly suggested to the editor that *MR* publish annotated resource guides or bibliographic essays on both the Armenian and Darfur experiences. No response yet.

Where I live, in Edina, Minnesota, the community newspaper lately ran a profile on someone who teaches at St. Thomas University and actively works toward ending the Darfur tragedy. I forwarded library-related items and invited her help in lobbying the Library of Congress and convincing our local libraries to promote the issue. I made a similar appeal to Taner Ackam, a Turkish scholar at the University of Minnesota. No responses yet.

It might be worth adding that in this overall area of crimes against humanity, LC has also steadfastly refused to craft a heading like NATIVE AMERICAN HOLOCAUST (1492–1900). Instead, they continue to employ INDIANS, TREATMENT OF. Which is like saying "Jews, Treatment of" rather than "Jewish Holocaust."

Also needed: a cross-reference from "Rwanda Genocide" to the standard form, GENOCIDE — RWANDA.

There's no reason for exultation in any of what I've shared with you. But perhaps it does demonstrate that there are various ways for libraries to address and explore serious issues. And that it often won't happen unless you *make* it happen.

Huh?, Fines and Fees, Self-Censorship (Continued)
(U*L 145, 2007)

A contribution to the July 2007 *Library resources & technical services* concludes with these two paragraphs:

> Complexities and variations of linguistic structures across languages and cultures have a significant effect on name and subject access across languages. Thus, study of linguistic and cultural approaches to developing cross-lingual and cross-cultural knowledge organization systems is critically needed. The major research gaps in current literature concern addressing issues in relation to developing interoperable guidelines for cross-linking of names and developing common conceptual mapping criteria that are interoperable across languages and cultures for cross-lingual subject access.
>
> This underlies the necessity of future studies in morpho-syntactic variation across languages for cross-lingual name access and an examination of lexicalization patterns based on semantic, syntactic, and pragmatic linguistic analysis for cross-lingual subject access. Drawbacks in word segmentation and transliteration schemes dealing with nonroman languages also call for reexamination of transliteration schemes and for the development of a morpho-syntactic parser for automatic word segmentation.

And a paper to be presented at a University of Wisconsin–Milwaukee library conference in May 2008 is titled: "Transgressive deconstructions: feminism and postcolonial trespasses on post-structural methodology."

Do these people *want* to be understood? Or is such language intended solely for members of their respective mystery cults? This is certain: it's not accessible English. And it's more likely to produce headaches than enlightenment.

The first policy objective in ALA's "Library Services for the Poor" is to promote "the removal of all barriers to library and information services, particularly fees and overdue charges." Echoing that mandate, the Nov.-Dec. 2006 *LG Communicator* reports:

> **Fines and fees** were a surprise report given to the [Los Angeles Public Library] Board of Library Commissioners on October 12, with them discussing it and then passing it at the same meeting. The Guild response was unable to be presented at the next meeting, since it

was cancelled, and the meeting after that, since it was cancelled, and the meeting after that, yes, it too was cancelled. So, in between we wrote to our elected officials and asked that they reconsider since so many of the changes will negatively affect fixed income and lower income patrons, including students, and will be very detrimental to maintaining our collections. We are still awaiting responses.

(The Librarians Guild, AFSCME Local 2626, publishes the *LG Communicator* bimonthly at 514 Shatto Place, 3rd Floor, Los Angeles, CA 90020.)

Julian Aiken, in the September 2007 *American Libraries,* argued that "more than half of our public libraries are not conforming to Article V of the Library Bill of Rights" by restricting collection access to minors. That's a major delinquency, dramatically undercutting the profession's continuous breast-thumping about our unwavering devotion to "intellectual freedom." But it's not only Article V being breached in the real world. What about Article II: "Libraries should provide materials and information presenting all points of view on current and historical issues"? As noted in my U*L 143 column, a whole universe of graphically erotic materials has effectively, if informally, been banned from American libraries, despite unquestioned user demand and solid production qualities. Here's even more evidence: only four academic institutions subscribe to *Adult video news,* the leading industry journal and review source. That's right. Four. Including no public libraries. Further, the GLBT Round Table *Newsletter* (v. 19, no. 2) on page 7 announced the findings of an online survey conducted among members of the Leather Archives & Museum regarding their "kinky reading." Respondents were asked about their favorite BDSM books and magazines and whether they could find such items at local libraries. The overall result: "They are not borrowing kinky books from their local libraries." Indeed, "only a few were sure libraries in their communities carried kinky materials." A mere "12 percent of respondents knew they get kinky materials at their public libraries; 8 percent reported a private library carried such materials; 12 percent reported being able to get these items at their college or university libraries." Of the three most favorite kinky fiction titles, just one — Patrick Califia's *Macho Sluts* — was held by a substantial number of libraries, according to WorldCat: 68. However, only five of the 68 were public libraries. John Preston's *I Once Had a Master* and Mason Powell's *Brig* are practically inaccessible, being owned by no more than 9 institutions, most of them academic. This is the score for the three top "specific fetish" nonfiction books:

- Joseph Bean's *Soaked! A Watersports Handbook for Men:* 2 holding libraries, both private.
- Larry Townsend's *Leatherman's Handbook:* 22 owning libraries, 5 public
- Hardy Haberman's *Family Jewels: A Guide to Genital Play and Torment:* 4 libraries, 3 private, 1 academic

Finally, the tally for library-owned "BDSM magazines":

- *Instigator Magazine:* 0
- *Bound & Gagged:* 4, 2 private, 2 academic
- *Drummer:* 9, including 1 public and 2 private

Not in *My* Library!

Until these numbers, as well as the holdings of erotic videos and graphic novels, vastly improve, let's not hear any more smug pronouncements concerning how deeply committed we are to the Library Bill of Rights and everyone's freedom to read.

"Controversial" Cataloging
(U*L 146, 2008)

What have I just read? Christopher Hitchens' *God Is Not Great: How Religion Poisons Everything* (Twelve, 2007). I largely agreed with his arguments and conclusions. Which wouldn't be especially noteworthy except that it directly relates to how the Library of Congress cataloged the work. LC did furnish this somewhat redundant note:

SUMMARY: "A case against religion and a description of the ways in which religion is man-made"—Provided by the publisher.

And mandated solely one access-point, apart from the prime title:

1. Religion—Controversial literature.

It's the subheading that rankles. I didn't find the book controversial. I found it congenial. Indeed, any tome that approached religion positively, favorably, I—and many others—would deem "controversial." So what's going on here? *Library of Congress Authorities* specifies that the subdivision, CONTROVERSIAL LITERATURE, is to be used "under names of individual religious and monastic orders, individual religions, Christian denominations, and uniform titles of sacred works for works that argue against or express opposition to those groups or works." The result of this practice is two-fold: to segregate or ghettoize criticism of religious entities and holy books, and to make it appear—by extension—that pro-religious material is *not* "controversial," but rather normal, mainstream, non-contentious, and acceptable. The remedy, of course, is simply to drop the subhead, CONTROVERSIAL LITERATURE, from the thesaurus, so that apologetic and critical works intermingle under major headings like RELIGION, CHRISTIANITY, ISLAM, and JUDAISM. (Hennepin County Library, in Minnesota, made such a correction at least two decades ago.)

The bib-record for Hitchens' volume could also have been made more useful in other ways. A more detailed (and searchable) note might have been easily crafted:

PARTIAL CONTENTS: A note on health, to which religion can be hazardous.—Arguments from design.—Revelation: the nightmare of the "Old" Testament.—The "New" Testament exceeds the evil of the "Old" one.—The Koran is borrowed from both Jewish and Christian myths.—The tawdriness of the miraculous and the decline of Hell.—Does religion make people behave better?—There is no "Eastern" solution.—An objection anticipated: the last-ditch "case" against secularism.—A finer tradition: the resistance of the rational.

And these further subject headings and added entries would not only more fairly represent the work but also heighten and simplify access to it:

2. God. 3. Miracles. 4. Bible—Criticism and interpretation. 5. Koran—Criticism and interpretation. 6. Secularism. 7. Atheism. 8. Health—Religious aspects. II. Title: How religion poisons everything. III. Title: Religion poisons everything. IV. Title: God is great.

Incidentally, while equipped with a mostly comprehensive and helpful index, these entries are oddly missing:

Darfur, 190
Lord's Resistance Army, 189–90
Rusesabagina, Paul, 192

The LC treatment of the University of Minnesota Press title, *Transgender rights* (2006), qualifies as yet another example of gross under-cataloging, which no amount of data manipulation or cyber-fixing will compensate for.

These are the original note and tracings:

Includes bibliographical references and index.
1. Transsexuals—Civil rights. 2. Transsexuals—Legal status, laws, etc. 3. Sex and law. I. Currah, Paisley, 1964– II. Juang, Richard M. III. Minter, Shannon.

This is how the actual content might have been better disclosed and rendered more accessible:

Notes: Contains material on transgender family law, binary sex categories, employment discrimination, intersex children's rights, transgender communities, transgender marriage, and "The International Bill of Gender Rights."
Subjects: 4. Intersex children—Civil rights. 5. Transgender people—Civil Rights. 6. Transgender people—Legal status, laws, etc.
Added entries: IV. Title: International Bill of Gender Rights.

While it's gratifying to observe that LC has instituted more than two dozen personally-recommended subject headings and changes over the past 4 years—among them, AMERICAN DREAM, ANTI-RACISM, COMMUNITY-SUPPORTED AGRICULTURE, CONFLICT DIAMONDS, GOD (CHRISTIANITY), KRUMPING, MORAL PANICS, MIXED MARTIAL ARTS, PLUTOCRACY, QUEER THEORY, SEX TOYS, SEXUAL FREEDOM, SINGLE PAYER HEALTH CARE, WICCA, TWO-SPIRIT PEOPLE, MOUNTAINTOP REMOVAL MINING, ZINES, INTERSEX PEOPLE, TRANSGENDERISM, INTERSEXUALITY (replacing HERMAPHRODITISM), INTERSEX CHILDREN, TRANSGENDER PEOPLE, DILDOS, and STRAP-ON SEX—these suggestions (as of late November 2007) have not yet been implemented:

*Recommendation +Date
AFRO-BRAZILIANS (replacing
  BLACKS—BRAZIL) 7-22-04
ALTERNATIVE PRESS (replacing
  UNDERGROUND PRESS) 2-1-05

ANAL FISTING 9-27-05
ANARCHO-PRIMITIVISM 6-26-06
ANARCHO-FEMINISM 11-27-05
ANTI-ARABISM 2-25-06
ARMENIAN GENOCIDE, 1915–1923

(replacing ARMENIAN MASSACRES, 1915–1923) 9-26-05
BUTCH AND FEMME (LESBIANISM) 8-24-05
CULTURE WARS (presently a UF under CULTURE CONFLICT) 12-26-04
DRAG QUEENS (presently a UF under FEMALE IMPERSONATORS) 8-24-05
EROTOPHOBIA 11-7-05
EROTIC GRAPHIC NOVELS 2-10-07
FEMINIST ZINES 11-27-05
GI MOVEMENT 12-12-05
GI UNDERGROUND PRESS 12-12-05
GENDERQUEERS 7-20-06
INDIVIDUALIST FEMINISM 12-20-05
INFOSHOPS 7-31-04
GAY PULP FICTION 8-2-06
LESBIAN PULP FICTION 6-21-06
LIVING APART TOGETHER 6-26-06
NATIVE AMERICAN HOLOCAUST (1492–1900) 2-1-05
POLYAMORY (presently a UF under NON-MONOGAMOUS RELATIONSHIPS) 11-4-04
QUEER ZINES 7-20-06
RECOVERED FACTORY MOVEMENT 8-5-05
LESBIAN BIKERS 1-22-07
SECOND-WAVE FEMINISM 11-27-05
SLOW MOVEMENT 7-25-05
SWEATSHOP-FREE PRODUCTS 11-8-02
THIRD-WAVE FEMINISM 11-27-05
TRANSHUMANISM 7-2-04
STUDENT ANTI-SWEATSHOP MOVEMENT 11-02
FAT STUDIES 7-28-06
AFFRILICHIANS/AFRILICHIANS/ BLACK APPALACHIANS (cross-references to AFRICAN AMERICANS–APPALACHIAN REGION) 7-17-07
APSALOOKE INDIANS (replacing CROW INDIANS) 7-2-07
ASSISTED DYING (replacing ASSISTED SUICIDE) 7-29-07
COLLEGE DISORIENTATION GUIDES 6-26-07
CRITICAL LIBRARIANSHIP 5-16-07
DARFUR GENOCIDE, 2003– (replacing SUDAN — HISTORY — DARFUR CONFLICT, 2003–) 3-13-07
FREEGANISM 6-28-07
GSAs in SCHOOLS (cross-reference to GAY-STRAIGHT ALLIANCES IN SCHOOLS) 7-25-07
SEXUAL SLAVERY 3-13-07
BOLLYWOOD FILM MUSIC 8-14-07
BOLLYWOOD FILMS 8-14-07
FEAR OF ISLAM/FEAR OF MUSLIMS/ HATRED OF ISLAM/HATRED OF MUSLIMS/ISLAMIC PHOBIA/ ISLAMPHOBIA (cross-references to ISLAMOPHOBIA) 2-15-07
HOMOPHILY 9-13-07
SOUSVEILLANCE 9-13-07
FOLKSONOMY 9-25-07
THEOFASCISM 10-15-07
ISLAMOFASCISM 10-15-07
WATER SPORTS (SEXUALITY) 11-6-07
EXTRAORDINARY RENDITION 11-9-07
WATERBOARDING 11-13-07
PATIENT DUMPING 11-16-07

Unhappily, even though rightly substituting TWO-SPIRIT PEOPLE for the previous BERDACHES, the new scope-note narrowly limits its assignment to material on Indian men who assume female dress and roles, rather than correctly applying it to *all* GLBT Native Americans.

Not in *My* Library!

Anyone wishing to support, emend, oppose, or expand these recommendations should directly contact the Cataloging Policy & Support Office, Library of Congress, Washington, DC 20540-4305. (Identifying assignment-candidates for specific new headings would be particularly welcome.)

Flawed Indexing, Erotica Selection, Subject Heading Currency, Undercataloging
(U*L 147, 2008)

As yet another sorry example of library publishers failing to provide adequate index access, these are missing entries or omitted pagination relating to merely one chapter in Libraries Unlimited's 2007 *Cross-cultural perspectives on knowledge management*:

Biased classification, 84–5, 89
Biased subject headings, 84–5
Borges, J. L., 84
Butler, T., 88
Classification bias, 84–5, 89
Descartes, R., 83–4
Dewey Decimal System (DDC), 89
Heidegger, M., 87–8
Interoperability, 83

KD. *See* Knowledge discovery
Knowledge discovery, 81–2, 85, 87, 91
Newspeak, 84, 92
Ontology, 82, 84, 87
Orwell, George, 84
Philosophical Language Concept, 83–4
Subject heading bias, 84–5
Suchman, L., 88
Svenonius, Elaine, 82

Such shoddiness does little to strengthen our credibility as expert information stewards.

My columns in U*L 143 and 145 identified erotica as a major area of self-censorship. Librarians who truly want to improve their sex-connected wares may find Tristan Taormino's "Pucker up" series in the *Village voice* at once useful and entertaining. For instance, her 12-4-07 offering included:

> Porn-loving lesbians are in luck: Adult movies by, for, and featuring real dykes are enjoying resurgence, so you can stuff the stockings of the queer women in your life with lots of DVDs this year. The Feminist Porn Award–winning *In Search of the Wild Kingdom* ($34.95, blowfish.com), is a mock-umentary about San Francisco queers. Early to Bed's *Special Delivery* ($29.95, early2bed.com) and Comstock Films' *Ashley & Kisha* ($27.95, comstockfilms.com) both star real-life couples; Belladonna's *Evil Pink 2* features super-hot girl/girl sex ($37.95, smittenkittenonline.com).

For the intellectual perverts and perverted intellectuals on your list, give them some smutty reading/gazing material, like *Stacked Decks: The Art and History of Erotic Playing Cards* ($24.95, blowfish.com); *The Best of Best American Erotica,* edited by Susie Bright ($14); Michael Grecco's *Naked Ambition;* or *LA. Bondage,* by photographer Dave Naz ($39.95).

Another gift for getting off is more porn: It keeps on giving! My recommendations are: *Afrodite Superstar* ($29.95, goodvibes.com), the debut title for Candida Royalle's new line of erotica for couples of color; *Dave Navarro: Broken,* the rock star's directorial porn debut from Tera Patrick's production company ($24.95, gamelink.com); *Not the Bradys XXX* ($25.95, adultdvdempire.com), the sex comedy of the year; *Pipe Dreams* ($35.99, shop-vivid.com), superstar Janine's final movie (barring a comeback, of course); and *Babysitters* ($25.95, adultdvdempire.com), the Digital Playground flick that takes the company's sexy contract stars and manages to breathe new life into an old concept.

Here's a supplement to my last-issue litany of personally-recommended-but-not-yet-created Library of Congress subject headings:

*Recommendation	*Date	*Recommendation	*Date
FEMINIST FAIRY TALES	1-31-08	SHOP STEWARD-DETECTIVES	12-10-07
SEXISM IN PUNK CULTURE	12-23-07	WIDOWER-DETECTIVES	12-10-07
CLOSETED LESBIANS	12-23-07	WORKING CLASS FICTION	12-10-07
BIKE MECHANICS	12-23-07	JANITOR-DETECTIVES	12-10-07
SEX WORKERS	12-23-07	PERENNIALISM (RELIGION)	12-19-07
BEARDED WOMEN	12-22-07	BIOPIRACY	1-7-08
FREAK SHOW PERFORMERS	12-22-07	SHOPDROPPING	1-7-08
SCRAPBOOKING	1-23-08	AFRO-CUBANS (replacing BLACKS — CUBA)	1-23-08
MEDICAL THRILLERS	12-10-07		
MOSS, LENNY (FICTITIOUS CHARACTER)	12-10-07		

In the meantime, LC did establish EXTRAORDINARY RENDITION (although without any syndetic connection to anti-terrorism policy), LESBIAN MOTORCYCLISTS, PATIENT DUMPING, and LIKES AND DISLIKES. Please feel free to join the fun by expressing your own opinions on headings that need to be innovated or changed. Send suggestions and complaints to Cataloging Policy & Support Office, Library of Congress, Washington, DC 20540-4305. Your input can tangibly help to correct the problem succinctly described in *On the record; report of the Library of Congress Working Group on the Future of Bibliographic Control* (January 9 2008), p. 19:

> At present, the process of maintaining LCSH and of creating new or revised headings can be slow to meet the needs of those working with emerging concepts in both published and archival materials.

Lastly, this is a recent effort to expand subject and genre access to fiction, the letter having been sent to LC on 12-10-07, thus far with no result:

Dear Colleagues,
To date, critical care nurse and mystery writer Timothy Sheard has produced three novels: *This won't hurt a bit* (2000), *Some cuts never heal* (2002), and *Race against death* (2006). All three feature Lenny Moss, a hospital custodian, widower, and shop steward in Philadelphia. Apparently, LC assigned no subject headings to the first volume, and only these to the second and third:

Indexing, Erotica Selection, LCSH Currency

Philadelphia, (Pa.)—Fiction
Hospitals—Employees—Fiction

This spartan, superficial treatment severely limits access to Sheard's widely-hailed series, effectively making the works impossible to find under significant genres and topics, as well as the principal character. I therefore recommend that the "Philadelphia" and "Hospitals" tracings be retrospectively applied to *This won't hurt a bit,* and that each of the trio also be assigned these rubrics:

Moss, Lenny (Fictitious character)—Fiction
Medical thrillers
Working class fiction
Widower-detectives—Philadelphia (Pa.)—Fiction
Shop steward-detectives—Philadelphia (Pa.)—Fiction
University hospitals—Philadelphia (Pa.)—Fiction

In addition, to reflect specific content, *Some cuts never heal* deserves

Transplantation of organs, tissues, etc.—Fiction

And *Race against death* should be rendered accessible under

Heat waves (Meteorology)—Philadelphia (Pa.)—Fiction
Medical malpractice—Philadelphia (Pa.)—Fiction
Medical students—Philadelphia (Pa.)—Fiction

Such expanded treatment will entail creating several new subject headings:

MEDICAL THRILLERS
UF Medical mystery stories
    Medical suspense stories
    Thrillers, Medical
BT Mystery stories
    Suspense stories
MOSS, LENNY (FICTITIOUS CHARACTER)
UF Lenny Moss (Fictitious character)
SHOP STEWARD-DETECTIVES
UF Detectives, Shop steward
    Steward-detectives

Union steward-detectives
BT Detectives
    Shop stewards
WIDOWER-DETECTIVES
UF Detectives, Widower
BT Detectives
    Widowers
WORKING CLASS FICTION
UF Fiction, Working class
    Working Class Novels
BT Fiction

The "Working class" form was established and employed over two decades ago at Hennepin County Library (Minnesota).

With heartiest Yuletide greetings.

Darfur Redux, LC Cataloging Rescue, Subject Heading Currency
(U*L 148, 2008)

On April 2d, I sent this query to Michael P. Dowling at the American Library Association's International Relations Office (50 E. Huron St., Chicago, IL 60611):

Dear Colleague,
Please advise what the ALA International Relations Committee and International Relations Office have done — or plan to do — to implement ALA's 2006 "Resolution on the Darfur Genocide."

On May 27th, Dowling replied:

Dear Mr. Berman:
Since the June 2006 ALA "Resolution on the Darfur Genocide," the publishing industry, both print and media, have produced numerous books and videos that libraries have purchased. Many libraries across the country have created resource guides on Darfur, from Hunterdon Central Regional High School http://central.hcrhs.k12.nj.us/imc/darfur to Columbia University http://www.columbia.edu/cu/lweb/indiv/africa/cuvl/darfurbib.html to the Boston Public Library http://maps.bpl.org/teacher_resources/.

In addition to resources, libraries have been putting on live and media programming on Darfur: Pasadena Public Library "Darfur: A Genocide We Can Stop" and San Diego Public Library "All about Darfur." ALA units have provided some programming on Darfur at the ALA Annual Conference in Washington D.C. last year — SRRT's "Darfur: The Library's Responsibility and Our Community's Need" and EMIERT's trip to the Holocaust Museum, which included an exhibition on Darfur.

The Office of Intellectual Freedom links to resources on Darfur and Genocide on its Hot Issues for Young People page: http://www.ala.org/ala/oif/forvoungpeople/hotissues/hotissues.cfm and ACRL links to http://www.crisisgroup.org/home/index.cfm.

In addition, I have forwarded your query to the Africa Subcommittee to see what further activities they may suggest.

I responded on May 30:

Dear Michael Dowling,
While delighted that *some* libraries have done something to highlight the Darfur Genocide, I remain disturbed and disappointed that:

- solely one ALA unit has conducted a conference program on the topic, and apparently none has produced a useful resource guide for the benefit of materials selectors, scholars, and citizens
- one high school, one public library, and one university are cited for creating online mediagraphies, and two public libraries are named as presenting in-house programs—within a national universe of over 100,000 libraries.
- an assertion is made about the "numerous books and videos that libraries have purchased" without any corroborating evidence whatever: which "books and videos"? and how widely held? has anyone performed a WorldCat search to determine which institutions, if any, secured films like *Darfur Diaries, Devil Came on Horseback, Journey to Darfur, Sand and Sorrow, Darfur Now,* and *On Our Watch;* relevant Congressional hearings and such books as *Darfur: Genocide Before Our Eyes* (2005), *Darfur's Sorrow* (2007), *Darfur: African Genocide* (Xavier), *Not on Our Watch* (2007), *Darfur Diaries* (2006), and *Genocide in Darfur* (2006)?
- evidently ALA's own International Relations Committee and IRO have done almost nothing to implement the 2006 resolution. What about surveying your members concerning *their* bibliographic, collection development and programming activities? why not commission a basic resource guide to be made available both online and in hard copy? how about asking the Library of Congress to improve subject access to Darfur Genocide materials by instituting the attached reform I proposed a year ago? and how about offering aid and support to advocacy groups like the Save Darfur Coalition, Genocide Intervention Network, American Jewish World Service, Amnesty International, and Sudan Divestment Task Force?

On April 3rd, I directed this plea to ALA's Executive Board, with copies to the boards of most divisions:

Dear Colleagues,

Beginning years ago with the screwball plan to stop classifying materials at the Library of Congress and instead shelve them by height and continuing through the more recent Calhoun Report, termination of series' authorities, LC Working Group recommendations, and presently underway reorganization involving new acquisitions duties for professional catalogers, it is manifest that core, essential LC cataloging operations—which truly benefit the national and even global library communities—are in the process of being diluted and dismantled.

In his 3-14-08 paper, "'On the Record' but Off the Track," the distinguished reference librarian Thomas Mann carefully and cogently describes and assesses the ongoing assault on LC cataloging practices by the LC management itself, an attack importantly motivated by a romantic, unrealistic devotion to "digitization."

Echoing Mann's recommendations, I urge the American Library Association to regard what's happening at LC as a serious crisis affecting libraries everywhere. Specifically, I suggest that:

- ALA declare that maintenance and improvement of LC's cataloging activities be ranked as a far higher priority than digitization of its collections.
- ALA firmly oppose departmental reorganization and job description revisions that, in Mann's words, "minimize (or even eliminate)" catalogers' "need for subject expertise," as well as burdening them "with acquisitions responsibilities that properly belong to other professionals."
- ALA strongly support the enlargement of LC cataloging staff, together with the funding to permit it, in order to compensate for increasing retirements and to allow such access-enhancing changes as more timely creation of subject headings, more

extensive cross-referencing and bibliographic note-making, and restoration of series control.

Please do not delay on these actions. What's at stake is basic access to and utilization of library resources. Isn't that what we're all about?

With thanks in advance,
Sanford Berman
ALA Honorary Member
Margaret Mann Citation Winner

As of 6-4-08, there had been no acknowledgment or progress report.

Here's a 2d supplement to my inventory of personally-recommended-but-not-yet-created Library of Congress subject headings:

*Recommendation	+Date	*Recommendation	+Date
SLOW MEDICINE	5-7-08	UNREASONABLENESS	2-21-08
FOOD SOVEREIGNTY	5-7-08	SEX WORKERS	4-2-08
BUDDHIST CHRISTIANS	5-7-08	ART ZINES	4-2-08
ATHEIST PARENTING	5-22-08	COMPILATION ZINES	4-2-08
HUMANIST PARENTING	5-22-08	PERZINES	4-2-08
PESTERING	2-21-08	CRITICAL CATALOGING	4-28-08
FOLLOWING RULES	2-21-08	ECO-THRILLERS	2-12-08
DEFERENCE	2-21-08	INDUSTRIAL POLLUTION	2-12-08
FARM BOYS	2-21-08		

Meanwhile, LC *did* establish SCRAPBOOKING, BIOPIRACY, SECOND WAVE FEMINISM, THIRD WAVE FEMINISM, and PUBLIC SEX. To support, critique, or extend any of these suggestions, contact Cataloging Policy & Support Office, Library of Congress, Washington, DC 20540-4305.

One Book, Many Missed Opportunities, or Why Cataloging Matters (When It's Done Right)
(U*L 149, 2008)

This is from the entry for "passing" in Philip H. Herbst's *Color of words: an encyclopedia of ethnic bias in the United States* (Intercultural Press, 1997), page 177:

passing. A denial of one's ancestry in order to be accepted as a member of a dominant group, thus overcoming barriers of discrimination. "We all ordered fish and settled down comfortably to shocking our white friends with tales about how many Negroes there were passing for white all over America" (Langston Hughes, *Laughing to Keep from Crying*, 1952, 6). See also Nella Larsen's novel, *Quicksand and Passing*, 1989.

Passing has occurred throughout history. For example, in extremely anti–Semitic countries, Jews have passed as members of other groups; and in racist societies, light-skinned black people have passed as white people. The expression *to pass* emerged in the United States around the 1920s, after the rapid migration of black people during World War I from the rural South to the North, to cities where their racial ancestry was not known. Because U.S. society defines a person of any degree of known black ancestry as black, passing becomes an escape hatch for those seeking assimilation into white society. Considered by many African Americans as a betrayal of heritage, passing may be less common among black people today, though it is difficult to know.

Two years earlier, the Library of Congress had added to its subject heading list:

150	Passing (Identity)
550	Identity (Psychology)
670	Work cat.: 95040106: Passing and the fictions of identity, 1996
670	Random House.
670	LC database, Oct. 15, 1995.
670	American heritage: **b** v. 46, p. 46–52, Feb.-March 1995.
680	Here are entered works on the practice of identifying oneself as a member of a racial, religious, ethnic, or other group not one's own by concealing one's ancestry or background.

Not in *My* Library!

Bliss Broyard recalls a fruitless and frustrating catalog search in her *One drop: my father's hidden life — a story of race and family secrets* (2007), pages 64–66:

> During the months following my father's death, after I got off from work I would take the subway from Scudder to the Boston Public Library on the nights it was open late. The library was usually bustling: professionals browsed through the career section, high school students giggled behind piles of textbooks, and lonely office workers read magazines before heading home.
>
> In 1990 the card catalog was not yet computerized, and the massive wooden filing cabinet that housed the thousands and thousands of alphabetized index cards itemizing the book collection stood in the center of the main room. When I extended the *P* drawer, it jutted three feet out from the cabinet, and as I hunched over it, searching through the cards for an entry about "passing," I was acutely aware of all the other patrons having to move around me to cross the room. If someone approached to use a neighboring drawer, I would become as nervous as if I were searching for a title on masturbation.
>
> All I could find under the entry for "passing" were books about football and college study guides. I tried looking up "mulatto" (which I learned came from the word "mule") and was directed to "miscegenation," a term that I'd never come across during my schooling. It sounded like something illegal, and, of course, it was. In a book on the subject, I discovered that in many states until the late 1960s, and in Louisiana until 1972, marriage between members of different races was against the law. I wondered briefly if my parents' marriage in New York State in 1960 had been unlawful, making me illegitimate on top of everything else. Then I read on and discovered that it was mostly southern states that outlawed intermarriage.

If not already apparent, the primary theme of Broyard's 2007 opus is "passing," especially as conducted by her critic-intellectual father, Anatole Broyard. Rear-cover blurbs unmistakably identify the major topic:

> Bliss Broyard's account of discovering that she is black, after a childhood of unwittingly "passing" at a tony prep school and a snooty yacht club, is among the most elegant and nuanced examinations of race I've encountered, an exquisite rendering of how color is simultaneously a meaningless abstraction and the all-pervasive marker of identity in America. *One Drop* transcends race, going to the essence of what it means simply to be.
> —Diane McWhorter, Pulitzer Prize-Winning Author of
> *Carry Me Home: Birmingham, Alabama —*
> *The Climactic Battle of the Civil Rights Revolution*

> Anatole Broyard's life becomes in these pages not only a record of how a man buries his blackness and constructs his whiteness, but also a testament to the mercurial and performative nature of race. Bliss Broyard has bravely and eloquently taken her father's legacy of passing and turned it inside out, making whole what was fragmented, making clear all that was hidden. At once a deeply personal memoir and an incisive social history.
> —Danzy Senna, author of *Caucasia*

Here is the LC CIP record:

Library of Congress Cataloging-in-Publication Data
Broyard, Bliss.
    One drop : my fathers hidden life — a story of race and family secrets / Bliss Broyard.—
1st ed.

One Book, Many Missed Opportunities

Includes bibliographical references and index.
  1. Broyard, Bliss—Family.   2. Authors, American—20th century—Biography.   I. Title.

Obviously, Broyard couldn't find anything in the catalog in 1990 under PASSING because LC hadn't yet established that heading. (Needless to say, it should have been innovated much earlier.) The supreme irony, however, is that Broyard wouldn't be able to find her own 2007 memoir under PASSING *now* inasmuch as LC failed to assign it to a work that unquestionably required it. In short, LC had the precisely right rubric in its vocabulary arsenal, but did not apply it, rendering *One drop* unfindable under PASSING (IDENTITY).

So, in addition to the two assigned subject tracings, there should have been

  3. Passing (Identity).

Further, the work might have been made more usefully and completely accessible by adding:

  4. Broyard, Anatole Paul, 1920–1990.
  5. Fathers and daughters—Personal narratives.
  6. Interracial persons—Identity.
  7. Family secrets—Case studies.
  8. African-American critics.
  9. African-American intellectuals.
  10. Racism—United States.
  11. Race awareness—United States.
  12. Women authors—United States—Personal narratives.

Some time ago—presumably for reasons of economy—LC stopped including or closing dates in personal name-forms, except to distinguish between otherwise identical names. That was a foolish, user-unfriendly decision since dates themselves convey potentially important information to readers. And catalogs, like it or not, **do** function in this regard as reference sources. It would be wise to reinstate the full-dating practice, as exemplified by the suggested Anatole Broyard heading. In like vein, "1966–" should be attached to the Bliss Broyard form.

LC's present descriptor, RACIALLY MIXED PEOPLE, does not represent current popular nor scholarly usage. INTERRACIAL PERSONS would be at once more familiar and less awkward.

Two of the standard LC headings noted above merit extra cross-references:

AFRICAN AMERICAN CRITICS
UF   Afro-American critics
       Black critics—United States

AFRICAN AMERICAN INTELLECTUALS
UF   Black intellectuals—United States

Madison Smartt Bell states

> By tracing two centuries' worth of the most subtle intricacies of racism, *One Drop* does a great deal to puncture the whole illusion of race.

Which supports the suggested RACISM—UNITED STATES.

Not in *My* Library!

Finally, only the prime title merited an LC tracing or added entry. But these permuted or variant forms could significantly help searchers locate the volume when they don't quite remember the "proper" title or subtitle:

II. Title: Single drop.
III. Title: My father's hidden life.
IV. Title: Father's hidden life.
V. Title: Story of race and family secrets.
VI. Title: Family secrets and race.
VII. Title: Race and family secrets.

Adage for critical catalogers: No matter who cataloged it first, try to make it better. (You usually can.)

Cats, Cataloging, Fines, and BBW (Banned Books Week)
(U*L 150, 2009)

Inspired by Vicki Myron and Bret Witter' s *Dewey: the small-town library cat who touched the world* (2008), a current bestseller, I suggested to the Library of Congress a new subject heading:

LIBRARY CATS
UF Cats in libraries
      Cats, Library
      Library pet cats
      Pet library cats
BT Cats as pets
      Libraries

Readers who like the idea can support the proposed descriptor by directly contacting LC (Cataloging Policy & Support Office, Library of Congress, Washington, DC 20540-4305). Even more helpful: identify books and films, including fiction and poetry, to which the innovated form can be retrospectively applied.

On June 24, 2008, I recommended that LC create a SOCIALIST FEMINISM rubric, noting that Hennepin County Library in Minnesota had done so in the early 1980s. Not long afterward, they did it, prompting this heartwarming letter from Helen Gilbert, Managing Editor at Red Letter Press (4710 University Way NE, Suite 100, Seattle, WA 98105):

> Thanks for the exciting news that you won over the Library of Congress to your recommendation for a subject category on "Socialist Feminism!" As a socialist feminist publisher, we truly appreciate your efforts to give our message more visibility and validity in the public eye.
>
> We applaud your work to make library institutions reflect the world's continuously changing, ideologically and socially diverse reality.

Another heading-campaign began on 12-11-08 with this missive to LC:

Dear Colleagues,
    I strongly recommend establishing a genre heading for
URBAN FICTION
UF Gangsta lit

Not in *My* Library!

  Street lit
BT African-Americans—Fiction
  Fiction

  The attached *New York times* report, "Urban fiction goes from streets to public libraries," cites numerous authors whose works may be assigned the new form.

  This "fast-growing genre," says the NYT's Anne Barnard, is "written mainly by black authors about black characters" and is "variously known as urban fiction, street lit or gangsta lit." Although gritty and graphic, Barnard reports that "public libraries from Queens, the highest-circulation public library in the country, to York County in central Pennsylvania are embracing urban fiction as an exciting, if sometimes controversial, way to draw new people into reading rooms, spread literacy and reflect and explore the interests and concerns of the public they serve." Barnard mentions Donald Goines and Iceberg Slim as early practitioners of the genre. In 2001, as documented in "What prisoners aren't allowed to read and why" (*Librarians at liberty,* December 2001, p. 1, 4–7), a Midwestern county library worker who serviced the Adult Correctional Facility and Juvenile Detention Center was ordered by a JDC official to no longer make "books authored by Donald Goines available to our residents." She explained that "these books contain graphic and vulgar sexual descriptions." In protest, the library worker argued that the ban "prohibits high-demand titles that encourage reading, and that speak to JDC residents and inner city populations in unique and powerful ways... Many Goines readers at JDC are not otherwise avid readers. This prohibition eliminates a significant source of reading materials for these prisoners," some of whom had not actually been "tried or convicted of anything." That's one library that urban fiction didn't get into.

  According to the 12-19-08 *Star tribune,* Hennepin County Libraries will institute a uniform fine schedule in January 2009 for all its 41 Minneapolis and suburban branches. This means, among other things, that "libraries in Minneapolis ... will start charging five cents a day on all formats of overdue teen and children's items and picture books just as suburban branches do." The Interim Library Director asserts that "streamlining of fees is designed to create fairness, to eliminate confusion, and to encourage customers to return materials on time." That's not, however, the genuine reason for assessing overdue fines. As noted by reporter Tim Harlow, this is: "Overdue fines generated $1.6 million for the library system last year."

  Most medium and large public libraries nationwide have become dependent upon fine revenues. They are fee-junkies. They *want* that money. If "customers" at Hennepin, for instance, really returned "materials on time," HCL would lose almost two million bucks. That's what it's all about. If "fairness" were an authentic concern or objective, no libraries would charge fines, knowing that such levies directly discriminate against low-income users. (Indeed, the American Library Association's Policy 61 specifically urges "the removal of all barriers to library and information services, particularly fees and overdue charges.") For more information and opinion on library fines and classism, and an earlier dispute over HCL's attempt to raise juvenile charges, see "Berman's bag:

Must 'the Poor' Always Be Among Us?," U*L, no. 117 (2000), p. 11–18; "Berman's Bag: 'Not in My Library,'" U*L, no. 125 (2002), p. 17–23; and "Classism in the Stacks: Libraries and Poor People," *Street Spirit*, February 2006, p. 6–7.

Here's another take on the fraud called Banned Books Week, posted 9-30-08 on effinglibrarian's blog:

> Yay, it's Banned Books Week. But not for ugly books. Only pretty, popular books get celebrated this week.
>
> The ALA BBW press kit says, "Banned Books Week 2008 will kick off in Chicago, with a Read-Out! The event will feature popular banned or challenged authors and local Chicago celebrities..."
>
> See? No one cares if unpopular books are banned or challenged or reconsidered or whatever you want to call it. I would love to see the list of books that people have asked libraries to remove that were discarded without argument or protest. The librarian just looked at it and said, "you're right, that's crap and doesn't belong in our library; I don't know what I was thinking when I ordered it. Thanks for pointing it out."
>
> A couple of weeks ago on the TV show *House*, the eponymous doctor was reading what looked like some bad porn novel with a title like *Bondage Women in Prison;* you know the ones with no cover art and filled with typos like vajina and oreola ... like the ones I have on my bookcase over here. What if someone saw that episode and came in to get that book? And it was a real book. And no other library in the country owned it, but it was available from your book vendor? Would you buy a copy to fill the request?
>
> No, you'd make some excuse about books requiring recommendations from a prominent review source even though half the books you buy are prepubs or mass-markets or popular titles with no reviews except on Amazon. You probably wouldn't buy a copy and no one would care.
>
> I bet that happens in libraries every day. No one defends those books. Or reads them out loud at public events. But that's a banned book celebration I'd circle on my calendar.

A nice dissection of BBW hypocrisy. As an even more recent TV allusion: *Desperate Housewives* lately revealed that Bree's son is into a serious relationship with a man who once appeared in a gay porn video. The presumably fictitious vid is clearly shown (well, the packaging, anyway). It's titled *Rear Deployment*. Let's assume that such a film had splendid production values. And that hundreds of library patrons requested it. Like the *House* example, chances are that no public library would buy it or even request it on ILL. Not necessarily because of "crappiness," but rather due to its explicit (and probably unapologetic) sexuality. The problem, in short, is not quality." It's erotophobia.

Postscript: Should anyone wonder how LC handled the *Dewey* book, it got two subject tracings: 1. Dewey (Cat). 2. Cats—Iowa—Spencer—Biography.

More Classism in the Stacks
(U*L 151, 2009)

On 11-12-08, Arin Greenwood posted an article on the Washington *City Paper* website ("D.C. libraries: not a homeless shelter, especially in the West End"). Summarizing a West End Library Friends report, the piece contains such compassionate, progressive nuggets as:

> The West End Library should be open and welcoming to every person who wants to use it. However, the consistent use of the branch as a day center by the downtown homeless population, not unique to the West End, is a major deterrent to other patrons wishing to use the branch. Therefore, the Committee has made and implemented several recommendations that will mitigate the use of the branch by those without a home base. These recommendations rearrange the reading room, brighten the interior and exterior of the building, and suggest programming to attract more of the non-homeless patron.

That's a quote from the report itself. Says the writer: "Here's what the library's friends find so offensive about the homeless library users...: the 'lack of adequate hygiene, 'that library patrons feel unsafe among the homeless, and that 'the reading rooms and tables are often occupied exclusively by homeless people and their possessions.'" According to Greenwood, "the report seeks an end to 'additional homeless programs offered in the library that are unrelated to core library functions.'" In the opinion of the DC Library Renaissance Project director,

> the West End Library followed the report by doing what libraries around the country are doing when faced with this same issue: It put blinds on street-facing windows so that homeless people couldn't sit inside while watching their belongings; it broke up big groups of tables and chairs into smaller conglomerations so that homeless people couldn't congregate en masse as easily; and it allowed users only a little bit of time on the computers at a time.

To be fair, much of the essay is not only critical of the Friends' bigotry and elitism, but also suggests that a new branch head by no means shares those attitudes. Nor do some of the nearly 30 library users who responded to the article. Here's one:

> Libraries are for people. They are for everyone. The so called "Friends" report is totally invalid. They say that they took a survey of West Enders, but the survey was only given to

people who the "Friends" wanted to give it to. I don't think the West End Friends represent the community's interest. They're simply the richest part of the community that's throwing a temper tantrum that people they don't like are alive and in their city... For God's sake, people who don't have a home can't kill a library.

Under the caption, "Question: library fines," *librarian.net* on 8-9-07 ran 39 comments. These are a few, affirming the contention in U*L 150 that overdue charges are at once duplicitous and discriminatory:

4. *Laura* Says:
Several years before I got here my library system lowered all fines to 10 cents a day for everything. While that's better than higher fines, I've always felt that fines unfairly target families with small children. A preschooler might check out a large stack of picture books, while a single adult might get only one or two books. A family with multiple children might mean multiple stacks of picture books. I don't have a solution to this, other than eliminating fines all together, but it bothers me.

5. *Doug Henderson* Says:
Why do you charge fines? I think that libraries that charge fines are double taxing their constituents. I do not believe the overdue rate is significantly greater at libraries that don't charge fines. If you tell your users that you charge fines simply to raise revenue that is fine. If you tell them you are doing it to get folks to return items quicker I think it is questionable.

6. *Jay Datema* Says:
Northern Illinois University Libraries (IL) had no fines—seemed to work for them. Sorry, don't know any of the data details.

7. *Jamie Anderson* Says:
For a big system, sadly fines are a large revenue source. The system I used to work at took in in excess of $100,000 per year. That money went directly to the City, which then reapplied that amount to the library's operating budget for the following year.

When the library introduced email notification of upcoming due dates, there was about a 17 percent drop in fine monies generated. This caused some worry in the City's Finance department.

8. *Dawn* Says:
My new library system does not charge fines, which surprised me at first, but makes a lot of sense now that I am used to it. Patrons can renew books up to five times, but if they don't do it within a certain time period, it turns into a lost book and check out is frozen. It seems to work great. I think that the revenue that comes from fines couldn't possibly pay for the amount of time staff has to spend dealing with them.

10. *Andrew* Says:
My experience is that where there are overdue fines for books, it discourages patrons from coming back to the library, and, in some cases, they just don't return their books if they're going to "have to pay for it anyway." Either way, it's bad.

I remember when I was young, my local library charged fines according to the number of notices they had to send through the mail, to cover processing costs (ie. 50c per notice). I thought that was a fair system.

But in a public library, I have the strong view that the only reason a patron should have to pay for anything is if they've damaged/destroyed a book due to blatant neglect. And no, a chewed kid's book doesn't count—it happens, just like a well-loved paperback will have pages falling out in no time.

22. *Marianne* Says:

In 1991 I did a survey of Vermont public libraries and found that only 37.5 percent charged fines, 18 percent had conscience boxes, and 45 percent did not charge fines at all. The larger the library, the more apt it was to charge something. Some librarians and trustees feel charging fines "promotes responsibility and serves as a "threat." In my view, the possibility of fines just keeps people who need the materials the most from borrowing stuff in the first place. It is an antiquated practice that should be abolished!

25. *Chuck Munson* Says:

There is no reason for libraries to charge fines like they traditionally do. If they need the money, they should go to their funding sources and ask for more funds. Fines discriminate against poor people. Why is a public library in such a hurry to get a book back in three weeks? If nobody wants it and I return it eventually, why bother with the fines? The people running the library may think that $25 in fines isn't much money, but for a poor person or an unemployed person, $25 is a lot of money. If you have a grocery budget of $75–100 a week, how in the world is it fair for a library to levy fines, even if they are capped at $25?

I'm an avid book reader and librarian. I'm also a working class person without much money. I've gotten so tired of public library fines over the years that I just stopped using libraries. I'd buy books, borrow them from friends, or just read stuff on the Internet. If I'm soured on public libraries, how many other people stopped going because of fines?

The DC West End Friends rejected homeless people's services as "unrelated to core library functions." Well, last year the ALA/SRRT Poverty Task Force surveyed American Library Association members regarding their knowledge of — and compliance with — Policy 61 (Library Services to Poor People). As fully reported in the 1-24-09 *Librarian at the kitchen table* blog, many respondents seemed to mirror the Westenders' ignorance concerning professional policy and the ALA's declared commitment to servicing poor people as a "core library function." These are the "action items" distilled by the Task Force from the survey results:

- Add class to article V of the Library Bill of Rights.
- Ask the ALA Office for Intellectual Freedom to partner with the HHPTF and adopt ALA Policy 61 by including it in their Intellectual Freedom Manual.
- Ask the ALA Office for Intellectual Freedom to educate librarians and the general public about the nature and importance of services to the poor as an issue of intellectual freedom in libraries.
- Ask the ALA Public Information Office and the Library Administration & Management Association (LAMA) to advocate for library services for poor people and to include poor people in library decisionmaking.
- Ask ALA to appoint a staff member devoted to increasing awareness of ALA Policy 61 and needs of the poor and working class. Allow this staff member to work with all interested parties without regard to ALA member status since many librarians actively serving poor people cannot afford ALA membership.
- Provide pro-active advocacy columns (implement the @ Your Library Campaign) to *American Libraries* and Office for Literacy and Outreach Services.
- Provide a toolkit similar to the Office for Intellectual Freedom's toolkit for libraries interested in serving the poor.

More Classism in the Stacks

- Ask libraries who serve the poor to post their information and resources to the Library Success "Services for the Poor and Homeless" wiki page.
- Offer ALA distinguished service awards to libraries that successfully serve the poor.
- Seek financial assistance for award winning libraries who serve the poor.

Worthy objectives. Now let's make them real!

Cataloging Stink, Truth in Materials Selection, CEO Pay
(U*L 152, 2009)

On March 18th, I sent this missive to LC's Cataloging Policy & Support Office (Washington, DC 20540-4305):

Dear Colleagues,
This is about James Moody (aka Stink). Well, it's also about Judy, his older sister, both of them being key characters in books by Megan McDonald. I'm frankly pumped up, having just read several chapters from *Stink and the incredible supergalactic jawbreaker* (2006) to my granddaughter's third-grade class at Red Pine Elementary in Eagan, Minnesota.

First, these two protagonists deserve fictional-character headings:

MOODY, JAMES
UF   James Moody
     Stink Moody

MOODY, JUDY
UF   Judy Moody

Which should be assigned to all appropriate titles, of course with a FICTION subhead. (For starters, the jawbreaker title plus *Stink: the incredible shrinking kid* (2005) merit both character rubrics.)

Second, the "shrinking" tome rightly got a BROTHERS AND SISTERS—FICTION tracing, but the jawbreaker work didn't. It should have.

Third, since Stink is notably (and importantly) short, seven, and in second grade, these traits (or conditions) should be represented by such subject tracings as:

SHORT BOYS—FICTION
SEVEN-YEAR-OLD BOYS—FICTION

SECOND-GRADERS—FICTION

Inasmuch as those primary descriptors don't appear yet in LCSH, they require new forms:

SHORT BOYS
UF   Boys, Short
BT   Boys

SECOND-GRADERS
UF   2nd-graders
BT   Elementary school children

SEVEN-YEAR-OLD BOYS
UF   Boys, Seven-year-old
BT   Boys

Fourth, as the LC "Summary" correctly indicates, President James Madison figures significantly in the "shrinking" book and so should get a MADISON, JAMES, 1751–1836—FICTION tracing.

Fifth, to enhance title access, such added entries should be assigned as:

II. Title: Incredible shrinking kid.
III. Title: Shrinking kid.
II. Title: The incredible super-galactic jawbreaker.
III. Title: Super-galactic jawbreaker.

Sixth, the "Stink" stories unmistakably depict a bossy older sister. Which should produce a subject access point like BOSSINESS IN GIRLS—FICTION. This might engender a new form:

BOSSINESS IN GIRLS
UF Bossy girls
BT Girls

Seventh, the "shrinking kid" story extensively involves Newton, a class pet. Two more subject tracings would helpfully and accurately represent that narrative facet: CLASS PETS—FICTION and NEWTS AS PETS—FICTION. In turn, a new form needs to be created:

CLASS PETS.
UF Pets, Class
    Classroom pets
BT Pets

Eighth, and lastly, the "super-galactic" volume demands three additional heading assignments: CONSUMER COMPLAINTS—FICTION, JAWBREAKERS—FICTION, and CHILDREN'S LETTERS. Because the latter two descriptors don't appear yet in LCSH, I suggest establishing:

CHILDREN'S LETTERS.
UF Child letters
    Children's correspondence
    Letters, Children's
BT Children's writings
    Letters

JAWBREAKERS
UF Jaw breakers
BT Candy

Stinkily,
/s/ Sanford Berman
4400 Morningside Road
Edina, MN 55416

In U*L 143, I ranted about "the selection taboo on visual sex," observing that "if librarians aren't (yet) willing to overcome the taboo, they should at least muster the honesty to admit it." Well, at least one library has. According to the Fall 2008 GLBTRT Newsletter, the Nampa (ID) Public Library board approved "a policy which barred ... buying movies rated NC-17 or X." At about the same time, the Bloomington (IL) Public Library removed the DVD, *Shortbus*—an unrated film featuring explicit sex—from its collection. Press reports don't indicate whether Bloomington's selection policy specifically bars graphic erotica. Maybe they should follow Nampa's example, because although the Idaho library's lately-adopted policy is itself manifestly censorious and deplorable, the candor in stating it — admitting it — is actually refreshing and commendable.

Of course, the tempest over sex in the library is hardly something new. Celeste West and Joani Blank discussed it from a sex-positive feminist perspective in 1983 (*Collection building*, v. 5, no. 1, reprinted in *Alternative library literature, 1982/1983*, p. 160–3). Said Joani:

> It seems even "liberated" librarians are afraid of confrontation. They fear that the world is full of Mrs. Grundys who will sweep down on a library, fire everybody for moral turpitude, and cut the funds forever.

And Celeste remarked:

> I'd say that's true; librarians are deathly afraid of the real or imagined censor to whom they ascribe immense power. There is almost a compulsion for libraries to project themselves, much as the school or church, as bastions of public decency ... I think librarians "select out" quality, explicit sex books like yours [published by Down There Press] because they are very puritanical people or else they are cowards. Or, god help us, both.

Perhaps unexpectedly, the furor over excessive CEO pay has library ramifications. Here's what *Nation* columnist Katha Pollitt wrote in the 3-23-09 issue (p. 12):

> I stopped donating to the New York Public Library when it gave its president and CEO Paul LeClerc a several-hundred-thousand-dollar raise so his salary would be $800,000 a year. Writing my modest check to the Friends of the Library made me feel pathetic, like one of the Southern Italian peasants in Carlo Levi's *Christ Stopped at Eboli* who gave Christmas presents to the local landowners instead of the other way around. If the library needed money, why didn't it start by asking LeClerc to give back, say, half a million dollars a year? That would buy an awful lot of books — or help pay for raises for the severely underpaid librarians who actually keep the system going.

Liberated Foreword, Unrequited LC Letters
(U*L 153, 2009)

In mid–2007, publisher Matt Stark invited me to contribute a foreword to Adam Keim's *History of the Quatrefoil Library,* just issued by the Friends of the Bill of Rights Foundation. I complied, with relish, also submitting numerous editing suggestions to correct mistakes and enhance readability. Further, I recommended a somewhat snappier title: "*We're Here. We're Queer. We're Stacked. Check Us Out!*"— *a History of the Quatrefoil Library.* (The quote-marked words represent an actual chant voiced during Gay Pride parades in Minneapolis.) Another unsolicited idea was to include among the appendices a list of most-borrowed or requested books, videos, and periodicals. After initial praise and thanks for the foreword, Stark abruptly announced that he would not run it unless all the cataloging-related passages were deleted. Believing them vital to my argument about how mainstream librarianship has ill-served GLBT people, I refused to drop them. So here, unexpurgated, is my original foreword to Klein's chronicle of one of North America's largest GLBT lending libraries, located in St. Paul (http://www.qlibrary.org):

> The 20-year history of Quatrefoil Library is variously a tale of outstanding vision, determination, inventiveness, generosity, collaboration, and love. It's also a model of grassroots, community-spirited, do-it-yourself achievement. Indeed, the Quatrefoil story could well serve as a handbook, a guide, for undertaking similar ventures elsewhere.
>
> These pages chronicle a stunningly successful effort by an impressive number of persons who devoted much of their time, creativity, energy, and treasure to meet the recreational and information needs of the Twin Cities GLBT population, providing books, videos, periodicals, and other materials, as well as a safe haven, to members of sexual minorities who are otherwise often disparaged and marginalized, sometimes even brutalized. The Quatrefoil project has been a continuing means of celebrating and legitimizing a whole history and culture, and of strengthening and affirming GLBT pride and self-esteem. It has been necessary, in part, because mainstream media and libraries have largely failed to do the job. They have mostly slighted, trivialized, or simply ignored the GLBT experience. Public libraries, for instance, unlike Quatrefoil, stock no lesbian and gay pulp fiction, not much (if any) material on "kinky sex," few queer zines, and almost no graphic erotica of whatever persuasion, clearly betraying the American Library Association's own "Library Bill of Rights," which nobly proclaims that "books and other library resources should be provided

for the interest, information, and enlightenment of all the people of the community the library serves" and that collections should represent "all points of view on current and historical issues." Further, academic and public libraries alike have long limited, or tainted access to GLBT materials and themes by employing biased subject headings and cross-references, failing to create descriptors that promptly and fairly reflect GLBT topics, and routinely undercataloging GLBT items. It was only in 2007 that the Library of Congress finally recognized TWO-SPIRIT PEOPLE, but even so failed to extend its application to all GLBT Native Americans, not merely the men previously termed "Berdaches." Likewise INTERSEXUALITY tardily replaced HERMAPHRODITISM only last year, while TRANSGENDERISM and TRANSGENDER PEOPLE (previously see-references to TRANSSEXUALITY and TRANSSEXUALS) similarly became primary rubrics very recently. And still unrecognized as useable, valid headings—meaning that no one can make an effective subject search for these topics in most catalogs—BUTCH AND FEMME, DRAG QUEENS, EROTOPHOBIA, WATER SPORTS (SEXUALITY), GENDERQUEERS, GAY PULP FICTION, LESBIAN PULP FICTION, TRANSPHOBIA, and CULTURE WARS.

No wonder, then, that GLBT people have needed to do it themselves, to meet their own intellectual and cultural needs through responsive, sensitive institutions like Quatrefoil Library.

These missives, all directed to the Cataloging Policy & Support Office, Library of Congress (Washington, DC 20540-4305), have thus far elicited no action or response:

April 28, 2008

Dear Colleagues,

With the imminent publication of K. R. Roberto's *Radical Cataloging* (McFarland), a new subject heading is required:

CRITICAL CATALOGING
SN   Here are entered materials on cataloging principles and practices that emphasize fairness, comprehensibility, and maximum access, as well as timeliness and user-responsiveness.
UF   Alternative cataloging
     Radical cataloging
     Socially responsible cataloging
     User-friendly cataloging
BT   Cataloging
     Critical librarianship [proposed 5-16-07]

The innovated form may also be retrospectively applied to several titles cited in the attached "Cataloging Criticism and Alternatives: A Source List," works by Hope Olson, and my *Cataloging Special Materials: Critiques and Innovations* (1986), *Subject Cataloging: Critiques and Innovations* (1984), and *Worth Noting* (1988).

May 22, 2009

Dear Colleagues,

Not long ago I recommended establishing subject headings for ATHEIST PARENTING and HUMANIST PARENTING. Now I suggest also creating

PUNK PARENTING
UF   Parenting, Punk
BT   Parenting
     Punk culture

Assignment-candidate: Jessica Mills' *My mother wears combat boots a parenting guide for the rest of us* (2007).

Liberated Foreword, Unrequited LC Letters

June 15, 2009

Dear Colleagues,

At present, MANIFEST DESTINY (UNITED STATES) appears in the Library of Congress subject heading list as merely a "see"-reference (UF/450) *to* MESSIANISM, POLITICAL—UNITED STATES. This effectively buries the concept, which clearly deserves its own status as a primary descriptor. So I now recommend deleting the 450 and establishing a new form:

MANIFEST DESTINY
SN Here are entered materials on a 19th century doctrine that the United States had the duty and right to expand its territory and influence throughout North America and beyond.
BT American exceptionalism [proposed 6-9-97]
    Imperialism, American [Hennepin County Library form, incorporating LC's "United States—Territorial expansion"]
    Messianism, Political—United States
    United States—Colonies [proposed 1971 to replace "United States—Insular possessions" and "United States—Territories and possessions"; also HCL form]

Authority: *Concise Columbia encyclopedia* (1983), p. 513; *American Heritage dictionary of the English language* (1992), p. 1093; Philip H. Herbst, *Color of words: an encyclopaedic dictionary of ethnic bias in the United States* (1997), p. 141.

June 9, 2009

Dear Colleagues,

Based on the attached documentation, including abundant citations for assignment-candidates, I suggest innovating a subject heading for

LITERARY DARWINISM
SN Here are entered materials on a branch of literary criticism that studies literature in the context of evolution through natural selection, specifically gene-culture evolution.
UF Darwinian literary criticism
    Darwinism, Literary
BT Evolutionary psychology
    Literature—History and criticism
    Natural selection

/s/ Sanford Berman

Nation Gets It Wrong, More Unrequited LC Letters, LCSH Currency
(U*L 154, 2010)

Even the "good guys" sometimes fabricate history to make a point.

On 9-16-09 I sent this missive, never published, to *The Nation* (33 Irving Place, NYC 10003):

Dear Friends,

An editorial, "The Ambush of Van Jones" (9-28-09), names Jocelyn Elders as one of a "long line of would-be public servants ... deprived of public office because right-wing demagogues have targeted them and distorted their views." That's much too simple. First, Elders wasn't a "would-be" public servant. She was already Surgeon General. Yes, critics—like the Christian Coalition and Concerned Women of America—accused Elders of sabotaging children's "innocence and modesty" by publicly declaring in 1994 that sex education should address masturbation. But when her remarks first appeared in a news report, it was HHS Secretary Donna Shalala and White House Chief of Staff Leon Panetta who rebuked her. And President Bill Clinton who forced her to resign. Right-wing demagogues? No. More like "liberal" wimps.

With best wishes,

For further details on Elders' forced resignation, see Martha Cornog's *Big Book of Masturbation* (Down There Press, 2003), p. 288–89. According to Cornog, "the Clinton Administration did not want to be associated with masturbation," not even as a safe sex-behavior.

These letters sent to LC's Cataloging Policy and Support Office (Washington, DC 20540-4305) have so far produced no action or reply:

June 26, 2007

Dear Colleagues,

Based on the attached July-August 2007 *Utne* report, "Dissent 101: Unsanctioned Student Guides Offer Advice on the Real College Experience," I suggest creating this subject heading:

COLLEGE DISORIENTATION GUIDES.
 SN Here are entered materials on unofficial guides for new college students that typically address issues

like gender, race, campus corporatization, hate crimes, militarism, student rights, sexual orientation, and labor, fair trade, and anti-sweatshop activism.
UF Disguides

Disorientation guides, College
Freshman disorientation guides
BT Alternative press publications
College student orientation
Student movement

With best wishes...,

April 30, 2009

Dear Colleagues,
Having lately read Dr. Seuss' *Lorax* to third-graders at Red Pine Elementary School in Eagan, Minnesota, as a commemoration of Earth Day, I warmly suggest improving access to this valuable work by adding these subject tracings to the catalog record:

ECO-POETRY
INDUSTRIAL POLLUTION — POETRY
DEFORESTATION — POETRY
GREED — POETRY
GROWTH (ECONOMICS) — POETRY
ENVIRONMENTAL DEGRADATION — POETRY
UNNECESSARY THINGS — POETRY

Based on Seuss' usage, these two cross-references could prove helpful:

GROWTH (ECONOMICS)
UF Biggering (Economics)
    Getting bigger (Economics)

The "eco" and "unnecessary" forms need to be established:

ECO-POETRY
UF Ecological poetry
    Environmental poetry
BT Poetry
UNNECESSARY THINGS
UF Things, Unnecessary
    Unnecessary products
    Unneeded things
BT Consumption (Economics)
    Products
    Property

INDUSTRIAL POLLUTION was earlier recommended on 2-12-08.
Because they have become nearly iconic, a metaphor for ecocide, it would also be worth creating a descriptor for TRUFFULA TREES and assigning it to *The Lorax* with a POETRY subhead.
With earth-friendly greetings...,

The sole subject heading assigned in the original CIP: STORIES IN RHYME.

8-16-09

Dear Colleagues,
Hennepin County did it years ago. Maybe decades. Now it would be helpful for LC to do it likewise: establish (and assign) a genre heading for

GAY LOVE STORIES
UF Gay romance stories
    Love stories, Gay
    M/M love stories
    Male/male love stories
    Romance stories, Gay
BT Gay men — Fiction
    Love stories

Data on two assignment-candidates attached.
With best wishes,
P.S. Needless to add, lesbian romances deserve a similar treatment.

October 24, 2009
Dear Colleagues,
Last week I noticed that a PBS 4-hour special program, *Latin Music USA,* devoted a whole segment to "Reggaeton," a genre that has spawned many performers and recordings, as well as some controversy. To make this music more accessible through library catalogs, I recommend establishing a subject heading for

REGGAETON MUSIC
UF   Regueton music
BT   Music, Popular — Puerto Rico

Attached: Historical data, usage-examples, and numerous assignment-candidates, especially CDs and videos.
With autumnal greetings,

Lately, a Library of Congress staffer complained on the Web that LC was being unfairly chastised for not creating subject headings in a timely fashion.

This year they established CONSPIRACY THEORIES, as reported by Jenna Freedman (http://ljenna.openflows.com/lcsh/20093week 37):

(C) 150 Conspiracy theories [May Subd Geog]
   680 Here are entered works on theories that postulate that certain events or phenomena occurred as a result of conspiracies among interested parties. Works on a particular event that is considered by some to be the result of a conspiracy are entered under the heading or headings appropriate for the event.
   550 History — Errors, inventions, etc.

This heading is so needed at the Library of Congress. It's shocking it's taken this long. Thank you to the Vanderbilt University cataloger who proposed it for *Voodoo histories: the role of the conspiracy theory in shaping modern history*!

That staffer "explained" that LC simply couldn't create descriptors because someone *thought* they should, but rather on the basis of actual, catalogable works that merited new headings. No relevant work, no new rubric.

In 1984 — TWENTY-FIVE YEARS AGO — Hennepin County Library in Minnesota cataloged George Johnson's *Architects of fear: conspiracy theories and paranoia in American politics,* a 1983 volume. That title triggered a new subject heading, CONSPIRACY THEORIES, duly reported to LC and other colleagues in *HCL cataloging bulletin,* no. 71 (July/August 1984), p. 7. Subsequent *Cataloging bulletin* issues announced further usage-examples and assignments. Copies went gratis to LC.

Says Jenna: "It's shocking it's taken this long." Yes. Shocking. And irresponsible.

More (Attempted) LCSH Input, Geopolitics Versus Historical Truth
(U*L 155, 2010)

These missives went to LC's Cataloging Policy & Support Office (Washington, DC 20540-4305):

February 10, 2007

Dear Colleagues,

I suggest innovating and retrospectively assigning this genre heading:

EROTIC GRAPHIC NOVELS
UF   Adult graphic novels
       Graphic novels, Erotic
BT   Erotic comic books, strips, etc.
       Erotic fiction
       Graphic novels.

The new form can be immediately applied to Melinda Gebbie/Alan Moore's *Lost Girls* (Book one, 1995; books 1–3, 2006).

With warmest regards,

/s/ Sanford Berman

11-18-08

Dear Colleagues,

Lately, the Library of Congress introduced a genre heading for DOCUMENTARY COMIC BOOKS, STRIPS, ETC. Assuming that form was intended to denote and identify the non-fiction equivalents of GRAPHIC NOVELS, I warmly recommend changing it to the much less cumbersome and unfamiliar

GRAPHIC NON-FICTION
UF   Documentary comic books, strips, etc.
       Non-fiction, Graphic
BT   Comic books, strips, etc.

The altered descriptor may be retrospectively assigned to Howard Zinn's *People's history of American empire; a graphic adaptation* (2008) and Will Eisner's *Plot: the secret story of the protocols of the Elders of Zion* (2005).

Incidentally, the two assigned subject tracings for the Eisner volume should be subdivided by COMIC BOOKS, STRIPS, ETC. And the work merits at least two further access points:

3. Forgeries—Comic books, strips, etc.
4. Literary hoaxes—Comic books, strips, etc.

With warmest regards,
/s/ Sanford Berman

12-15-09

Dear Colleagues,
   I recommend establishing a new subject heading:

CYYBERCHONDRIA
SN   Here are entered materials on the baseless fueling of fears and anxiety about common health symptoms due to information gleaned from the Internet.

SF   Internet-fueled health anxiety
     Web-fueled health anxiety
BT   Health information—Internet resources
     Hypochondrias

   Attached: Usage-examples and citations for online and other assignment-candidates.

With best wishes,
/s/ Sanford Berman

2-2-10

Dear Colleagues,
   I recommend creating a subject heading for

GROUP POLARIZATION
SN   Here are entered materials on the tendency for people to develop attitudes or make decisions that are more extreme when in a group, rather than doing so alone or independently.

UF   Choice shift (Group polarization)
     Polarization, Group
     Risky shift (Group polarization)
BT   Attitude change
     Polarization (Social sciences)
     Social groups
     Social psychology

   Attached: usage-examples, definition, and assignment candidate citations from *Wikipedia, Google books,* and the 11-2-09 *New Yorker* (Elizabeth Kolbert's "Things people say").

With best wishes,
/s/ Sanford Berman

2-23-10

Dear Colleagues:
   Based on the attached *Harper's Magazine* article and many Google citations, I suggest creating a subject heading for

PROSPERITY GOSPEL
SN   Here are entered materials on the belief that God wants His children to enjoy health, happiness, and wealth now and not as an eternal reward in Heaven.

UF   Gospel of prosperity
     Gospel of wealth
     Wealth gospel
BT   Wealth—Religious aspects—Christianity

With best wishes,
/s/ Sanford Berman

More LCSH Input, Geopolitics Versus Truth

As an update to my remarks in U*L 139 ("'Genocide' or Merely 'Massacres'?—the Politics of Subject Cataloging," p. 15–18) and 144 ("Obsessions," p. 26–28), on March 5, 2010 I directed this letter to Howard L. Berman (U.S. House Foreign Affairs Committee, Washington, DC 20515):

> Dear Representative Berman,
> On December 5, 2009, I wrote President Barack Obama:
>
> This may seem a small and superficial matter. Yet it directly deals with the issue of conducting foreign relations on the basis of firm principles like truthfulness and support for victims of oppression and mass murder. To get to the point: your predecessor dismissed the U.S. Ambassador to Armenia because that envoy spoke in public about the "Armenian Genocide." Successive administrations have denied that unquestionable genocide in order not to offend Turkey, an ally whose government steadfastly maintains that the willful expulsion and extermination of Armenians in Anatolia from 1915 to 1922 never happened. Or that it was their own fault. I now learn that you, too, have decided not to use the G-word.
>
> Has truth become a negotiable commodity, a geopolitical pawn? Are Armenians never to achieve the same kind of recognition of their historic calamity as Jews and Rwandans? All because we fear to offend the descendants of the original perpetrators? Pretty sad. And shameful. I, for one, expected more honesty and integrity from an Obama presidency.
>
> The President never responded. Two years earlier, on 10-22-07, I urged Speaker Pelosi to schedule a House vote on declaring the 1915–1922 events a genocide. I believe she failed to do so.
>
> Yesterday, *BBC World News* reported that the House Foreign Affairs Committee had again approved a genocide resolution. I applaud that action. By copy of this letter, I once more urge Speaker Pelosi to permit a vote. And I encourage my own Representative, Erik Paulsen, to support this long overdue statement that the destruction of some 1.5 million Armenians almost a century ago should rightfully be termed what it was: genocide.
>
> On a directly-related matter: Since 2005, I have been petitioning the Library of Congress to replace its globally-employed subject heading, ARMENIAN MASSACRES, with the more accurate and historical ARMENIAN GENOCIDE. Thus far, LC has adamantly refused to make this simple change although they have the authority and technology to do so. Therefore, I request that the House Foreign Affairs Committee and Rep. Paulsen recommend to the Library of Congress that the present inaccurate and misleading descriptor be replaced by the Genocide form sanctioned by scholars, historians, and human rights advocates.
>
> With thanks in advance for your timely response,
> /s/ Sanford Berman
> cc: Hon. Nancy Pelosi
>   Hon. Erik Paulsen
> Enclosures

Hardly any surprise, but as of April 9th, there hadn't been any "timely response." In fact, no response at all, not even an acknowledgment. Press reports, however, suggest that the Genocide declaration will be shelved by the House leadership, even though the Swedish Parliament had defied its own government one week after the House committee action, prompting the *New York Times* to exclaim: "Sweden labels mass killing of Armenians genocide." That led me to transmit a short plea to Berman, Pelosi, and Paulsen:

Not in *My* Library!

March 18, 2010

Dear Representatives,

If the Swedes can do it, so can we! Please let the whole House vote on H. Res* 252. It's shameful that the United States remains among the genocide-deniers.

Tangentially, I attended a program on March 30th at the Minneapolis Community and Technical College. The topic: Youth in Cuba Today. The presenters: two Federation of University Students leaders, one 24, the other 30 (not exactly "youths"). One speaker, in the course of reciting the Cuban Revolution's many successes, explicitly declared that the island is not beset by "racial discrimination." Later, someone asked how Cuba addresses "Africanness," and was assured by the same speaker that a particular saint's day is widely observed and emphasizes African elements, and that Afro-Cuban drum groups are common, enjoying official support. Unable to contain myself, I observed — from the audience — that it was fine to celebrate Africanness. I applauded it. However, I wondered why, since 60–70 percent of the Cuban population is Black, did Afro-Cubans experience 70 percent unemployment compared to 30 percent for Whites, and why did Blacks constitute 85 percent of the prison population. The immediate reply was to impugn my numbers and their source.

But I noted that the statistics derived from a state-published document authored by the chief economist. Then the "defense" was to explain the disparities as a "legacy," not something for which the Cuban revolutionary leadership could possibly be held responsible. Despite a wealth of visual, statistical and anecdotal evidence, the presenters simply could not manage to say the word, "racism." Yet until something is called by its right name, it cannot be corrected. Armenians continue to undergo spiritual and emotional torment because Turkish nationalists and bureaucrats refuse to acknowledge what befell their ancestors, refuse to say "genocide." And Afro-Cubans are unlikely to experience full citizenship and equality until Cuban political (and "youth") leaders recognize that racism permeates their society.

I'll readily furnish more documentation on both situations, Turkish and Cuban, on request.

LCSH Currency (Continued), Libraries and Politics, Retiring the R-Word, Celeste West Tribute
(U*L 156, 2010)

The Library of Congress lately replaced the utterly antiquarian subject heading, COOKERY, with the less-quaint, post–Victorian COOKING. That LC should have favored modernity and familiarity over nostalgia and sentimentality surely merits applause. Less praiseworthy, however, is how long it took to make that commendable switch.

They could have done it sooner. Much sooner.

Although it then involved changing many permutations and cross-references, Hennepin County Library in Minnesota substituted COOKING for COOKERY in 1976. HCL duly reported that term-shift to LC and others through its bimonthly *Cataloging bulletin*. If anyone hasn't done the math yet, that was 34 years ago. Thirty-four years to finally permit more contemporary and findable language in library catalogs. Such a lag is not worth celebrating. It's to bemoan. And bewilder.

My still-unsuccessful efforts to persuade the Library of Congress *to* jettison the subject form, ARMENIAN MASSACRES, in favor of ARMENIAN GENOCIDE, betray a stark departure from professional "neutrality" and integrity. They manifestly won't make the change because they fear political consequences. The Obama Administration and House leadership don't want to antagonize Turkey by honestly labeling what happened to Armenians in the early 1900s as "genocide." Unhappily, that's not the only case of LC failing to uphold basic tenets of ethical conduct and intellectual freedom. Emily Parker reports in the 5-16-10 *New York Times book review* (p. 35) that Chinese-Canadian writer Denise Chong last year published *Egg on Mao*, which "tells the true story of Lu Decheng, who threw paint-filled eggs at Mao's portrait in Tiananmen Square during the 1989 protests." The cover "features a photo of Chairman Mao's paint-splattered face underneath the bold type: 'The Story of an Ordinary Man Who Defaced an Icon and Unmasked a Dictatorship.'" Parker thinks that "Chong had underestimated the fear of offending Beijing—not in China but in the West." The author was shunned by a Canadian nonprofit and a TV station. But this is the kicker: "the nervousness," says Parker, "wasn't limited to Canada. The United States Library of Congress declined an invitation to hold an event with Chong, suggested by the Canadian Embassy." Why? According to "a library employee involved in the discussions ... the political sensitivity of the book was one factor ... along with the library's relationship with the National Library of China." Hardly a stunning commitment to promoting diversity of opinion and unfettered speech. Again, politics trumps principle.

When Rahm Emanuel early in 2010 referred to liberal activists as "retarded," he didn't mean it as a compliment. Later, Rush Limbaugh talked about "retards in the White House." That, too, was not intended as praise. (Indeed, Rush repeated "retard" 40 times for emphasis.) On the 2-23-10 "Joy Behar Show," guest Bill Maher declared "retard" an important word to use, although admitting that he wouldn't say it directly to a developmentally disabled person. That's like declaring "nigger" to be okay as long as it's not said to a Black person. Joy did not dissent. My respect for both has now tanked.

The R-words are almost always employed as slurs, insults, putdowns. It's not a matter of "political correctness" to retire those terms from our collective vocabulary. It's a matter of elemental decency and respect. And despite Rahm, Rush, Joy, Bill, and even Stephen Colbert publicly embracing such invectives, others—perhaps more thoughtful and caring—have decided to scrap them. For instance, the West Virginia House of Delegates recently and unanimously approved a measure to erase "mentally retarded" from the state's law books, replacing that negative and hurtful phrase with "intellectually disabled." Said Republican John Ellem, minority chair of the House Judiciary Committee: "I think everyone would pretty much agree that the term 'mentally retarded' or 'retard' is pretty stigmatizing. We can lead by example, and say that at least in state code, we're not going to use this derogatory or stigmatizing term any more." Maryland made a similar switch in 2009. Connecticut lately renamed its Dept. of Mental Retardation the "Dept. of Developmental Services." Massachusetts and Missouri have done likewise. Good for them! Farewell to the R-words. They won't be missed.

Revolting Librarians. Synergy. Booklegger Magazine. Celeste West generated these monuments of critical librarianship. In the Fall 2004 *Counterpoise,* I described her as "the most awesome, electric, and incisive voice ever in library literature."

Celeste died in January 2008. To celebrate her life, influence, and achievement, Library Juice Press this year published *She was a booklegger: remembering Celeste West,* co-edited by Toni Samek, K. R. Roberto, and Moyra Lang. It's a welcome memorial. However, it prompts three friendly suggestions for a revised edition or second printing:

- While bibliographic references abound and half the volume contains "Selected Writings by Celeste West," this should have been the occasion for compiling a comprehensive, annotated resource guide to everything by and about the iconic and hugely significant CW, including—for instance—her contributions

to *Collection building* and *Alternative library literature.* Such a Festschrift demands that sort of thorough bio-bibliography.
- The index could be better. For example, Eric Moon is cited once (p. 26), but his appearance on p. 171 goes unnoted. And there are no entries for myriad persons and topics, among them Bill Katz, Jesse Shera, *Library literature*, Ed Badajos, Burton H. Wolfe, *Tits and clits comix,* Paul Dunkin, COSMEP, Robert Calvert, war tax resistance, Joyce Crooks, Joan Dillon, Joan Goddard, Barbara Deming, Allen Ginsberg, medicine, health care, conservation, Nancy Schimmel, literary-industrial complex, Anne Woodsworth, Noel Peattie, Carol Starr, Elizabeth Joseph, Sonia Johnson, Meredith Small, Emma Goldman, Buddhism, celibacy, Cockettes, conglomerate media, Laughing Buddha Maria, Clown Conservatory, breast cancer, suicide, bipolar illness, Hopalong Cassidy, and Lone Ranger.
- The Library of Congress CIP entry deserved to be complemented by an "Alternative Cataloging-In-Publication" record that pointedly included subject tracings for CRITICAL LIBRARIANSHIP, ANARCHAFEMINISTS, ALTERNATIVE PRESS, and COUNTERCULTURE.

The Kids Are Not All Right
(U*L 157, 2010)

Being an American Library Association honorary member, I regularly get ALA hardcopy periodicals in the mail. (These have become fewer as round tables and divisions switch to strictly online publications.) A recent arrival, the Summer/Fall 2010 *Children and libraries*, contained an unexpected gem: Patricia Mendell and Patricia Sarles' "'Where did I *really* come from?'; assisted reproductive technology in self-published children's picture books." Maybe "gem" doesn't quite describe it. Because it's a rare and disturbing account—published outside the standard tech services venues—of actual library users identifying a real, immediate need for bibliographic access, then petitioning the Library of Congress to meet that need by establishing a specific subject heading and retrospectively assigning it to some 13 titles, only to be curtly and officiously rebuffed. This carefully documented case illustrates longstanding complaints about LC practice, including unresponsiveness, imperiousness, and a failure to achieve subject heading currency.

Mendell, a practicing psychotherapist and founding member of the American Fertility Association, and Sarles, a school librarian, begin their report and bibliography this way:

> For those wanting to become parents but unable to conceive naturally, reproductive medicine has offered alternative routes to having a baby. The most difficult decision for parents who decide to use alternative family-building options is whether to tell their child that he or she was born with the assistance of a donor and/or surrogate. Parents want to know what to say when their child starts asking "Where did I come from?"
> Parents often are concerned about what language to use in discussing disclosure and conception and how their child will react once told. Because most children's understanding of reproduction evolves over time, so will the questions they ask about their origins. While there are many excellent books that have helped parents address the question of natural conception, only in the last twenty years has there been a gradual increase in books about third party reproduction, and in particular, in those written for children. What is there, if anything, and how do librarians locate these materials for their patrons?

For both professional and personal reasons, the authors sought to locate works on donor offspring, ultimately discovering that while many books on the topic had been cataloged by LC, none had been assigned the rubric DONOR OFFSPRING. And topical access overall was inadequate and inconsistent. Their frustrating search prompted them to ask: "How does a librarian find books on certain subjects if there are no subject headings for those books?"

An approach to LC by means of the Ask a Librarian correspondence form that stated the search problem and declared that over 40 books had been identified as either being about donor offspring or having donor offspring as main characters produced this reply:

> We have not had the need to establish a heading for the children of sperm donors, as we have not cataloged any items that specifically focus on that topic. The existing headings have been adequate for the items that we've cataloged. We establish new headings only as they are needed for cataloging new works being added to our collection.

The authors promptly supplied the titles of 13 books in the LC catalog, 7 for kids, 5 for YAs, and 1 for professionals. They never got an answer.

The article, a model of cataloging criticism, includes 2 tables: "Keywords and subject terms used in the search" and "Subject headings currently employed by LC." Further, annotated booklist entries specify subject descriptors that were (or would be) assigned to each item. The authors pointedly observe that a "lack of uniformity in subject headings, as well as the absence of the LC subject heading 'donor offspring,' makes it difficult to search for books on this subject." To make the issue at once practical and personal, they quote a donor-offspring mother:

> Considering that there have been well over one million donor offspring born, this sends the message that children like my son do not exist because the Library of Congress has not established an official subject category for these children and their families.

Having become seriously distraught over the Mendell/Sarles experience, I sent this missive to LC's Cataloging Policy & Support Office (Washington, DC 20540-4305):

August 31, 2010

Dear Colleagues,
 Based on the extensive documentation in the Summer/Fall 2010 *Children and libraries* (p. 18–29), I recommend the overdue establishment of a subject heading for

DONOR OFFSPRING
UF   ART offspring
    Assisted reproductive technology
        offspring
    Children of egg donors
    Children of gamete donors

Children of sperm donors
Donor egg offspring
Donor sperm offspring
Egg donor offspring
Sperm donor offspring

The new form may be retrospectively assigned to the numerous titles cited by Mendell and Sarles, as well as the recent feature film, *The kids are all right*.

With best wishes,
/s/ Sanford Berman
Sanford Berman
4400 Morningside Road
Edina, MN 55416

NOT IN *MY* LIBRARY!

Still-fuming wrap-up: To claim that a new subject isn't warranted because there's nothing in the collection to assign it to when desperate (and responsible) searchers have precisely noted at least 13 such works—well, that's slovenly, unresponsive, condescending, or worse. Maybe there should be a big sign posted in LC (and other) cataloging departments: WHO-IN-HELL ARE WE CATALOGING *FOR*?

Remembrance of Things Past, Interview Excerpts
(U*L 158, 2011)

From 1962–1966 I supervised U.S. Army Special Services libraries in Karlsruhe, Worms and Mannheim-Sandhofen, West Germany. I'd earlier been a GI stationed in Heidelberg, but this later stint was in civvies. An unexpected (and truly heartwarming) holiday card lately reminded me of that army library period. A former GI, now retired, wrote, in part:

> I found some information about you on the internet, so I'm assuming you are the Sanford Berman who I knew as a librarian when I was stationed at Taukkunen Barracks in Worms, Germany, from late 1964 until 1966 when our infantry unit moved to Baumholder...
>
> For many years I have wanted to tell you what an important part you played in the formation of my political consciousness. Your wise moral counsel with regard to peace and justice will remain with me forever. For me and my friends your library was a place, a safe haven, where we could listen to protest music by Joan Baez and Bob Dylan and where we could explore anti-war literature without fear of reprisal.
>
> I'm the person who printed the typed stencils for "Yin Yang," our independent magazine, on a hand cranked copying machine. I wanted to contribute some work to it, but alas, Yin Yang didn't last that long. Just participating in it was very important to me.

To amplify those most welcome recollections, here are passages from a foreword I did for Ken Wachsberger's 1993 *Voices from the underground volume 2 — a directory of sources and resources on the Vietnam era underground press* (Mica Press), immediately following my account of an epiphany experienced at an early–60s poetry reading in DC by Allen Ginsberg, Leroi Jones (now Amiri Baraka), Gregory Corso, and Peter Orlovsky:

> Fire marshals ended the program prematurely, but that evening's experience so profoundly affected me (although I confess to already having been powerfully influenced by reading Henry Miller in clandestine, Paris-printed paperbacks while a GI in Germany) that later, working as an army librarian in Europe, I managed (by means of genuinely "creative financing") to get whole anthologies of Beat writing as well as several issues of *City Lights Journal* into the libraries I supervised (which incidentally prompted a censorship attempt

by a Southern Methodist chaplain who wore paratroop boots while conducting Sunday services). One month I also mounted a counter-top "Beat Lit." display featuring a photo of Allen at his shaggiest and most unkempt, not exactly the type of gung-ho role-model exhibit my civilian "brass" encouraged in barracks libraries.

And we did our *own* poetry readings at base service clubs. GIs and I shared work we had written ourselves, together with a large dose of Whitman, William Carlos Williams, Corso, Ginsberg, Garcia Lorca, Brecht, Yevtushenko, Lawrence Ferlinghetti, Vachel Lindsay, and Hans Magnus Enzensberger, among others.

Finally, in early 1966, we went the whole way. That February, *Yin Yang* appeared. "An independent journal of art, ideas, and imagination, published from time to time by Coleman Barracks Library" in Mannheim-Sandhofen, West Germany, it contained poems, graphics, plays, photos, and short stories, by me and about a dozen soldiers. GIs composed three-fourths of the editorial board. That first issue proved sufficiently candid, if not actually brash, "liberating," and un-military, that a Lt. Colonel visited me in the library office to report that "some people" thought it "subversive" and to deliver a not-so-veiled warning about publishing another number.

Even as he cautioned us, the master pages for the March issue rested quietly in an office drawer. (In fact, the "Good News" Colonel practically sat on them as he spoke.) Later they *became* the March issue, featuring splendid, mind-warping collages and photographs by Norman Morris (a truly inspired and utterly unique artist whose permanent legacy to Coleman Barracks was a totally-rearranged/redecorated display case) and Jim Caccavo (afterwards a celebrated war photographer and teacher), ironic poetry by Ed Badajos (within a few years to become a major surrealist cartoonist and author of both *Filipino Food* and *Dick!*), and "unspeakable" verse like this excerpt from "Rotation to Freedom," by John S. Cunningham, who planned after discharge to attend college in Baltimore and get active in the Civil Rights movement:

> There will be reason
> as well as purpose,
> for the deeds I do.
> No more asking, Why?
> I'll get answers that make more sense
> than "authority" or
> "jurisdiction!"
> But, most important,
> I'll be free.
> Hallelujah!

Whether those two issues of *Yin Yang* influenced the later GI underground press, I don't know. But I happily nominate them as among the first of the genre.

Continuing in this mode of self-reflection (or is it self-advertisement?), Alycia Sellie interviewed me for her December 2010 zine, *The borough is my library*. These are excerpts:

BIRTH AND EDUCATION
Arrived (or erupted) October 6, 1933 at Belmont Hospital in Chicago. (That experience apparently convinced my parents, Sam and Dorothy, not to beget any more little darlings. Yes, I'm an only child. And do not feel deprived or slighted because of no siblings. Just the opposite.)

Attended a series of grammar schools in north Chicago until, at age 8, in 1942, the family migrated to Los Angeles. (Why travel westward almost immediately after Pearl Harbor? For work. My dad labored in the shipyards as a sheet metal worker during the war. Later he became a supermarket employee, joining the Retail Clerks International Association, or RCIA, now the UFCW. He ultimately served as president of the union retirees club and once testified before Congress in favor of unions being able to negotiate on behalf of retired members.)

My schools in L.A.: Virginia Road Elementary (where mulberry trees grew, providing leaves to feed my pet silkworms), Mt. Vernon Jr. High (the site of my triumph as 7th grade spelling champ, though I subsequently tanked over "antidisestablishmentarianism," or something similar, not because I couldn't spell it, but rather due to excessive confidence and consequently foolish speed), Susan Miller Dorsey High (I played Editor Webb in a school production of Thornton Wilder's *Our Town*) and UCLA — rah rah rah — my majors being Poli. Sci., English, and Anthropology. (While an undergrad, I TA'd for Frances Clarke Sayers' children's lit. course, co-founded the campus SDA — Students for Democratic Action — and derived much insight and inspiration from Stanley Diamond's Anthro class.)

Postgrad: the Catholic University Library School, Washington, DC, where it took 4 years to garner an MSLS, produce a massive, two-volume thesis, *Spanish Guinea: an annotated bibliography,* and stay impervious to such nonsense as the book selection teacher — a robed monk who also held the post of Censor Librorum for his order — advising us not to acquire any material by or about Paul Robeson in order to avoid contributing to the "international Communist conspiracy."

DO YOU REMEMBER WHAT YOU THOUGHT ABOUT LIBRARIANS BEFORE YOU JOINED THE PROFESSION?

I most fondly recalled Saturday morning story hours at a Chicago branch library. That experience predisposed me to view librarians favorably. (Mostly I still do.)

WHY DID YOU DECIDE TO BECOME A LIBRARIAN?

Unsurprisingly, a *Bottom line* interviewer posed almost the same question in 2003: "If you had the opportunity to do it all over again, would you still choose a career in this profession? Why or why not?" And this is what I replied:

Well, the unvarnished truth is that librarianship wasn't my first career choice. I thought I wanted to be a foreign service officer, maybe graduating to ambassador, traveling widely and spreading the American gospel. That aim ended when, after returning to the States from Germany where I'd been an Army draftee for two years, I failed the foreign service oral exam, plunged into correspondence school piecework labor, and finally enrolled in the District of Columbia Public Library's work-study program (i.e. work full time, study whenever you can). I'm convinced that chance governs much of the universe, and chance surely directed my career path, which I don't regret. Not at all. In fact, I later observed foreign service personnel in action overseas, especially Europe and Africa, thankfully concluding that I hadn't become one of them: essentially soldiers in suits. What frankly propelled me toward DCPL's program was the experience of working as a messenger clerk (page) for about three years at a Los Angeles Public Library branch. That's where I doubtless got the bug, even though my first-ever task was to mop up kid pee near the fairy tale shelves. Is there anything more satisfying than making it possible for people — irrespective of class or appearance or age — to learn, to laugh, to reflect, and to relax in their own public space and without being exhorted to do this or buy that?

WHO ARE YOUR LIBRARY HEROES: DID YOU HAVE LIBRARY MENTORS, OR HAVE YOU HELPED MENTOR OTHER LIBRARIANS?

It may seem extremely conceited. Or ignorant. Or both. But I can't honestly name any "heroes" or formal mentors. However, I gladly cite the late Marvin Scilken, founder/editor/publisher of the *U*n*a*b*a*s*h*e*d Librarian* and longtime Director of the Orange

(New Jersey) Public Library, as a model and goad. In particular, he practiced and promoted local deviation in cataloging and classification to achieve greater access to library resources and enhance user comfort. For instance, he routinely "exploded"—that is, spelled out—catalog record abbreviations so that ordinary people could understand them. And he freely added subject headings to standard, centrally-supplied records to expand findability. Some of those tracings were for fictional characters, a practice we happily copied and enlarged at Hennepin County Library.

More to follow. In the meantime, for a purely visual treat (or massive embarrassment), see "Grandpa Berman makes funny" on YouTube.

More Interview Excerpts, Atheist Deficit, What Rosa Said
(U*L 159, 2011)

Here are more questions and answers from Alycia Sellie's December 2010 *Borough Is My Library*:

HOW DO YOU SEE THE RELATIONSHIP BETWEEN SOCIAL JUSTICE, ACTIVISM, AND LIBRARIANSHIP?

It's intimate. And I was tempted to simply leave it with that pithy, perfunctory comment. But to elaborate or exemplify "intimacy" a little: Whether you're a designated materials selector or not, when you encounter a book, DVD, magazine, or CD from outside the mainstream — perhaps something reviewed in *Counterpoise* or *Multicultural review*—that would help diversify the library collection and possibly appeal to otherwise marginal or alternative (that is, frequently neglected or overlooked) groups and persons, recommend it for acquisition.

When you discover that works are undercataloged, need contents notes for further clarity and searching, or have been shelved where likely browsers won't find them, either correct the situation yourself (if a tech services staffer) or suggest improvements to the appropriate colleagues. When you encounter relevant information, regardless of format, that might interest community or campus organizations, or faculty or coworkers, alert them to it. When serious policies are being considered that could impact staff or users—like raising fines and fees or commercializing, if not privatizing, services—insist on staff and user input before managers make those decisions.

If the library isn't abiding by standards relating to intellectual freedom and poor people's services, for example, raise that issue in meetings and other fora. If material can't be located or identified in the catalog under, say, DONOR OFFSPRING (think *The kids are all right*) and it turns out that the Library of Congress hasn't established such a subject descriptor: 1) ask your own institution to innovate and assign the rubric, and/or 2) petition LC to do so.

IS THERE ANY PROJECT OR INITIATIVE THAT YOU'D ESPECIALLY LIKE TO SEE CONCLUDED, NOW THAT YOU'VE REACHED THE LATE SEVENTIES?

Yes. Five years ago, in October 2005, I and others launched a campaign to get commemorative postage stamps issued for Eugene V. Debs and Mother Jones. Many letters and postcards have been sent to the USPS Stamp Development Committee favoring the proposal, some from unions and labor history groups, but largely from ordinary citizens who fervently believe that such recognition for Jones and Debs is long overdue. While it may sound somewhat corny and melodramatic, I'm now 77, with cardiac and a few other disorders. In short, I don't have much time left. And my single wish before death is to be able to see, buy, and use stamps honoring Debs and Jones. That's it. Nothing else.

If any friends, colleagues, and zine readers want to join the campaign, just mail a supportive statement to: Citizens Stamp Advisory Committee: Stamp Development, U.S. Postal Service, 475 L'Enfant Plaza SW (Room 3300), Washington, DC 20260-3501.

YOUR ACTIVITIES HAVE BEEN WELL DOCUMENTED. IS THERE SOMETHING YOU'RE PROUD OF THAT MOST PEOPLE DON'T KNOW ABOUT?

This: In 1994, I created the Lorraine O. Berman Memorial Scholarship Fund which "annually supports a scholarship for a female law student of color." Administered by the University of Minnesota Foundation, the endowment is currently worth $128,538, with $6,305 to be granted this year.

YOU'VE LATELY EXAMINED THREE ARTICLES BY EMILY DRABINSKI: "GENDERED S(H)ELVES; BODY AND IDENTITY IN THE LIBRARY," "CLASSIFICATION AS TEXT: LEGIBLE IDEOLOGIES, RESISTANT READINGS," AND "TEACHING THE RADICAL CATALOG." WHAT IS YOUR RESPONSE?

These are a few comradely, if also scattershot, comments:

- Of course, gender, class, religious, ethnic, and other bias has widely impacted library classification and subject heading schemes, as well as such cataloging practices as note-making, access-point provision, and abbreviation use. However, not all cataloging defects or delinquencies stem from bigotry or malign intent. Some derive, almost certainly, from institutional torpor, timidity, and arrogance.
- Why not just scrap or substitute something else for admittedly flawed systems like LCC, LCSH, and DDC? Because, frankly, there's too great an investment in them. Which is to say that replacing any one of them would produce a costly, service-wrecking mess. Not to mention a colossal headache for staff and users alike. We're too far along to simply start over. But even if we're stuck with them, it doesn't mean that these tools or systems can't be remolded, massaged, and tweaked to perform better. What I seem to detect in many system-critiques is a sense of despair and hopelessness, leading to a kind of paralysis.
- The idea of teaching the "critical catalog" and warning users of pervasive assumptions and prejudices is laudable. But it's unlikely to make materials ("knowledge objects") any more accessible, and while it may raise social and political consciousness, it will reach only a fragment of library users nationwide. The vast majority of users frequent public, school, and junior college institutions,

not private, research, and university operations. So in a way that "remedy" appears a bit elitist. And not very effective.
- Here's an outright heresy: Hardly anyone outside academia (and cataloging departments) actually "reads" classification schedules (that is, DDC and LCC). Call numbers for most users are primarily a means to retrieve works already identified in the catalog or to browse among affine materials. Apart from academia, "mark and park" is what classifying's all about.
- Even within the confines of given structures—LCSH, LCC, DDC—there can be dynamic and helpful change. And local libraries, in any event, can—with a modicum of determination, wit, and independence—overcome or bypass system deficiencies. If, for example, works on transsexuals have been seriously separated on the shelves by virtue of assigning disparate class numbers, it can be decided to routinely classify such materials in only one designated place. (That's what Hennepin County Library did decades ago regarding AIDS. Everything on the topic got classed in the same range and so could be found in the same location.) If users seek items on "butch and femme" and the collection contains relevant material, but none of it can be detected through a catalog subject search because LC hasn't yet recognized that topic—well, innovate and retrospectively assign a butch/femme rubric locally, or at least demand that LC establish the descriptor. In the cited example of a book about a Black quarterback and his racist experience in pro football, the possibilities for accurate and comprehensive access need not be restrained by a "first cut" like QUARTERBACKING (FOOTBALL) or such additional tracings as RACISM IN SPORTS, AFRICAN-AMERICAN ATHLETES—SOCIAL CONDITIONS, or DISCRIMINATION IN SPORTS. Should LC or network catalogers have failed to do so, why not modify or add AFRICAN-AMERICAN FOOTBALL PLAYERS and RACISM IN FOOTBALL (which might require innovation)?
- "Berman's approach suggests there is some 'right' language that could be universally understood and applied. The politics of language are rarely so tidy." Well, often they are tidy. If it's accepted that ethnic and other groups should be called by their self-preferred names, and the evidence is persuasive for what those names are, then LAPPS become SAMI, BUSHMEN transmute into SAN, and GYPSIES morph into ROMANIES (or ROMA). To make the point that language—in this case, an ethnonym—can be impossibly iffy, LC's Chief of the Cataloging Policy & Support Office is quoted as saying that after changing GYPSIES to ROMANIES in 2004 "we received complaints from several individuals and a few organizations that opposed our discontinuing usage of the term Gypsies." In short, that woefully overdue name-switch was questioned due to remarks by a frequently inflexible, insensitive, and unresponsive LC boss. Massive documentation supporting the ethnonym-change could (and should have been) examined before uncritically accepting the essentially snide and

clueless words of Barbara Tillett. Much supporting data had been cited or reproduced since the 70s in the *HCL cataloging bulletin*.
- Last gasp: cataloging should be predicated on 3 principles: findability, intelligibility, and fairness. Perfection, neutrality, and objectivity may often elude us. But it's still worth trying.
- As a gloss to those remarks about why our principal cataloging and classification schemes should not be totally scrapped, Nicholas Lemann, in the September 2010 *New Yorker*, makes an analogous point about schools:

> The story line on education, at this ill-tempered moment in American life, expresses what might be called the Noah's Ark view of life: a vast territory looks so impossibly corrupted that it must be washed away, so that we can begin its activities anew, on finer, higher, firmer principles. One should treat any perception that something so large is so completely awry with suspicion, and consider that it might not be true — especially before acting on it.
>
> We have a lot of recent experience with breaking apart large, old, unlovely systems in the confidence of gaining great benefits at low cost. We deregulated the banking system. We tried to remake Iraq. In education, we would do well to appreciate what our country has built, and to try to fix what is undeniably wrong without declaring the entire system to be broken. We have a moral obligation to be precise about what the problems in American education are — like subpar schools for poor and minority children — and to resist heroic ideas about what would solve them, if those ideas don't demonstrably do that.

As more evidence of the pervasiveness of self-censorship in libraries — an intellectual freedom problem of much greater magnitude than Huck Finn and Harry Potter "challenges" — Tracy Black reports in the April 2011 *Freethought Today* that "area public libraries" in Amarillo, Texas, "have very few books for atheists. The catalogue shows just two copies of *The God delusion* for the entire area. The high schools are even worse. A search for 'atheism' doesn't bring up a single book, yet any given library has dozens of devotionals, bible studies, and Christian living books."

Rosa Luxemburg, murdered by the Freikorps (later Hitler's Brownshirts) on January 15, 1919, was a revolutionary socialist frequently jailed for what she said: for instance, opposing World War I. Vivian Gornick, reviewing a collection of her letters in the May 2, 2011 *Nation*, describes Rosa as "a diehard democrat" who "never for a moment" thought "democracy should be sacrificed to socialism." In 1918, after the Bolsheviks had assumed power in Russia and just 6 months before her death, she wrote from a prison cell these eloquent words:

> [Lenin] is completely mistaken in the means he employs. Decree ... draconian penalties, rule by terror.... Without general elections, without unrestricted freedom of press and assembly, without a free exchange of opinions, life dies out in every public institution and only bureaucracy remains active.... Freedom only for the supporters of the government, only for the members of one party, no matter how numerous, is no freedom. Freedom is always freedom for the one who thinks differently.

Even though she wasn't addressing librarians directly, we should wholeheartedly embrace and promote her declaration. These are truly words to live by. Vielen Dank, Rosa!

No to Government Secrecy and Repression!
(U*L 160, 2011)

On January 20, 2011, I sent this message to Attorney-General Eric Holder, my U.S. House member, and both Minnesota Senators:

Dear Attorney-General, Congressman, and Senators,
PFC Bradley Manning has been subjected to inhumane solitary confinement and forced drugging for about 9 months. He has not been tried and convicted of any crime. If he has, indeed, released "classified" information on this country's unlawful and deathly wars in Iraq and Afghanistan, he deserves high praise, not torture and imprisonment. I urge all of you to seek Bradley Manning's immediate release and the dropping of charges against him. Should that prove unfeasible, at least insist that PFC Manning no longer be regarded as POI and that he be treated humanely. Finally, he is entitled to a fair and speedy trial. The way he has been treated so far is a disgrace to our purported commitment to prevent and oppose detainee abuse.

On a related matter, the FBI has in recent months conducted raids against peace activists and threatened them with Grand Jury indictments. These are transparently acts of intimidation, intended to stifle anti-war speech and demonstrations. They recall the deplorable COINTELPRO campaigns of the 60s and 70s. Please end these First Amendment travesties. And try to muster the decency and dignity to apologize for such wanton transgressions of human rights and intellectual freedom. Yours for robust dissent (not to mention peace and justice)....

To date (June 2011), none of the four addressees has replied. In the meantime, full charges against PFC Manning were released on March 2nd. They include "aiding the enemy," a capital offense. Here's an update and request from the Bradley Manning Support Network:

One year ago today, on May 26, 2010, the U.S. government quietly arrested a humble young American intelligence analyst in Iraq and imprisoned him in a military camp in Kuwait. Over the coming weeks, the facts of the arrest and charges against this shy soldier would come to light. And across the world, people like you and I would step forward to help defend him.

Bradley Manning, now 23 years old, has never been to court but has already served a year in prison—including 10 months in conditions of confinement that were a clear violation of the international conventions against torture. Bradley has been informally charged with releasing to the world documents that have revealed corruption by world leaders, widespread civilian deaths at the hands of U.S. forces, the true face of Guantanamo, an unvarnished view of the U.S.'s imperialistic foreign negotiations, and the murder of two employees of Reuters News Agency by American soldiers. These documents released by WikiLeaks have spurred democratic revolutions across the Arab world and have changed the face of journalism forever.

For his act of courage, Bradley Manning now faces life in prison — or even death.

But you can help save him — and we've already seen our collective power. Working together with concerned citizens around the world, the Bradley Manning Support Network has helped raise worldwide awareness about Manning's torturous confinement conditions. Through the collective actions of well over a half million people and scores of organizations, we successfully pressured the U.S. government to end the torturous conditions of pretrial confinement that Bradley was subjected to at the Marine Base at Quantico, Virginia. Today, Bradley is being treated humanely at Fort Leavenworth, Kansas. Thanks to your support, Bradley is given leeway to interact with other pre-trial prisoners, read books, write letters, and even has a window in his cell.

Of course we didn't mount this campaign to just to improve Bradley's conditions in jail. Our goal is to ensure that he can receive a fair and open trial. Our goal is to win Bradley's freedom so that he can be reunited with his family and fulfill his dream of going to college. The U.S. government has already spent a year building its case against Bradley, and is now calling its witnesses to Virginia to testify before a grand jury.

What happens to Bradley may ripple through history — he is already considered by many to be the single most important person of his generation. Please show your commitment to Bradley and your support for whistle-blowers and the truth by actively supporting his defense.

With your help, I hope we will come to commemorate all those who risk their lives and freedom to promote informed democracy — and as the birth of a movement that successfully defended one courageous whistle-blower against the full fury of the U.S. government.

To learn more and find out what you can do, go to: www.bradleymanning.org

According to the July 2011 *Nation* ("Widening War on Wikileaks"), the Justice Department's aggressive investigation of Manning and WikiLeaks has escalated. Grand jury subpoenas have been issued to David House, cofounder of the Bradley Manning Support Network; Tyler Watkins, Manning's former boyfriend; and Nadia Heninger, a cryptologist who worked with WikiLeaks' volunteer Jacob Appelbaum. Kevin Gosztola warns that "along with other Obama-era prosecutions of whistleblowers, including the recently collapsed case against ... NSA official Thomas Drake, the targeting of WikiLeaks has the potential to deter journalists and others who might expose corruption and government abuse."

Courage to Resist (484 Lake Park Avenue, No. 41, Oakland, CA 94610) hosts the Bradley Manning Defense Fund. Donate online at couragetoresist.org/bradley or mail tax-deductible checks, noting "Manning Defense" on the memo line. CTR also issues a national newsletter and in May produced an action-oriented, extremely useful *Organizing Toolkit*, replete with sample petitions, letters, and press releases.

Send contributions for the Julian Assange and WikiLeaks Defence Fund to "FSI-Julian Assange Defence Fund," c/o Finers Stephen Innocent LLP, 179 Great Portland Street, London, UK W1W 5LS.

For more information and views, see: Elizabeth DiNovella's "Getting the secrets

No to Government Secrecy and Repression!

out," an omnibus review in the May 2011 *Progressive*, p. 43–44; Gaitlin Davis' inventory of "WikiLeaks online resources," *Counterpoise,* Summer/Fall 2010, p. 83; and Marjorie Cohn's "Bradley Manning: American hero," reprinted from the 9-19-10 *Huffington Post* in *Counterpoise,* Summer/Fall 2010, p. 33–4.

Sources on the FBI crackdown against antiwar protestors: Margaret Sarfehjooy, "Double standards apply to peace activists," *Worldwide WAMM,* January 2011, p. 4; and James Walsh, "Papers left behind by FBI decried by antiwar activists," *Star tribune,* May 19, 2011. Also: Committee to Stop FBI Repression (stopFBl.net).

Apart from individual action by librarians traditionally and ethically committed to open government, transparency, and free speech, it would be helpful (and encouraging) for the American Library Association and other professional groups to explicitly and firmly defend WikiLeaks and whistleblowers, including Bradley Manning, and denounce FBI raids and grand jury hearings that palpably have less to do with fighting terrorism than with stifling dissent.

Word Peeves, "Content-Enriched Metadata," No "Sexting" Allowed
(U*L 161, 2011)

Maybe no one else cares. But I do. So here, like it or not, are three practices in current speech and writing that routinely annoy me—and may imperil the utility and grace of our shared language:

- The dictionary defines "preventative" as "a variant of preventive." Why the extra "ta" has been inserted into a perfectly clear and useful word is not explained. THERE IS NO SOUND REASON TO SAY OR WRITE "PREVENTATIVE." It's superfluous, a garbage-word that accomplishes nothing apart from mindlessly elongating "preventive."
- When nearly everything is "interesting," then nothing is. Yet "interesting" or "interestingly" pervades the linguistic cosmos. It's not merely ubiquitous, omnipresent, it's also somewhat condescending. Why not let readers, listeners, and viewers decide *themselves* whether something truly fascinates or engages them? And why do we need to be informed that the author or speaker finds something "interesting"? Can't we assume that they wouldn't waste their (and our) time on it otherwise? Since this is now no more than a space-filler, a time-killer, let's drop it. Interesting idea, right?
- Especially on PBS, narrators or hosts gravely warn viewers that "what follows contains very graphic images." Well, first—and most obviously—visual images *are* graphic, making the phrase a redundancy. Of course, what the earnest TV announcer really means to say is that they're going to run pictures that may upset or unsettle you. More particularly, there could be scenes of dismembered bodies, mass graves, executions, or starving children. Well, if *that's* what the TV producers fear will horrify and sicken us, then why not dispense with the awkward and unhelpful euphemism and just flat-out state, for instance, "this report includes footage of prisoners being tortured"? Tell it like it is. We can handle it.

Word Peeves, No "Sexting" Allowed

In a 1983 *Reference Librarian* piece, "Where have all the Moonies gone?," I wrote (under the caption, "Descriptive cataloging: notes"):

> Non-archival libraries don't need some standard notes like "Includes index" or "Includes bibliography." However, other sorts of notes could prove extremely useful in helping potential readers decide whether they truly want a particular item, but these are less frequently supplied. For instance, HCL catalogers added this note to the record for Gloria Kaufman's *Pulling Our Own Strings: Feminist Humor and Satire*: "Includes anecdotes, songs, cartoons, poetry, essays, jokes, and comic routines." And they regularly make notes about sequels and cycles; e.g., "The 2d volume of the author's Dirshan The God-Killer saga, the 1st of which is The Lerious mecca, the 3d, Sword for the empire, and the 4th, The maneaters of Cascalon." Further, "Includes more than 50 photos, some in color, and over 70 traditional designs and projects to piece by machine and quilt in your lap," seems more likely to aid erstwhile borrowers than LC's cryptic collation for the same work: "ill. (some col.)."

Seven years later, I contributed the satirical "Tips on cataloging and classification for library users: a generic handout" to *Public image* (October 1990) It included these remarks:

> Don't expect the catalog to tell you that Kathleen Hirsch's *Songs From the Alley* (1989) is an "in-depth account of the ... life histories of two homeless women," that Michael R. Kelsey's travel guide, *Hiking and Exploring Utah's Henry Mountains and Robbers Roost* (1987) includes a section on "the life and legend of Butch Cassidy," or that *Not Necessarily the New Age* (1988) contains 18 essays by Carl Sagan, Philip J. Klass, Martin Gardner, and others on such topics as karma, past-life regression, Shirley MacLaine, UFO abductions, Brad Steiger, and New Age music. This information *could* be conveyed in notes within the bibliographic or catalog record, but—you guessed it—LC almost never does it. And neither do we. And if we don't *note* the contents, we—quite consistently—also don't permit subject or author access to them, meaning—for instance—that under Butch Cassidy's name there will be no entry for the Kelsey travel guide and under Sagan's nothing referring to *Not Necessarily the New Age*.

Then, in the June 1998 *Librarians at liberty,* I observed (below the rubric, "Descriptive cataloging: missing notes"):

> There is no longer any "controversy" over the utility of full, partial or composed notes in bibliographic records. They often convey (in greater detail than the title alone) what is actually inside a work and may even indicate the author's tone or approach, ultimately saving the searcher's time. Additionally, they greatly facilitate keyword searching in online catalogs. Apparently, LC only creates such notes for about 4 percent of adult nonfiction titles and this year totally *stopped* making them for juvenile fiction.

Now, in the September 2011 *College & research libraries,* Yuji Tosaka and Cathy Weng report on a study, "using circulation data from a medium-sized academic library, of the effect of content-enriched records on library materials usage." Their findings "show that enhanced records were overall associated with higher circulation rates and that keyword search was the most frequently used search option directly associated with circulation." The researchers conclude

> Libraries have invested resources and efforts in making content-enriched data available for end users. This seems to have been an encouraging trend. We would like to see such data

being used to full advantage to support users' information needs in a robust and creative way. As we learned from our study, however, there is still a great distance between where content-enriched access is today to where it can be tomorrow. Only by continuing to provide content-enriched metadata and content-enriched access can users easily retrieve the library resources they need. The library community should commit to keeping the OPAC relevant in an evolving scholarly information landscape, where the quantity and variety of resources have proliferated on a massive scale. Enabling content-enriched access is a crucial part of keeping library catalogs relevant and making library materials easily discoverable among the myriad other resources in the larger digital environment.

Even though it took 28 years since my original plea, the *C&RL* note-making study and endorsement are most welcome. What comes next? Well, LC, networks, and individual libraries must zealously and consistently *add* such notes. No search (and other) benefits will magically accrue from "enhancements" that haven't been made in the first place.

It's nice to report that over the past year the Library of Congress established 7 subject headings I suggested: HACKTIVISM, GLEE CLUBS, SHOW CHOIRS, LOCAVORES, TRANSPHOBIA, DIGITAL RIGHTS MANAGEMENT, and MBALAX (MUSIC). Not so nice is LC's inexplicable failure to create dozens of other descriptors—all recommended with scope notes, usage examples, cross-references and assignment candidates—among them:

ELECTRONIC CIGARETTES	YARN BOMBING
FREE CULTURE MOVEMENT	DONOR OFFSPRING
BULLSHIT (THE ENGLISH WORD)	LAUGHTER YOGA
HOLY YOGA	PROSPERITY GOSPEL
AERIAL YOGA	GARBAGE HOUSES
BENEFIT CORPORATIONS	LITERARY DARWINISM
FINANCIAL SPECULATION TAX	PUNK PARENTING
DUMPSTER DIVING	SEXTING
PADDLEBOARDING	SEX-POSITIVE FEMINISM
IMPACT INVESTING	CLASS PETS
EVOLUTIONARY MEDICINE	POSTFEMINISM
EVOLUTIONARY PSYCHIATRY	FOLKSONOMY
STREET SOCCER	

Really Banned Books, Another Word Peeve, Clint's Fantasy, OWS Library Trashed, PFC Manning's Gift
(U*L 162, 2012)

Most titles publicized yearly by the American Library Association as "banned" have not truly been removed from schools, libraries, and bookstores. Nor have they been either destroyed or prohibited by government entities like cities, states, provinces, or countries. They have commonly been "challenged" and sometimes switched from one curriculum level to another or dropped from a reading list. Well, here are two candidates for the next Banned Books report that fully deserve to be there:

- According to Martha C. Nussbaum ("Gandhi and South Africa," *Nation*, October 31, 2011), "at the end of March, the Indian state of Gujarat banned the printing and distribution of Joseph Lelyveld's *Great Soul Mahatma Gandhi and His Struggle with India* (Knopf)." The uproar stemmed from claims "that *Great Soul* portrays Gandhi as a bisexual or homosexual."
- In 2003, says Nussbaum, "Macalester College's James Laine published *Shivaji: Hindu King in Islamic India*, which mentions but does not endorse a rumor that the revered seventeenth-century Hindu hero Shivaji might have been an illegitimate child, thus impugning the purity of his equally revered mother. The book was banned in India upon its publication for containing material that promotes social enmity, an interdiction lifted only in 2010 by the Supreme Court. Meanwhile, a Sanskrit scholar who had assisted Laine was assailed, and mobs ransacked the archive in Pane, where Laine had done his research, destroying priceless manuscripts."

In U*L 161, I denounced as needless and superfluous the word "preventative." The same applies to "orientate" and "orientated." Orient is a verb. Orient gains no extra or special significance by adding "ate" to it. It's a pointless, wasteful elongation. So let's banish it to the rhetorical dumpster.

Not in *My* Library!

Leonardo Di Caprio plays G-Man Hoover in Clint Eastwood's biopic, *J. Edgar*. Early on, the film makes the extravagant claim, not subsequently challenged, that the soon-to-be FBI Director not only worked at the Library of Congress, but also developed their cataloging system. Maybe with some help, but not much. On screen, J. Edgar performs a feat of biblio-magic, asking his date (later to become his secretary) to name a topic that interests her. She says "indiscretion." He then proceeds to the LC card catalog, selects a 3-by-5, lifts it from the drawer (as if there were no metal rod), disappears briefly behind nearby bookstacks, and beamingly reemerges with a volume in hand that satisfies the request. Wow! Except that almost none of it is believable. If J. Edgar found anything relevant in the catalog it was because "Indiscretion" appeared as the first word in a book title. That term is not currently an LC subject heading and probably wasn't in the early 1900s either. So it was a lucky title-find serving as a topical descriptor. Hardly the gateway to identifying all or most of the library's holdings on the desired subject. And it's wholly laughable that Di Caprio would so speedily retrieve the physical volume, when the overwhelming likelihood is that it would have been shelved deep within the closed stacks, not within a few steps of the catalog. (Those nearby materials would probably have been reference books.) Director Eastwood has not contributed much to explaining or dignifying librarianship with such cinematic bullshit. (For a critique of Eastwood's political spin, see Beverly Gage's "Real J. Edgar," *Nation*, 12-19-11, p. 4, 6.)

On 12-6-11, I sent this letter to *American Libraries*:

> Dear Colleagues,
> Not long ago, nearly everyone went berserk when a deranged Florida minister publicly torched his own copy of the Koran. On November 15th, the NYPD, acting on orders from Mayor Bloomberg, tossed into dumpsters 5,000 books comprising the Occupy Wall Street People's Library. That's bibliocide on a massive scale, wantonly conducted by government itself. Yet the public and media do not evidence much outrage. ALA's next "banned books" inventory should include every title trashed by Bloomberg's storm troopers. Will it?

(A slightly altered version appeared in the Jan./Feb. 2012 issue, p. 8.) The American Library Association's intellectual freedom gatekeepers have for years refused to acknowledge Cuban book-burning, the court-ordered destruction of "independent library" collections. Let's see what they do about the Library Plaza atrocity.

William Scott, in the December 12th *Nation* ("The People's Library lives," p. 5) says "the collection of more than 5,000 donated books of every genre and subject, all free for the taking, was created not only to serve the Occupy Wall Street protesters; it was meant to provide knowledge and reading pleasure for the wider public as well, including residents of Lower Manhattan. It was also a library to the world at large, since many visitors to the park stopped by the library to browse, to donate books of their own, and to take books for themselves." Scott writes that Mayor Bloomberg promised "that the library was safely stored and could be retrieved," but in fact "only about 1,100 books were recovered and some of those in unreadable condition. Four library laptops were also destroyed, as well as all the bookshelves, storage bins, stamps and cataloging supplies and the large tent that housed the library."

An English professor at the University of Pittsburgh, Scott declares

> I love books—reading them, writing in them, arranging them, holding them, even smelling them. I also love having access to books for free. I love libraries and everything they represent. To see an entire collection of donated books, including many titles I would have liked to read, thoughtlessly ransacked and destroyed by the forces of law and order was one of the most disturbing experiences of my life.

Later on November 15th and into the next day, supporters replenished the People's Library with hundreds of donations. However, on the 16th, at 7:30 P.M., the library was again "raided and thrown in the trash... The NYPD first barricaded the library by lining up in front of it, forming an impenetrable wall of cops. An officer then announced through a bullhorn that we should come and collect our books, or they would be confiscated and removed. Seconds later, they began dumping books into trash bins that they had wheeled into the park for that purpose. As they were throwing out the books, a fellow OWS librarian asked one of the NYPD patrolmen why they were doing this. His answer: "I don't know."

Now the OWS Library operates three mobile units, continuing to service occupiers and demonstrators with free books. Scott reports that "the people we met at our mobile units ... went out of their way to express their joy that we were still here. They also struggled to articulate their feelings of loss, frustration, anger, disgust, and outrage over the seizure and destruction of the library." He eloquently concludes

> Although we often shout, "This is what democracy looks like!" on our marches, it's also something we can say every day to those who pay a visit to the OWS library. In fact, it's something that the People's Library, by its very presence—in any location, in any form, with any number of books is perfectly capable of saying for itself.

PFC Bradley Manning will be court-martialed. He could ultimately be imprisoned for life. Or executed. As an update to my U*L 160 column on government secrecy and repression, here are excerpts from an October 11, 2011 statement, "In solidarity with the Occupy Movement":

> We share a common commitment to exposing the corruption of corporate power upon our democratic system. Organizers with the Bradley Manning Support Network have been on the ground at Occupy Wall Street, Oakland, DC, Boston, Chicago, SF and elsewhere.
>
> We condemn the government's crackdown on our fellow citizens around the country. There is no excuse to silence those who speak freely, assemble peacefully, and seek to petition their government. We also stand for the right of the press to operate free from government harassment. For over 16 months, the Obama administration has withheld the freedom of PFC Bradley Manning in retaliation for allegedly exposing evidence of abuse via WikiLeaks and other media outlets. The administration's unprecedented pursuit of whistleblowers like Manning has created a severe chilling effect on those who seek to expose and correct wrongdoing.
>
> Similarly to the Arab Spring, the Occupy movement can draw from information revealed by WikiLeaks that exposes corporate manipulation of our foreign policy. An October 2009 diplomatic cable shows how U.S. diplomatic officials shared sensitive intelligence with Shell

to give the oil corporation unfair economic leverage in Nigeria. Shell executives privately boasted to U.S. diplomats that its agents had managed to infiltrate all of the major Nigerian government ministries. Another series of cables illustrate how diplomatic officials successfully squashed a proposed increase in the Haitian minimum wage. Pressure from U.S. diplomats on Haitian officials enabled major American clothing companies like Levi's and Hanes to continue exploiting sweatshop labor in Haiti. Other cables show that Chevron executives worked in tandem with U.S. officials to avoid paying $18.2 billion in court-ordered damages after the energy giant acquired Texaco, which had dumped billions of gallons of waste in indigenous areas.

Taken as a whole, the material allegedly revealed by PFC Manning shows that an unjust accumulation of informational power runs parallel to widespread economic and political inequalities. In both the United States and abroad, 99 percent of the people are kept in the dark, while corporate elites use restricted information to manipulate government policies for their personal profit.

Our struggle for Bradley Manning's freedom is a struggle for everyone's freedom. The Occupy movement's fight for true democracy is everyone's fight. That is why we're standing in solidarity, in person, as we occupy everywhere.

The December 2011 Courage to Resist national newsletter also argues that the U.S. withdrawal from Iraq may have been accelerated by a damning cable released by WikiLeaks with the probable help of Manning. Bradley should get a medal, not a noose.

Post Office Crisis, LC Letters
(U*L 163, 2012)

On 2-28-12 I wrote my congressional representative and senators:

Please advise what you are doing to prevent the United States Postal Service from being decimated or privatized.

USPS — which delivers mail to everyone, everywhere at a fixed, affordable price — is utterly essential to an egalitarian, democratic society. It underpins a free press, especially in the form of magazines and newspapers. It supports small business, as Michael I. Niman explains in the enclosed "Going Anti-Postal" (*Humanist*, March/April 2012). And it uniquely facilitates communication among the many millions of Americans without Internet access. Further, post offices and letter carriers directly contribute to community building and social bonding. In short, USPS is an institution to be treasured, not trashed.

One immediate measure to protect USPS would be to lift the bizarre requirement that it prefund portions of its retirement 75 years into the future.

Yours for a vibrant, continuing Postal Service,

Later, on 3-9-12, I forwarded more documentation on why and how to preserve and improve USPS: the March 2012 *Hightower Lowdown* (P.O. Box 3109, Langhorne, PA 19047; hightowerlowdown.org). Titled "The Post Office is not broke — and it hasn't taken any of our tax money since 1971," the whole issue is dedicated to "answering the lies that privatization zealots and FedEx are peddling."

These three letters, all directed to the Cataloging Policy & Support Office, Library of Congress, Washington, DC 20540-4305, have so far elicited no response:

October 30, 2011

Dear Colleagues,

The current subject heading, COMMONS, is not broad or deep enough to denote the emerging concept and movement that defines "Commons" as "everything that belongs to all of us," including not only forests, atmosphere, rivers, fisheries, lakes, grazing land, and such public spaces as parks, but also literature, arts, media, information, the Internet, and other cultural elements as well as public services like education, health care, and transportation, not to mention libraries.

I suggest adding an expansive scope note to the present descriptor, now limited strictly to real estate, so that COMMONS may be applied to the growing number of materials dealing with the broader concept and movement. If desirable to retain the current land-related citations in one place, the rubric could be transformed with a gloss to reflect the more specific scope, e.g., COMMONS (REAL PROPERTY). In that event, the new, unglossed form should be provided with an array of "see also" references, among them

BT	Cooperation		Internet
	Ownership		Public libraries
	Property		Public schools
	Sharing		Public transportation
NT	Commons (Real property)	RT	Commercialization
	Free culture movement [recommended earlier]		Privatization

With best wishes,
/s/ Sanford Berman
Enclosures:
Jay Walljasper, "Struggle for the commons," *Nation*, 10-17-11, p. 24–26; "Commons," *Wikipedia*, 10-12-11

February 24, 2012

Dear Colleagues,

At present, LCSH includes this form:

OPEN AND CLOSED SHOP — LAW AND LEGISLATION — UNITED STATES
UF   Right to work laws

Since "right to work" legislation is currently a "hot" election year topic, it would be helpful to maximize access to that subject. So I warmly suggest examining the titles now appearing under the "open and closed" descriptor. If *all* of them actually deal with RTW, the "open and closed" rubric should be replaced with:

RIGHT TO WORK LAWS
SN   Here are entered materials on state statutes under which the union shop is prohibited, as are maintenance of membership, preferential hiring, and other contract clauses requiring union membership.
UF   RTW laws
BT   Union-busting.

Should there be some assigned titles that do not strictly deal with RTW, the present "open and closed" descriptor could be retained, but all truly RTW material should be reassigned to the new, more specific subject heading. The current 450/UF, "Right to work laws" would need to be deleted, and a "see also from" reference introduced from the "open and closed" heading *to* RIGHT TO WORK LAWS.

These changes should substantially improve finding materials on an issue of intense concern and debate.

With best wishes,
/s/ Sanford Berman

March 22, 2012

Dear Colleagues,

Larry Johnson, President of Minnesota Veterans for Peace Chapter 27, writes in the Spring 2012 chapter newsletter:

> Six months ago I tried to find books in the library on war profiteering. There was virtually nothing. I guess because the selective information system didn't want people to know too much about how you can sell to both sides, heavily overcharge the Pentagon for shoddy

equipment, and still keep doing business with the Pentagon, because "putting regulations on defense contractors might discourage free enterprise."

Johnson's trouble in locating relevant material may have been less due to deficiencies in the library collection than to a failure to helpfully identify such resources in the catalog. To remedy that problem, I suggest creating this subject heading:

WAR PROFITEERING
SN Here are entered materials on profits derived from selling weapons and other goods to parties at war.
UF Profiteering, War
      Profiting from war
BT Military-industrial complex
      War — Economic aspects
RT Military-industrial complex

Enclosed: *Wikipedia* entry, usage-examples, and citations for both print and online assignment candidates, including Smedley D. Butler's *War is a racket*.

With best wishes,
/s/ Sanford Berman

Another Real Banning, The Trashing of Both Hypatia and Her Library, Not-So-Funny Cataloging
(U*L 164, 2012)

In U*L 162 I nominated two India-related tomes for ALA's next Banned Books list and also bewailed Mayor Bloomberg's wanton destruction of the OWS Library in Liberty Plaza last November. Since then, Ronald A. Lindsay reported in the August/ September 2012 *Free Inquiry* (page 6) that "a new book by Muslim author and activist Irshad Manji was banned in Malaysia for being blasphemous and for causing 'disturbance to the public.'" So make that a third nomination. And that same magazine issue features Michael B. Paulkovich's remembrance of the terrible fate that in the 5th century befell both the Alexandrian Library and its heroic director. In New York City, a mayor ordered the bibliocide. In Alexandria, it was a bishop, Theophilus, intent upon demolishing all vestiges of "heathenism," who engineered the wrecking of everything produced by non–Christian intellectuals, freethinkers, and philosophers. This is what happened:

> The original library, holding almost a million books, was a center of ancient scholarship and knowledge. It burned accidentally around 48–47 BCE. After a move to the neighboring Serapeum, Alexandrian scholars quickly began to recover their collection, copying every written scroll or book they came across to build up their new repository...
> In 391 CE, furious Christian leaders stormed the library ziggurats (the Mithraeum and the Serapeum), toppling statues, slashing artwork, and burning every library text they found — hundreds of thousands of scrolls and books. They razed the most venerable temple of learning and knowledge of their day like drunken soccer hooligans after losing (or winning) the World Cup...
> Hypatia, the beautiful and brilliant head librarian, mathematician, and philosopher, continued teaching well after her library's destruction. In 415, Saint Cyril, pope of Alexandria, concocted vituperative lies and depicted Hypatia as a "sorceress" able to cast "magic spells." Cyril played the proverbial witch card, the Christian ace in the hole.
> Fanatical monks eventually caught up with Hypatia when she was about 60 years old. They ambushed her chariot on her trek homeward, dragged her through dusty streets, and tortured her to death by *skinning her alive*. Those Christian leaders then chopped up her body and burned her limbs, her torso, and her very recently detached cranium, flowing

with lush locks, plopping all onto their pious bonfire—all this to make sure, I suppose, that not only was she merely dead but really most sincerely dead.

For a dramatic, visual rendition of these events, see the 2009 film, *Agora*, starring Rachel Weisz.

Here are four letters sent this year to the Library of Congress Cataloging Policy and Support Office (Washington, DC 20540-4305), so far without any action or reply:

May 15, 2012

Dear Colleagues,
    I recommend establishing a subject heading for

STAND-YOUR-GROUND LAWS.
- SN   Here are entered materials on laws declaring that a person may use force in self-defense when there is reasonable belief of a threat. Such laws, also often called Castle Doctrine laws, frequently state that a person has no duty to retreat when their home is attacked or, indeed, to abandon a place where they have a right to be or to give up ground to an assailant.
- UF Castle Doctrine laws
     "Line in the sand" laws
     "No duty to retreat" laws
- BT Self-defense—Law and legislation
     Shooting—Law and legislation

Attached: a partial *Wikipedia* entry plus Google usage-examples and citations for online, government, and other assignment-candidates. Upcoming works on the Trayvon Martin Case will doubtless merit the new rubric.

May 25, 2012

Dear Colleagues,
    I recommend creating a subject heading for a two-decades old practice and philosophy:

ATTACHMENT PARENTING
- SN   Here are entered materials on a parenting philosophy based on principles of attachment theory in developmental psychology. Three basic elements are breastfeeding (sometimes into toddlerhood), co-sleeping (inviting babies into the parental bed), and babywearing (literally attaching infants to their mothers via slings).
- UF Parenting, Attachment
     Sears attachment parenting
- NT Babywearing
     Breastfeeding
     Co-sleeping
- BT Parenting
     Mother and child

Attached: *Wikipedia* entry; Kate Pickert's "Man who remade motherhood," *Time,* May 21, 2012, p. 33–9; Google usage-examples plus citations for print and online assignment-candidates.

Also suggested:

BABYWEARING
- SN   Here are entered materials on the practice of wearing or carrying a baby or child in a sling or other carrier.
- UF Baby wearing
     Wearing, Baby
- BT Attachment parenting
     Parenting

Not in *My* Library!

Attached: *Wikipedia* entry plus Google usage-examples and assignment-candidate citations, including Maria Blois' *Babywearing: the benefits and beauty of this ancient tradition* (2005).

/s/ Sanford Berman

June 14, 2012

Dear Colleagues,
 I recommend establishing a subject heading for

WAGE THEFT
SN   Here are entered materials on the practice of underpaying or not paying workers for their labor. This may involve stealing tips, making illegal paycheck deductions, and failing to pay overtime or the minimum wage, as well as classifying workers as "independent contractors" to avoid paying unemployment insurance, and denying legal meal breaks.
UF   Theft of wages
      Theft, Wage
BT   Employers—Malpractice
      Labor exploitation [HCL form]
      Stealing
      Wages
      Working poor people

Enclosed: *Wikipedia* entry plus abundant usage-examples and citations for print and online assignment candidates.

/s/ Sanford Berman

June 13, 2012

Dear Colleagues,
 I recommend establishing a subject heading for

STOP-AND-FRISK
SN   Here are entered materials on a police practice to temporarily detain and search people they deem suspicious
UF   Police stop-and-frisk
      Stopping-and-frisk¡ng
BT   Criminal procedure
      Searches and seizures

Enclosed: usage-examples plus citations for print, online and video assignment-candidates.

/s/ Sanford Berman

This is a recent LC Cataloging-in-Publication entry:

Smith, Jeanette C., 1946–
 The laughing librarian: a history of American library humor / Jeanette C. Smith ; forewords by Will Manley and Norman D. Stevens.
 Includes bibliographical references and index.
 1. Library science—United States—Humor.
 2. Librarians—United States—Humor.
 3. Libraries—United States—Humor. I. Title.

And here is what I wrote in response:

5-11-12
Cataloging Policy & Support Office
Library of Congress
Washington, DC 20540-4305

The Trashing of Both Hypatia and Her Library

Dear Colleagues,

Jeanette C. Smith's *Laughing librarian* deserves better, more useful cataloging than it got. So I suggest this treatment instead:

Smith, Jeanette C., 1946–

    The laughing librarian: a history of American library humor. Forewords by Will Manley and Norman D. Stevens.

    Illustrated with cartoons and comic strips.

    PARTIAL CONTENTS: Batgirl was a librarian: library superheroes.—Edmund Lester Pearson: the main guy.—Norman D. Stevens and the Molesworth Institute.—Will Manley: the bad boy.—Mad magazine: it's a mad, mad, mad, mad library.—The New Yorker: the smart set just loves to read.—Joyfully subversive.

    1. Library humor. 2. Librarian superheroes. 3. Pearson, Edmund Lester, 1880–1937. 4. Stevens, Norman D., 1932– . 5. Manley, Will, 1949– . 6. Mad Magazine cartoons. 7. New Yorker cartoons. 8. Critical librarianship—Humor. 9. Molesworth Institute. I. Manley, Will, 1949– II. Stevens, Norman D., 1932– . III. Title. IV. Title: Librarians laughing. V. Title: History of American library humor. VI. Title: American library humor: a history.

This will entail at least three new subject headings:

LIBRARY HUMOR

  UF   Humor, Library
         Librarians—Humor [now a primary form]
         Libraries—Humor [now a primary form]
         Library science—Humor [now a primary heading]
  BT   Humor

LIBRARIAN SUPERHEROES

  UF   Superheroes, Librarian
  BT   Librarians
         Superheroes

CRITICAL LIBRARIANSHIP [recommended 5-16-07, with suggested scope note, cross-references, and assignment-candidates]

/s/ Sanford Berman

P.S. From Page 103:

Because the quest for library humor leads everywhere and anywhere, Stevens compares it to sunken treasure. He states that many instances of library humor are not cataloged by the Library of Congress and are not included at all or are included inconsistently in indexes and abstracts. Brief pieces are ignored. Indexers and catalogers often do not recognize satire for what it is. When indexed, library humor is often listed under peculiar terminology such as Libraries—Anecdotes, Facetiae, Satire, Etc. Stevens calls for a direct "Bermanized" heading—Library Humor—named for cataloging reformer and activist Sanford Berman, but he concludes that this is unlikely to happen without the existence of a library humor round table in ALA to make it a major goal. While the Library of Congress has since changed its headings to "Libraries—Humor, Library Science—Humor, and Librarians—Humor," it has not established a direct Library Humor subject heading.

Response to Stevens' 1985 article was immediate. A letter to the editor from Berman, the head cataloger at the Hennepin County Library in Minnesota, appeared in the June 1985 *American Libraries.* Berman announced that the subject heading Library Humor would appear in the *Hennepin County Cataloging Bulletin #77* of July/August

1985. He used Stevens' article as the authority for establishing the heading, and he assigned it to works including *Tales of Melvil's Mouser* (Paul S. Dunkin, 1970), *Lighter Side of the Library* (Janice Glover, 1974), *Is That the Library Speaking?* (Ken Hornsby, 1979), *The Natives Are Always Restless* (Gerald Rafferty, 1964), *Library Humor: A Bibliothecal Miscellany to 1970* (Norman Stevens, 1971), and Berman's own biennial compilation, *Alternative Library Literature.*

Laureates Support PFC Manning, Self-Censorship Affirmed, J'Accuse LC of Untimeliness and Sloth, Let's Hear It for Robin Hood!
(U*L 166, 2013)

Because it deals importantly with issues of information policy, government secrecy, and whistleblowing, here's a statement lately released by three Nobel Peace Prize winners:

As people who have worked for decades against the increased militarization of societies and for international cooperation to end war, we are deeply dismayed by the treatment of Pfc. Bradley Manning.

We have dedicated our lives to working for peace because we have seen the many faces of armed conflict and violence, and we understand that no matter the cause of war, civilians always bear the brunt of the cost. With today's advanced military technology and the continued ability of business and political elites to filter what information is made public, there exists a great barrier to many citizens being fully aware of the realities and consequences of conflicts in which their country is engaged.

Responsible governance requires fully informed citizens who can question their leadership. For those citizens worldwide who do not have direct, intimate knowledge of war, yet are still affected by rising international tensions and failing economies, the WikiLeaks releases attributed to Manning have provided unparalleled access to important facts.

Revealing covert crimes in Iraq and Afghanistan, this window into the realities of modern international relations has changed the world for the better. While some of these documents may demonstrate how much work lies ahead in terms of securing international peace and justice, they also highlight the potential of the Internet as a forum for citizens to participate more directly in civic discussion and creative government accountability projects.

Questioning authority, as a soldier, is not easy. But it can at times be honorable. The words attributed to Manning reveal that he went through a profound moral struggle between the time he enlisted and when he became a whistleblower. Through his experience in Iraq, he became disturbed by top-level policy that undervalued human life and caused the suffering of innocent civilians and soldiers. Like other courageous whistleblowers, he was driven foremost by a desire to reveal the truth.

Private Manning said in chat logs that he hoped the releases would bring "discussion, debates and reforms" and condemned the ways the "first world exploits the third." Much of the world regards him as a hero for these efforts toward peace and transparency, and he has been nominated for the Nobel Peace Prize as a result. However, much as when high-ranking officials in the United States and Britain misled the public in 2003 by saying there was an imminent need to invade Iraq to stop it from using weapons of mass destruction, the world's most powerful elites have again insulted international opinion and the intelligence of many citizens by withholding facts regarding Manning and WikiLeaks.

The military prosecution has not presented evidence that Private Manning injured anyone by releasing secret documents, and it has asserted in court that the charge of "aiding the enemy through indirect means" does not require it to do so. Nor has the prosecution denied that his motivations were conscientious; it has simply argued they are irrelevant. In ignoring this context and recommending a much more severe punishment for Bradley Manning than is given to U.S. soldiers guilty of murdering civilians, military leadership is sending a chilling warning to other soldiers who might feel compelled by conscience to reveal misdeeds. It is our belief that leaders who use fear to govern, rather than sharing wisdom born from facts, cannot be just.

We Nobel Peace Prize laureates condemn the persecution Bradley Manning has suffered, including imprisonment in conditions declared "cruel, inhuman and degrading" by the United Nations, and call upon Americans to stand up in support of this whistleblower who defended their democratic rights. In the conflict in Iraq alone, more than 110,000 people have died since 2003, millions have been displaced and nearly 4,500 American soldiers have been killed. If someone needs to be held accountable for endangering Americans and civilians, let's first take the time to examine the evidence regarding high-level crimes already committed, and what lessons can be learned. If Bradley Manning released the documents, as the prosecution contends, we should express to him our gratitude for his efforts toward accountability in government, informed democracy and peace.

ARCHBISHOP DESMOND TUTU
MAIREAD MAGUIRE
ADOLFO PEREZ ESQUIVEL

In these columns and elsewhere, I've maintained — with plentiful examples — that the primary book-banners in libraries are librarians. Recently, in the November/December 2012 *Public libraries* (page 47), Linda Evans reviews Nye/Barco's *True stories of censorship battles in America's libraries* (ALA, 2012). As a result of conducting "Banned Books Exposed" programs at many state and regional library conferences over several years, during which they gathered firsthand stories "from librarians regarding censorship challenges," the authors concluded, in part, "that the most common form of censorship is often silence when materials are not purchased or are quietly withdrawn to avoid controversy." Why isn't this reality more often (if ever) explored in the Panglossian library press?

After "retiring" in 1999, I've continued to make recommendations to the Library of Congress for new or revised subject headings, as well as suggesting better cataloging treatment for specific titles. Much of this effort has been reported in this column. Well, in the period 2005–2012, LC *has* accepted some 83 proposals, notably including AMER-

PFC Manning, Self-Censorship, Untimeliness

ICAN DREAM, ANTI-RACISM, CONFLICT DIAMONDS, KRUMPING, MEN'S UNDERWEAR, MORAL PANICS, MIXED MARTIAL ARTS, PLUTOCRACY, QUEER THEORY, SEX TOYS, SEXUAL FREEDOM, SINGLE-PAYER HEALTH CARE, WEST VIRGINIA MINE WARS, 1897–1921, WICCA, ZINES, MOUNTAINTOP REMOVAL MINING, INTERSEX PEOPLE, INTERSEXUALITY, SEX SCANDALS, TRANSGENDER PEOPLE, DILDOS, EXTRAORDINARY RENDITION, PATIENT DUMPING, LIKES AND DISLIKES, SCRAPBOOKING, FOOD SOVEREIGNTY, BIOPIRACY, SECOND-WAVE FEMINISM, THIRD-WAVE FEMINISM, PUBLIC SEX, REPRODUCTIVE RIGHTS, SOCIALIST FEMINISM, PRISON-INDUSTRIAL COMPLEX, LIBRARY CATS, WATERBOARDING, WITCH HUNTING, POST RACIALISM, LESBIAN SEPARATISM, URBAN FICTION, MANIFEST DESTINY, CELL PHONE NOVELS, REGGAETON, PREDATORY LENDING, HACKTIVISM, GLEE CLUBS, SHOW CHOIRS, TRANSPHOBIA, MBALAX (MUSIC), DUMPSTER DIVING, and SEXTING. Wow! Impressive. Plenty of reason to rejoice. In fact, 83 reasons. However, during that same 7-year period, more than 160 recommendations—all documented, justified and provided with scope notes and cross-references—have *not* been implemented. Among the "rejects": AFRO-BRAZILIANS and AFRO-CUBANS (replacing BLACKS—BRAZIL and BLACKS—CUBA), ANAL FISTING, ANARCHO-PRIMITIVISM, ANARCHA-FEMINISM, ANTI-ARABISM, ARMENIAN GENOCIDE, 1915–1923 (replacing ARMENIAN MASSACRES, 1915–1923), BUTCH AND FEMME (LESBIANISM), CULTURE WARS, DRAG QUEENS, EROTOPHOBIA, GI MOVEMENT, GENDERQUEERS, INFOSHOPS, NATIVE AMERICAN HOLOCAUST (1492–1900), SLOW MEDICINE, MOTHERS' WRITINGS, ATHEIST PARENTING, HUMANIST PARENTING, TRANSHUMANISM, FEMINIST FAIRY TALES, CRITICAL CATALOGING, CRITICAL LIBRARIANSHIP, PESTERING, SEX WORKERS, BEARDED WOMEN, BOLLYWOOD FILMS, BOLLYWOOD FILM MUSIC, INDUSTRIAL POLLUTION, TECHNOLOGICAL SINGULARITY, POSTFEMINISM, JAWBREAKERS, VAMPIRE LOVE STORIES, LITERARY DARWINISM, LAUGHTER YOGA, GARBAGE HOUSES, EVOLUTIONARY MEDICINE, STREET SOCCER, YARN BOMBING, FREE CULTURE MOVEMENT, MORAL INJURY, BENEFIT CORPORATIONS, IMPACT INVESTING, RIGHT-TO-WORK LAWS, WAR PROFITEERING, LIBRARY HUMOR, STAND-YOUR-GROUND LAWS, ATTACHMENT PARENTING, BABYWEARING, WAGE THEFT, AIDS DENIALISM, STOP-AND-FRISK, DRONE WARFARE, HATE ROCK MUSIC, ANTIVACCINE MOVEMENT, and FAIRY GARDENING. Not only have these myriad recommendations been ignored—meaning that library users are denied catalog access to many useful, timely, and provocative topics—but no LC staffer has even condescended to acknowledge this almost monthly input, much less explain why, for instance, LC has refused to establish descriptors denoting widely-popular Bollywood films, the 500 years of genocide against Native Americans, and the contentious practice of drone warfare. So, although ordinarily patient and forgiving, I now disgustedly accuse LC of wanton unresponsiveness, bibliocide-by-cataloging, and a monumental lack of collegiality. What will this desperate accusation produce? Probably nothing. Yet I couldn't contain my unease and disappointment any longer.

Okay, here we go again: These two letters I sent to the Library of Congress Cataloging Policy & Support Office (Washington, DC 20540-4305) late last year:

Not in *My* Library!

October 23, 2012

Dear Colleagues,

I recommend establishing a subject heading for
ROBIN HOOD TAX

SN Here are entered materials on a financial transactions tax to raise funds to protect public services, combat poverty, and address climate change.

UF Robin Hood FTT
    Robin Hood financial transactions tax
    Wall Street transactions tax

BT Financial services—Taxation
    Transfer taxes

Enclosed: *Wikipedia* entry plus usage-examples and citations for both print and online assignment-candidates.

With warmest regards,

/s/ Sanford Berman
cc: Hon. Tom Harkin
    Hon. Peter DeFazio
    Hon. Keith Ellison

November 2, 2012

Dear Colleagues,

Please cancel my 7-12-11 recommendation to create a FINANCIAL SPECULATION TAX subject heading. Instead, I suggest adding these cross-references to the lately proposed ROBIN HOOD TAX:

UF FST
    FTT
    Financial speculation tax
    Financial transactions tax
    Securities speculation tax
    Securities transaction tax
    Speculation tax

BT Business—Taxation

With warmest regards,
/s/ Sanford Berman

Index

"Passim" (literally "scattered") indicates intermittent discussion of a topic over a cluster of pages.

abbreviations 90, 160
academese *see* jargon, academic
academic libraries 36, 55; *see also* library schools
access to stacks *see* closed stacks; open shelving
Acre Massacre, 1191 46
activism, community *see* community activism
adages and slogans *see* slogans and adages
added title entries 90, 130, 139
ADL *see* Anti-Defamation League (ADL)
Adult Video News 115
Afghan Massacre: The Convoy of Death 74–75
AFR *see* Automatic Field Recognition (AFR)
African Americans 127–29, 132, 163
Afro-Cubans 150
AFSCME: Local 2864 (HCL) 12, 54; Local 2910 (Library of Congress) 94; *see also* Librarians' Guild, AFSCME Local 2626
AIDS classification 163
Aiken, Julian 115
ALA *see* American Library Association (ALA)
Alexandrian Library 178
"Almost Banned Books" 50, 51
alternative cataloging-in-publication data *see* cataloging-in-publication data, alternative
Alternative Library Literature (Berman and Danky) 12
alternative press 11, 31, 50, 51, 55, 73–74, 140; cataloging treatment 89; excerpts 58–60 passim 67, 71–72, 95, 140, 178–79; on homelessness, hunger, poverty, and inequality 23–24, 33; *see also* G.I. underground press; library alternative press;

street newspapers; zines
"alternative press" (proposed subject heading) 93
alternative press publishers 131
Alternative Publishers of Books in North America (APBNA) 51
Alternatives in Publication Task Force (AIP) 16
American Federation of State, County, and Municipal Employees *see* AFSCME
American Indians in subject headings *see* Native Americans in subject headings
American Libraries (*AL*) 27, 31, 32
American Library Association (ALA) 1, 10–11, 167; Berman's honorary membership 10, 154; CC:DA 89; conference "grandstanding" 105; Council 28–29, 54, 55, 82, 101, 112; Cuban debate 62–63, 172; Darfur Genocide response 112–13; Ethics Committee and Ethics Code 28–29, 54–55, 82; Ethnic Materials Information Exchange Round Table (EMIERT) 124; Executive Board 125; GLBT Round Table 115; International Relations Committee and Office (IRC and IRO) 124, 125; library school accreditation 65–66; Library Services for the Poor (Policy 61) 10, 11, 12, 25, 114, 132, 136; Midwinter meetings 4, 7; Office of Intellectual Freedom (OIF) 124, 136; Patriot Act response 86; Social Responsibilities Round Table (SRRT) 11–16 passim 124, 136; Subject Analysis Committee (SAC) 11; Summer conference 2001, 13; *see also American Libraries*; Banned Books Week; *Children and Libraries*; resolutions, ALA

amnesties 42
Amnesty International 13, 62, 63–64, 69, 75
Anderson, Byron 51
Anderson, Jamie 135
Angelou, Maya 49, 50, 51
Anglo-American Cataloging Rules (AACR) 2
Anglo-American Cataloging Rules 2nd ed. (AACR2) 11, 89
Anglo-American Cataloging Rules 3d ed. (AACR3) 89
anticommunism in library school 82, 159
Anti-Defamation League (ADL) 106
arcane and pedantic writing 114
archives, gay and lesbian *see* gay and lesbian archives
archives, personal *see* personal archives
Armenian Genocide 95, 98–100, 105, 111–12, 149–50, 151
"Armenian massacres, 1915–1923" (subject heading) 98–100, 105, 111, 149, 151
army librarianship 157–58
arts periodicals 39
Asians in subject headings 81
Assange, Julian 166
assisted reproductive technology in subject headings 154–56
atheist books *see* freethought and atheist books
atrocities 74–75, 178–79
"attachment parenting" (proposed subject heading) 179
audiovisual materials 2; *see also* films; music CDs; videos
author statement (descriptive cataloging) 90
Automatic Field Recognition (AFR) 3
automation of library catalogs 1, 2–6
Avram, Henriette 5n

Index

BBW *see* Banned Books Week
Badajos, Ed 153, 158
Baker, Nicholson 10, 36, 46
Baker & Taylor 16, 110
Baltimore 58–59, 60–61
Banned Books Week 31, 49–51, 60–61, 72–73, 133, 171
banning of library users 44
Baraka, Amiri 15, 157
Barco, Kathy 184
Barnard, Anne 132
Barry, Matthew J. 44
Barsotti, Kate 90, 91
BDSM books and magazines 31, 115, 141
Beat poetry 157–58
Bechdel, Alison 109
Behar, Joyce 152
Behind the Green Door 109
Bell, Madison Smartt 129
"berdaches" (subject heading) 119, 142
Berman, Howard L. 149
Berman, Lorraine, memorial scholarship *see* Lorraine O. Berman Memorial Scholarship
Berman, Sam 158–59
Berman, Sanford: as army librarian 157–58; birth and education 158–59; "grandstanding" by 105; as HCL head cataloger 5; HCL Management Team experience 52–54; hiring at HCL 1–2; "informative mailings" of 16–17; interviews 10–17, 158–64; language peeves 114, 168, 171; letters 62–63, 81–83, 89–90, 144, 172; letters and mailings to LC 15, 48, 96–108 passim 122–23, 131–32, 138–39, 142–48 passim 183–86; letters to HCL 11, 112; letters to legislators 149–50, 165; "makes funny" on YouTube 160; postage stamp campaign 161–62; *Prejudices and Antipathies* 5, 11, 105, 106; scholarship funding 162; *Spanish Guinea: An Annotated Bibliography* 159; talks/presentations 92–94, 111–13; as U*L columnist 8; work history (pre-HCL) 159; works disappeared from HCL 32–33
"Bermanization" 181
Berry, John N. 81
best-seller rental programs 22
bias in subject headings 11, 14, 20, 22, 81, 83, 102–6 passim 117, 142
Bible "banning" 50
"bibliocide" 32, 46, 83–84, 172–73, 178, 185
bibliographic record maintenance *see* catalog record maintenance

bibliographic record notes *see* notes (bibliographic records)
bibliographies 57
The Big Book of Masturbation (Cornog) 144
Billington, James H. 27, 33, 99
bisexuals' library services *see* library services for GLBT people
Black, Tracy 164
black Americans *see* African Americans
Blake, Fay 10
Blank, Joani 140
blog posts 133
Bloomberg, Michael 17, 172, 178
boards, library *see* library boards
bomb-making 73, 77
bondage and discipline publications *see* BDSM books and magazines
Bondage Women in Prison (fictional title) 133
book aesthetics and browsability 43
book-burning 73, 172, 178
book catalogs (libraries) 2–6 passim
book de-emphasis 43, 67–68
book destruction *see* bibliocide
book illustrations, cataloging treatment of *see* illustrations in books, cataloging treatment of
book publishing, cost-cutting measures in *see* cost-cutting measures in publishing
book sales and CD sales 36, 58, 59–50, 95
book selection *see* materials selection
book series *see* Harry Potter books; Left Behind books; Lenny Moss books; Stink books (Megan McDonald)
book series cataloging *see* series cataloging
book theft 32
The Book Thing (Baltimore) 59
books, children's *see* children's literature
books, Christian fundamentalist *see* Christian fundamentalist literature
books, comic *see* comic books, strips, etc.
books, freethought and atheist *see* freethought and atheist books
books, rare *see* rare books
bookstores 59, 72
The Borough Is My Library: excerpts 158–64
bosses *see* management
Bowker *see* R. R. Bowker
boycotts 13

brackets 90
Bradley Manning Defense Fund 166
Bradley Manning Support Network 173
British Columbia 23
British Library 36
browsing 43, 90; *see also* closed stacks; open shelving
Broyard, Anatole 128, 129
Broyard, Bliss: *One Drop* 128–30
buildings *see* library buildings
Buschman, John 66
Bush, George W. 69, 149
"business model" librarianship 12, 58, 94, 107, 109
By What Authority 24

Caccavo, Jim 158
Canada 23, 26, 75
card catalogs 3–4, 128; in films 172
Carney, Stephen 54, 55, 56
Castro Ruiz, Fidel 63
catalog notes *see* notes (bibliographic records); subject headings: scope notes (public)
catalog record maintenance 3, 4
cataloging 14, 15, 19–20, 33, 161; of children's books 138–39, 145, 155; credos 19, 164; delusions about 27; of erotic graphic novels 110, 147; error in 3n2, 20, 49; of freethought/atheist books 117–18; of GLBT literature 83, 101–2, 145–46; HCL practices 83–84, 92–94 passim 106, 117, 146, 151, 163, 181; of libertarian books 96; outsourcing and downsizing 33–34, 77, 109; "local deviation" 160, 161, 163; of periodicals 93; of recorded music 73; of religious literature 117–18; rulebooks 2, 11, 89; of zines 92–94; of transgender books 118; *see also* "copy cataloging"; descriptive cataloging; fiction cataloging; Library of Congress: cataloging practices; MARC (machine-readable cataloging); series cataloging; subject headings; "undercataloging": case studies
cataloging-in-publication data, alternative 153
Cataloging-in-Publication (CIP) Program 15, 20
Catholic Agitator 23
Catholic University Library School 82, 159
cats in subject headings 131, 133
censorship 49–51, 72–73, 88, 109, 139–40, 157–58, 159; Cuba

188

Index

13, 62–64; HCL 6–7; India 171; library press 27–34; Malaysia 178; *see also* Banned Books Week; self-censorship
Censorship Battles in America's Libraries (Nye and Barco) *see True Stories of Censorship Battles in America's Libraries* (Nye and Barco)
CEO pay 140
Chaffee, James 10, 29, 42, 67–68, 87
challenges to library materials 31, 49–51, 133, 171
checking out library materials *see* circulation
Chevron 174
Chicago 158, 159
child mortality 25
children, only *see* only children
children, parenting of, in subject headings *see* parenting in subject headings
children, restriction of access for 115
Children and Libraries 154–56
children in photography books 72
children of egg or sperm donors in subject headings 154–56
children's fines *see* fines for children's materials
children's literature: cataloging of 138–39, 145, 154; library policy inequities 135; study and teaching of 159
children's services 52–53, 135, 159
Chong, Denise 151–52
Christian fundamentalist literature 82
Christian repression 159, 178–79
Christian slogans 44
Christianity in subject headings 148
Christocentrism 20, 54, 71–72, 106, 164
Christopher, Hearne, Jr. 79
church-state separation 44–45
CIP, alternative *see* cataloging-in-publication data, alternative
CIP Program *see* Cataloging-in-Publication (CIP) Program
circulation 31, 59, 169; manual practices 7; *see also* fines; interlibrary loans; renewal of library materials
citizen activities 10, 42, 67
City Lights Journal 157
City Pages 81
classical music 58, 59
classification of library materials 20, 162, 163
classism 19, 22, 26, 53, 78–79, 134–37
Clinton, Bill 144

closed stacks 90, 91, 115
clothing industry 174
Coca-Cola 29–30, 33
codes and coding 3
Codreanu, Sergin 71
COINTELPRO 76, 165
collection building 11, 161; library user input 67, 71–72
collection weeding *see* weeding of library materials
college libraries *see* academic libraries
College of St. Catherine 15, 86, 108, 111
collegiality 55, 184
Color of Words (Herbst) 127
comic books, strips, etc. 31, 147–48; *see also* graphic novels
commemorative stamp campaigns *see* postage stamp campaigns
commercialism 29–30, 33, 60, 68; *see also* privatization
Committee on Cataloging: Description and Access (CC:DA) 89–90
"commons" (subject heading) 175–76
communications/journalism periodicals 40
community activism 16
compact discs, music *see* music CDs
compiler main entry 90
computerization of library catalogs *see* automation of library catalogs
computerized scanning *see* scanning (computers)
conference presentations, library *see* library conference presentations
Congress *see* U.S. Congress
consensus, library management by 55
"conspiracy theories" (subject heading) 146
"content-enriched metadata" 169–70
contents notes *see* notes (bibliographic records)
contracting out *see* outsourcing
"controversial literature" (subject subdivision) 117
conversion programs 3, 6; Berman-to-Freedman 8–9
"cookery" (subject heading) 151
"cooking" (subject heading) 151
"copy cataloging" 33, 130, 160
Coretta Scott King Task Force 13
Cornog, Martha 144
corporate influence 29–30
corporate sponsorship 68
corporations, multinational *see* multinational corporations
Corso, Gregory 157

cost-cutting measures in publishing 57
Council on Library and Information Resources, Task Force on the Artifact in Library Collections 35–37
Counterpoise 10, 15–16
Courage to Resist 166
"critical cataloging" (proposed subject heading) iv, 142, 184
cross-references 19, 22, 48, 80, 113; examples 93, 123, 138–48 passim
Cuba 13–14, 62–64, 68–70, 75–76, 150, 172
cultural preservation 68
"culture wars" (proposed subject heading) 103–4
Cunningham, John S. 158
Cyril of Alexandria, Saint 178

Danky, James 16
Darfur Genocide 95–96, 100, 101, 112–13, 124–25
dashes 90
data entry 3
database-tampering 32, 83–84
DC Public Library *see* District of Columbia Public Library
deaccessioning of library materials *see* weeding of library materials
Debbie Does Dallas 109
Debs, Eugene V. 162
Deep Throat 109
democracy 52, 164, 166, 175; in library management 52–56 passim
Democracy Now! 74, 112
demonstrations *see* protests and demonstrations
Denver Public Library 78
descriptive cataloging 19, 89–90; *see also* notes (bibliographic records)
Desperate Housewives (TV program) 133
destruction of libraries *see* libraries, destruction of
Dewey Decimal Classification (DDC) 162, 163
Dewey: The Small-Town Library Cat Who Touched the World (Myron and Witter) 131, 133
Diamond, Stanley 159
Di Caprio, Leonardo 172
Dickinson College Library 55
digital divide 79
digital sources 36–37, 38
directors of libraries *see* library directors
"dirty laundry" airing 53, 55–56
discarded library materials 58–60, 95

INDEX

Disciplined Mind: A Critical Look at Salaried Professionals and the Soul-Battering System That Shapes Their Lives (Schmidt) 55–56
disinvestment 113
District of Columbia Public Library 134–36, 159
Diuguid, Lewis W. 78–79
Dr. Seuss *see* Seuss, Dr.
Dodge, Chris 16, 83–84
Dollars and Sense 24
dominance and submission publications *see* BDSM books and magazines
donated library materials 29–30, 84
"donor offspring" (proposed subject heading) 154–55, 161
Double Fold (Baker) 36
double standards 22–23
Dowlin, Ken 85
Dowling, Michael P. 124
Down There Press 140
Doyle, Tony 77
Drabinski, Emily 162–64
Drake, Thomas 166
Drexel University College of Information Science and Technology 65–66
Driscoll, Sally 12
"drone warfare" (proposed subject heading) 184
drugs, books about 73–74
drugs in subject headings 35
dumbing-down of library collections 35–41 passim
DVDs, browsability of 90
DVDs, erotic and sexually explicit 121, 122, 139

e-books 43
Eastwood, Clint: *J. Edgar* 172
economics 4–5n5, 21–26, 113, 174, 176–77, 186; *see also* labor-related subject headings; poor people; unions
editor main entry 90
education 24–25, 164; *see also* higher education; student use of libraries
Effing Librarian 133
Ehrenreich, Barbara 13, 46, 47
Eland, Tom 55
Elders, Jocelyn 144
electronic books *see* e-books
electronic scanning *see* scanning (computers)
Ellem, John 152
Emanuel, Rahm 152
employee reprimands *see* worker reprimands
English language usage: arcane and pedantic 114
environmental depredation 174

environmental impact reports 34
environmental periodicals 39
Epstein, Rob 84
equal signs 90
erotic films and videos 109, 121–22, 133
"erotic graphic novels" (proposed subject heading) 110, 147
erotica and erotophobia 109–10, 115, 121–22, 133, 140, 141
erotica, cataloging of 110, 147
error in cataloging *see* cataloging: error in
Ethnic Materials Information Exchange Round Table (EMIERT) 11, 12, 124
ethnonyms 6, 106, 119, 163
Evad, Dave 67
Evans, Linda 184
executives' pay 140
explosives manufacturing 73, 77

"false drops" (information retrieval) 48, 78
"fanzines" (subject heading) 92–93
fatwas 73
Favreau, Karen 82
FBI 165, 167, 172; *see also* COINTELPRO
fear of offending 111, 149, 151–52
fear of sexuality *see* erotica and erotophobia
Federal Bureau of Investigation *see* FBI
federal government *see* U.S. government
fees 22, 26, 90, 114–15
feminism in subject headings 96–97, 131
feminism, sex-positive 140
Fesenmaier, Steve 16, 40, 93
festschrifts 152–53
fiction, African American 132
fiction cataloging 11, 83, 84, 90, 102, 122–23, 138–39, 145, 160
fiction, pictorial *see* graphic novels
fiction, pulp *see* pulp fiction, lesbian and gay
film posters 41, 60
films 84; censored/removed from libraries 74, 139; face-making grandfathers in 160; Library of Congress in 172; weeding and sale of 40–41; *see also* DVDs; erotic films and videos
financial gifts *see* gifts, financial
fines 22, 26, 42, 43, 114–15, 132, 135; for children's materials 53
forced resignations/retirement 11, 144
foreign-language materials 58
foreign service 159
foundations and friends groups

see library foundations and friends groups
Franklin, Robert 18
Franklin Library (MPL branch) 66–67
Free Inquiry 178–79
free stores 59
Freedman, Jenna 2, 8, 17, 22, 146
Freedman, Maurice J. (Mitch) 1–7 passim 18
Freedman, Paula 7
freedom: Rosa Luxemburg on 63, 164; *see also* intellectual freedom
freedom of speech of library workers 10, 28–29, 52–56 passim 58, 81–82; curtailed by PATRIOT Act 61
Freedom to Read Protection Act 87
freethought and atheist books 71–72, 95, 164; cataloging of 117–18
Friedrich, Judith 83
Friends of Cuban Libraries 69
"friends of the library" groups *see* library foundations and friends groups
Fun Home (Bechdel) 109
fund-raising schemes 44–45
fundamentalist literature, Christian *see* Christian fundamentalist literature

Gandhi, Mahatma 17, 171
garment industry *see* clothing industry
"gatekeeper" role of librarians 82, 140
Gates, Robert F. 40–41
gay and lesbian archives 84–85
Gay and Lesbian Historical Society of Northern California 84, 85
gay and lesbian libraries *see* GLBT libraries
gay and lesbian library services *see* library services for GLBT people
gay and lesbian pulp fiction *see* pulp fiction, lesbian and gay
gay erotica 115, 133
gay, lesbian, bisexual, and transgender literature, cataloging of *see* GLBT literature, cataloging of
gay, lesbian, bisexual, and transgender people in subject headings *see* GLBT people in subject headings
Gebble, Melinda 109–10
Gehner, John 12, 17, 66–67
general material designations (GMDs) 90

Index

genocide 95–96, 98–100, 101, 111–13, 149–50
genre headings 11, 83, 84, 93, 102, 122, 123, 131–32, 145
G.I. underground press 157–58
gift library materials *see* donated library materials
gifts, financial 140
Gilbert, Helen 131
Ginsberg, Allen 157, 158
GLBT libraries 141
GLBT library services *see* library services for GLBT people
GLBT literature, cataloging of 83, 101–2, 145–46
GLBT people in subject headings 108, 118, 119, 142, 145–46
GLBT Round Table 11, 12; *Newsletter* 115, 139
global changes (catalog records) 4
"God (Christianity)" (subject heading) 106
Goines, Donald 132
Goodman, Amy 74, 112
Gordon, Bill 54
Gornick, Vivian 164
Gosztola, Kevin 166
government-church separation *see* church-state separation
government documents 34, 43
government, federal *see* U.S. government
governments, state *see* state governments
"Grandpa Berman Makes Funny" 160
"grandstanding" 105
"graphic images" warnings on television *see* television "graphic images" warnings
"graphic non-fiction" (subject heading) 147
graphic novels 31, 109–10, 147
graphic sexuality *see* sexuality, graphic
Great Soul Mahatma Gandhi and His Struggle with India (Lelyveld) 171
Greenfield, Marjorie 106
Greenwood, Arin 134
Gregorian, Vartan 91
Grier, Barbara 85
Griffin, Laura 93
Grimes, Andrea 93
Gross, Tina 77–78, 87
"Gypsies" (subject heading) 106, 163

Haiti 174
Hamilton, David 72
Hancock, Ian F. 106
handwritten records 3
Hanes 174
"Hansen's Disease" and "Hansen's Disease patients" (subject headings) 106
Harlow, Tim 132
Harper, Myrna 6
Harry Potter books 42, 49–50, 58, 60
Hasskarl, Mark 8
Haught, James A. 46
Hauptman, Robert 57
Hawaii Outsourcing Scandal 16, 18
Hay, Harry 85
HCL Cataloging Bulletin see Hennepin County Library Cataloging Bulletin
health insurance 25
height shelving *see* shelving by height
Helms-Burton Act 68, 69, 70, 75, 76
Henderson, Doug 135
Hennepin County Library (HCL) 1–7, 11–12; "biblio-Stalinism"/database tampering at 7, 32–33, 83–84; cataloging practices (Berman era) 83–84, 92–94 passim 106, 117, 146, 151, 163, 181; directors 2, 5, 6–7, 53, 112; fine income 22, 53, 132; letters to 11, 83–84, 112; librarians' union 12, 54; Library Board 32; management practices 52–54; periodical subscription cancelations 37–40
Hennepin County Library Cataloging Bulletin 6, 32, 106
Herbst, Philip H.: *Color of Words* 127
HERE *see* Hotel Employees and Restaurant Employees Union (HERE)
hierarchical organizations 52, 55, 56, 67
higher education 37, 159; scholarships 162; *see also* library schools
Hightower, Jim 59
Hightower Lowdown 175
Hill Reference Library *see* James J. Hill Reference Library
history 32, 36, 37, 55, 68, 127; periodicals 140
History of the Quatrefoil Library (Keim) 141
Hitchens, Christopher: *God Is Not Great* 117–18
Hochschild, Adam 17
Hoduski, Bernadine E. Abbott 8
Holder, Eric 165
holiday library closures 54
Holley, Robert P. 109
Holocaust, Jewish *see* Jewish Holocaust
"Holocaust, Native American" (proposed subject heading) *see* "Native American Holocaust" (proposed subject heading)
Holy Horrors: An Illustrated History of Religious Murder and Madness (Haught) 46
homeless library users 134–35
homelessness 2, 11, 21–26 passim 79; *see also* street newspapers
honorifics 90
Hoover, J. Edgar, in films 172
Horn, Zoia 10
Hotel Employees and Restaurant Employees Union (HERE) 13
House (TV program) 133
housing 25; *see also* homelessness
How to Make Love Like a Porn Star (Jameson) 82, 87–88
Hoy, Mike 73–74
Hoyer, Kristin 10–17
Hughes, Langston 127
human rights: Afghanistan 74–75; Cuba 13–14, 62–64
humor, library, in subject headings *see* "library humor" (subject heading)
hunger 24–25
Hunger, Homelessness, and Poverty Task Force (ALA) 12, 136
H. W. Wilson Library Periodical Award 6
Hypatia of Alexandria 178–79

I Know Why the Caged Bird Sings (Angelou) 50, 72
IBM Magnetic Tape Selectric Typewriter 6
ILLs *see* interlibrary loans
illustrations, banning of 6
illustrations in books, cataloging treatment of 169
income 25; *see also* executives' pay
independent librarians (Cuba) 62–64, 68–70, 75–76
indexes and indexing 46, 57, 79–80, 88, 118, 121, 153, 181
Indians in subject headings *see* Native Americans in subject headings
"individualist feminism" (proposed subject heading) 96
inequality 21, 26, 33, 79, 174; Cuba 150; *see also* double standards
Ingersoll, Robert G. 95
Innovative Interfaces, Inc. 3n2
institutional classism *see* classism
Institute of Library Research, University of California (ILR) 2–3, 4, 5, 6
intellectual freedom: Cuba 13–14, 62–64, 68–70, 72–74; *see*

INDEX

also censorship; freedom of speech for library workers
"intelligent design" (proposed subject heading) 47–48
"interesting" (word) 168
interlibrary loans 4n4
Internet 37, 67–68, 133
interracial people 127–30
Iraq War 69, 174, 183–84
Islamic authors *see* Muslim authors
Islamic death warrants *see* fatwas
"Islamic Salvation Front (Algeria)" (subject heading) 35, 90

J. Edgar 172
"Jackdaws Strut in Peacock's Feathers" (Berman) 14, 19
Jackie Eubanks Memorial Award 16
James J. Hill Reference Library 43
Jameson, Jenna 82, 87–88
Jansons, Inese 6n6
jargon, academic 114
Jenkins, Jerry B. 82
"Jesus bricks" 44–45
Jewish holidays 54
Jewish Holocaust 112, 149
Jewish identity hiding (passing) 127
"Jewish question" (subject heading) 81, 105–6
Joffee, Andrew 95
Johnson, Larry 176–77
Jones, Leroi *see* Baraka, Amiri
Jones, Mary ("Mother") 162
Jones, Violet 42, 60
Journal of Information Ethics 54, 77
journalists, prosecution of 111
juvenile fines *see* fines for children's materials

Kagan, Al 68–70
Kane, Bart 16
Kansas City (Missouri) Public Library 36, 43, 78–79, 90–91
Kansas Historical Society 36
Keim, Adam: *History of the Quatrefoil Library* 141
Kent, Robert 69, 70
keyword searching 14, 19, 47, 77–78, 87, 89, 94, 169–70
Kick, Russ 72–73
Kids Can Make a Difference Newsletter 24
King, Coretta Scott 13
King County Library System 44–45
"kinky" library materials *see* BDSM books and magazines
Knapp, John 3

Kristof, Nicholas D. 95
Krutch, Joseph Wood 57

labels, pejorative and stigmatizing 20, 81, 152
labor-management relations 52–56 passim 87
labor-related subject headings 176, 180
labor unions *see* unions
LaHaye, Timothy 82
Laine, James 171
Landers, Lora 6–7
Lane, Iris 59–60
Lang, Moyra 152–53
language peeves 114, 168
Latin Music USA (TV program) 146
Latinisms 17, 90
The Laughing Librarian (Smith) 180–81
law journals 40
law school scholarships 162
laws and legislation *see* Helms-Burton Act; "right to work laws" (proposed subject heading); "stand-your-ground laws" (proposed subject heading); USA PATRIOT Act
lawsuits 73
Lazere, Arthur 84
LBR *see* Library Bill of Rights
LC *see* Library of Congress (LC)
LCSH *see* Library of Congress Subject Headings (LCSH)
Leather Archives & Museum 115
Leclerc, Paul 140
Lee, Earl 16
Left Behind books 82
Lelyveld, Joseph 171
Lemann, Nicholas 164
Lenin, Vladimir Ilich 164
Lenny Moss books, cataloging of 122–23
"lepers" and "leprosy" (subject headings) 106
lesbian and gay libraries *see* GLBT libraries
lesbian and gay library services *see* library services for GLBT people
lesbian and gay literature, cataloging of *see* GLBT literature, cataloging of
lesbian and gay pulp fiction *see* pulp fiction, lesbian and gay
lesbian archives *see* gay and lesbian archives
lesbians and gays in subject headings *see* GLBT people in subject headings
Lesniaski, David 108–9
Levinson, Nan 15, 80
Levi's 174

LG Communicator 77, 114–15
LGBT libraries *see* GLBT libaries
LGBT library services *see* library services for GLBT people
LGBT literature, cataloging of *see* GLBT literature, cataloging of
LGBT people in subject headings *see* GLBT people in subject headings
libertarian books, cataloging of 96
librarian blog posts 133, 135–36
Librarian.net 135–36
librarians' "gatekeeper" role *see* "gatekeeper" role of librarians
Librarians' Guild, AFSCME Local 2626 34, 52, 73, 87, 114–15; *see also LG Communicator*
librarians, murder of *see* murder of librarians
librarianship, army *see* army librarianship
librarianship, "business model" *see* "business model" librarianship
libraries, academic *see* academic libraries
libraries, destruction of 172–73; *see also* "bibliocide"
libraries, public *see* public libraries
libraries, special *see* special libraries
library administrators' pay 140
library alternative press 6, 7–9, 12–13, 15–16, 159–60; excerpts 10–17, 158–64
library associations, state *see* state library associations
Library Bill of Rights 28–29, 38, 51, 54–55, 82, 116, 136, 141–42
library boards 32, 53, 114, 139
library buildings 42–43, 54, 68, 78–79, 87, 90–91; religious messages on 44–45; *see also* library hours
library catalog automation *see* automation of library catalogs
library catalogs, book-format *see* book catalogs (libraries)
library catalogs, card-format *see* card catalogs
library catalogs, creation and maintenance of *see* cataloging
library catalogs, keyword searching of *see* keyword searching
library cats 131, 133
library collection building *see* collection building
library collections, destruction of *see* "bibliocide"
library collections, open and closed *see* closed stacks; open shelving

192

Index

library collections, unprocessed *see* "unprocessed" collections
library conference presentations 77–78, 87, 98, 111; arcane and pedantic titles of 114
library destruction *see* libraries, destruction of
library directors: eschewed at MCTC 55; HCL 2, 5, 6–7, 53
library discards *see* discarded library materials
library foundations and friends groups 44, 68, 134–35, 140
library holiday closures 54
library hours 78
"library humor" (proposed subject heading) 181
Library Journal (*LJ*) 1, 27, 32, 81–82
Library Juice 103
library management *see* management
library materials, challenges to *see* challenges to library materials
library materials, circulation of *see* circulation
library materials, classification of *see* classification of library materials
library materials, discarded *see* discarded library materials
library materials, donated *see* donated library materials
library materials, preservation of *see* preservation of library materials
library materials, renewal of *see* renewal of library materials
library materials, sale of *see* book sales and CD sales
library materials, selection of *see* materials selection
library materials, sexuality in *see* sexuality in library materials
library materials, weeding of *see* weeding of library materials
library naming rights and opportunities *see* naming rights and opportunities
Library of Alexandria *see* Alexandrian Library
Library of Congress (LC) 14; "Ask a Librarian" forms 155; authority records 4–5, 8, 11, 14, 125; Berman letters and mailings to 15, 48, 96–108 passim 122–23, 131–32, 138–39, 142–48 passim 184–85; catalog card service 4n4; catalog records 14, 82–83; Cataloging Policy & Support Office (CPSO) 15; cataloging practices 1, 4–5n5, 15, 17, 33, 49, 94, 96, 103, 107–9 passim 117, 118, 122–33 passim

143, 146, 154–56, 169; commercial shilling by 29–20; in films 172; height-shelving proposal 27; MARC Project 1, 3; resistance to change 4–5n5, 22–23, 107, 108–9, 154–56, 163; vote of no confidence in 36; *see also* Cataloging-in-Publication (CIP) Program
Library of Congress Classification (LCC) 162, 163
Library of Congress Subject Headings (LCSH) 5n11, 14–23 passim 47–48, 81, 93, 96–113 passim 118, 122, 126–31 passim 142–46 passim 163, 170, 175–76, 184–85; antiquarian 5, 105, 151; arcane and unfamiliar 19, 35, 105; bias in subdivisions 117
library press 1, 81–82, 95–96, 103, 184; virtual censorship by 27–34; *see also* Hennepin County Library Cataloging Bulletin; library alternative press
library professional journals *see* professional journals
Library Resources & Technical Services 114
library revenue generation from fines *see* revenue generation from fines
library sales *see* book sales and CD sales
library school students 3, 66–67
library schools 65–66, 82, 86, 108, 111; Berman experience 159
library security guards *see* security guards
library services for children *see* children's services
library services for GLBT people 83, 101–2, 108, 118, 119, 141–42, 145–46; *see also* GLBT Round Table
library services for poor people 134, 136–37
Library Services for the Poor (ALA Policy 61) 114, 132, 136
library staff policy input 28, 29, 54, 55, 82, 161; lack of at HCL 37, 52, 53
library unions 12, 33–34, 52, 54, 94
library use by students *see* student use of libraries
library user challenges *see* challenges to library materials
library user records 87
library user requests 67
Library Users Association 84–85
library users, banning of *see* banning of library users
library users, homeless *see* homeless library users

library users' stories 128
library workers' freedom of speech *see* freedom of speech of library workers
"light bulbs" (subject heading) 105
Limbaugh, Rush 152
Lindsay, Ronald A. 178
literature *see* children's literature; fiction, African American; fiction cataloging; graphic novels; poetry; pulp fiction, lesbian and gay
Litwin, Rory 103
living wage 25
lobbying 105, 113
"local deviation" in cataloging 160, 161, 163
local records *see* municipal records
Long Haul: Speaking Out about Poverty 23
Loompanics Unlimited 73–74
The Lorax (Seuss) 145
Lorenz, Pare 40–41
Lorraine O. Berman Memorial Scholarship 162
Los Angeles 1–2, 23, 158–59
Los Angeles Public Library (LAPL) 34, 52, 73, 114–15, 159
"lost" books 43–44
Lost Girls (Moore and Gebble) 109–10, 147
low-income people *see* poor people
loyalty oaths 53–54
Lu Decheng 151
Luxemburg, Rosa 63, 164

Madison, James 139
Madison Zine Fest 92
magazine subscription cancelations 37–40
magazines, BDSM 115
Maguire, Mairead 184
Maher, Bill 152
main entry 90
Malincolnico, Michael 4, 5–6
management 29, 52–56, 87, 161; peer-based 55; *see also* library directors
"Manifest Destiny" (subject heading) 143
Mann, Sally 72
Mann, Thomas 94, 125
Manning, Bradley 17, 165–67, 173–74, 183–84
manual practices 7; *see also* card catalogs; handwritten records; typists and typing
Mao Zedong 151–52
MARC (machine-readable cataloging) 1–6 passim
Marcum, Deanna B. 99–100, 105
Marichal, Oden 75–76

193

Index

"mark-and-park" classification 163
Marriott Hotel, San Francisco, boycott 2001 13
masochism *see* BDSM books and magazines
Massachusetts 23
massacres 46, 74–75, 98–100
master's degree programs (library science) *see* library schools
masturbation 144
The Match! 58–60 passim
material designations *see* general material designations (GMDs)
materials challenges *see* challenges to library materials
materials selection 31, 82, 161; taboos 109–10, 115–16, 121; *see also* collection building
McDonald, Megan 138–39
MCTC *see* Minneapolis Community and Technical College
McElroy, Wendy: *Sexual Correctness* 96
McWhorter, Diane 128
media, news *see* news media
medical journals 39
Medical Subject Headings (MeSH) 106
"medical thrillers" (proposed subject heading) 123
"memory hole" 32, 37, 55
Mendell, Patricia 154–56
metadata, content-enriched *see* "content-enriched metadata"
Methamphetamine Manufacture Secrets see Secrets of Methamphetamine Manufacture
microfilm and microfilming 41, 60
Miller, Henry 157
minimum wage 25; Haiti 174
Minneapolis Community & Technical College 55, 150
Minneapolis Public Library (MPL) 66–67
Minnesota Library Association 86–87
miscegenation 128
mistakes in cataloging *see* cataloging: error in
Mitchell, Nancy 78
MLA *see* Minnesota Library Association
MLS programs *see* library schools
The Modern Temper (Krutch) 57
monks 159, 178
Moore, Alan 109–10
Moore, Maureen 33
Moore, Michael 46, 52
Morris, Norman 158
Mother Jones *see* Jones, Mary ("Mother")

"mountaintop removal mining" (proposed subject heading) 47–48
MPL *see* Minneapolis Public Library
MultiCultural Review 113
multinational corporations 174
municipal records 36
Munson, Chuck 136
murder of librarians 178–79
Murphy, Ed 21
music CDs 34, 58, 67, 73
music, classical *see* classical music
Muslim authors 178
Myron, Vicki: *Dewey* 131, 133

NAFTA in subject headings *see* North American Free Trade Agreement in subject headings
names of peoples *see* ethnonyms
names, self-preferred *see* self-preferred names
naming rights and opportunities 12, 68
Nampa (Idaho) Public Library 139–40
Nasrin, Taslima 73
The Nation 75, 140, 144, 164, 172–73
National Endowment for the Humanities 37
national health insurance 25
"Native American Holocaust" (proposed subject heading) 113
Native Americans in subject headings 6, 113, 118, 119
Nava, Michael 83
Nazi Holocaust *see* Jewish Holocaust
Neal-Schumann Publishers 1
neutrality 25, 58, 164; myth of 29–30, 44, 56, 151
New York Police Department 172–73
New York Public Library 3–5, 140
news media 25, 95, 112, 168; *see also* journalists
newsletters 6, 24, 36, 115, 139
newspapers, weeding and sale of 36, 40
Nickeled and Dimed: On (Not) Getting by in America (Ehrenreich) 46, 47
Nigeria 174
"nigger" (word) 152
Niman, Michael I. 175
Nobel Peace Prize winners 183–84
Nobody Listened (film) 76
Non-Book Materials: The Organization of Integrated Collections (Weihs) 2
North American Free Trade Agreement in subject headings 19, 47, 90
notes (bibliographic records) 14, 19, 89, 169–70; examples 83, 88, 117, 118, 169
notes, scope *see* subject headings: scope notes
Nowak, Mark 15
nude children in photography books 72
Nussbaum, Martha C. 171
Nye, Valerie 184
NYPD *see* New York Police Department
NYPL *see* New York Public Library

Obama, Barack 149
Occupy Wall Street library 17, 172–73
OCLC 3, 4, 7, 11, 50, 83, 109
OCR programs *see* Optical Character Recognition (OCR) programs
oil companies 174
One Drop: My Father's Hidden Life (Broyard) 128–30
Onion 17
only children 158
open hours, library *see* library hours
open shelving 90, 91
Optical Character Recognition (OCR) programs 8–9
oral histories 36
organizations, hierarchical *see* hierarchical organizations
"orientated" (word) 171
Orwell, George 32, 37
Oslo Accords in subject headings 35, 90
Ostrowsky, Ben 8
Our Saviour's Housing (Minneapolis shelter) 66–67
outsourcing 16, 20, 33–34, 42
Outspoken: Free Speech Stories (Levinson) 15, 80
overdue library materials, amnesties for *see* amnesties
overdue library materials, fines for *see* fines

Panetta, Leon 144
parenting in subject headings 179
Parker, Emily 151–52
parking fees 90
participatory management 55
passing (identity) 127–30
Patriot Act *see* USA PATRIOT Act
patron challenges *see* challenges to library materials
patron records *see* library user records

Index

patron requests *see* library user requests
patrons, banning of *see* banning of library users
patrons, homeless *see* homeless library users
patrons' stories *see* library users' stories
Paulkovich, Michael B. 178–79
pay of library administrators *see* library administrators' pay
Paya, Osvaldo 75
peace activists 176; FBI raids of 165; *see also* Nobel Peace Prize winners
Peattie, Noel 10
pedantic writing *see* arcane and pedantic writing
Pelosi, Nancy 149
peer-based management 55
pejorative labels *see* labels, pejorative and stigmatizing
Pelosi, Nancy 149
Pennington, Jerry 1, 2, 4, 5
People's Culture 36
People's Library *see* Occupy Wall Street library
Pérez Esquivel, Adolfo 184
periodicals: cataloging of 92–94; subscription cancelations 37–40; weeding of 43; *see also* library press; magazines; BDSM; newsletters; newspapers; professional journals; zines
personal archives 36, 84, 85
petition campaigns 53, 87, 161–62; *see also* Berman, Sanford: letters and mailings to LC
petroleum companies *see* oil companies
photography books 72
Pima County Public Library 43–44, 50–51, 58
Plotnik, Art 1, 2
poetry 157–58
police 172–73; in subject headings 180
political prisoners 13, 62–64, 69–70, 75, 76
political trials *see* trials, political
Pollitt, Katha 140
Polos, Susan L. 8
poor people 21–26 passim 66–67, 78, 79, 132, 134–37
"poor people" (LC subject heading) 22
Poor People and Library Services (Venturella) 66
"porn" films and videos *see* erotic films and videos
postage stamp campaigns 161–62
Postal Service *see* U.S. Postal Service
posters and poster collections 41, 60

poverty 21–26; *see also* homelessness; poor people
Prejudices and Antipathies (Berman) 5, 11, 105, 106
prescription drugs in subject headings 35
preservation, cultural *see* cultural preservation
preservation of library materials 35–41 passim 43, 60, 67–68
"preventative" (word) 168
prisoners, political *see* political prisoners
prisoners' reading 132
privacy infringement 61, 86–87
privatization 16, 24, 36, 175; *see also* outsourcing
professional journals 54, 77, 95–96, 103; arcane/pedantic language in 114; excerpts 154; *see also* law journals; medical journals
professionals' struggles against hierarchy and authoritarianism 55–56
Progressive Librarian (*PL*) 12–13
Project Censored 27
protests and demonstrations 13, 29–30
public libraries: Banned Books Week practices 60–61; censorious policies 6–7, 139–40; collection shortcomings 141; Darfur Genocide response 124; Denver 78; "embrace" of urban fiction 132; Hawaii 16, 18; Idaho 139–40; Kansas City, Missouri 36, 43, 78–79; Minnesota 42–43, 66–67; New York City 3–4, 140; Stephen Carney on 56; Tucson 43–44, 50–51, 58; Vermont 136; Washington 44–45; Washington, D.C. 134–36; weeding practices 58–59; *see also* Hennepin County Library; Los Angeles Public Library; San Francisco Public Library
public notes (authority records) *see* subject headings: scope notes (public)
public-private partnership 68
publishing, cost-cutting measures in *see* cost-cutting measures in publishing
pulp fiction, lesbian and gay 141
Punk Planet 67

Quebec 26
"queer zines" 93–94, 102, 119, 141

racial passing *see* passing (identity)
racism 127–29 passim 163; Cuba 150

Radcliffe, Charles: *Dancin' in the Streets* 82
radicalism 55–56; oral histories 36; *see also* alternative press
Ranganathan, S. R. 19
rare books 34, 36
Rear Deployment (fictional video) 133
Red Letter Press 131
Redmond Regional Library 44–45
religious literature, cataloging of 117–18
religious messages on library buildings 44–45
renewal of library materials 135
rental programs 22
repression, Christian *see* Christian repression
repression, workplace *see* workplace repression
reprimands 53
resignations, forced *see* forced resignations/retirement
resolutions, ALA: on Cuba 13, 62; on Darfur 101, 112, 113, 124, 125; on workplace speech 28–29, 54, 82
restricted access to library materials *see* closed stacks
"retarded" (word) 152
retirement, forced *see* forced resignations/retirement
revenue generation from fines 22, 53, 132, 135
rich people 21, 33
"rich people" (subject heading) 22
Richard I, King of England 46
"right to work laws" (proposed subject heading) 176
The River (Lorenz) 40–41
Rizzolo, James A. 4
Roberto, K. R. 142, 152–53
Roberts, Don 2, 7
Robeson, Paul 82, 159
Robin Hood 46
"Robin Hood tax" (proposed subject heading) 186
Rohlf, Robert H. 2, 5, 6–7
"Romanies" (subject heading) 106, 163
Rosemont, Franklin: *Dancin' in the Streets* 82
Rowling, J. K.: Harry Potter series 42, 49–51 passim 58, 60
R. R. Bowker 1
Rushdie, Salman 73
Rwanda Genocide 113, 149

Sack, Bette 42
sadism and masochism publications *see* BDSM books and magazines
Safety and Freedom Enhancement Act 87

INDEX

St. Paul Public Library 42–43
sales of books and CDs *see* book sales and CD sales
Samek, Toni 152–53
San Francisco Public Library 29, 42, 46, 67–68, 84–85, 93
Sanchez, Elizardo 75
Sarles, Patricia 154–56
scanning (computers) 8–9
Schmidt, Jeff: *Disciplined Mind* 55–56
scholarships 162
schooling *see* education
schools, library *see* library schools
Schuman, Patricia Glass 1, 2
science periodicals 39
Scilken, Marvin H. 7, 9, 159–60
Scilken, Polly 7
scope notes *see* subject headings: scope notes (public)
Scott, William 172–73
secrecy, workplace *see* workplace secrecy
Secrets of Methamphetamine Manufacture 73–74
security guards 91
"See" and "See also" references *see* cross-references
selection of library materials *see* materials selection
self-censorship 31, 109–10, 115–16, 121, 139–40, 184
self-preferred names 106, 163
Sellie, Alycia 17; interview of Berman 158–64
Senna, Danzy 128
series books *see* Harry Potter books; Left Behind books; Lenny Moss books; Stink books (Megan McDonald)
series cataloging 122–23, 125, 138–39, 169
Seuss, Dr. 145
sex education 144
sexism in subject headings 20
sexuality, graphic 31, 109–10, 115–16, 139–40, 141
sexuality in library materials 31, 82, 87–88, 115–16, 139–40; *see also* erotica and erotophobia
sexuality in subject headings 118, 119
Shalala, Donna 144
She Was a Booklegger (Samek, Roberto, and Lang) 152–53
Sheard, Timothy 122–23
Shell Oil 174
shelving by height 27
shelving, open and closed *see* closed stacks; open shelving
Sherman, Don 3
Shilts, Randy 84, 85

Shivaji: Hindu King in Islamic India (Laine) 171
Shortbus 139
Shut Up Shut Down (Nowak) 15
Silberstein, Stephen 3n2, 6
16mm films 41
slashes 90
Slim, Iceberg 132
slogans and adages 3n3, 44, 130
small press literature 31, 89
Smith, Donny 16, 17, 65–66
Smith, Jeanette C.: *The Laughing Librarian* 180–81
Smith, Wayne 75–76
Social Responsibilities Round Table (SRRT) 11–16 passim 124, 136; Hunger, Homelessness, and Poverty Task Force (HHPTF) 12, 136
social sciences periodicals 39–40
"socialist feminism" (subject heading) 131
soldiers 157–58; *see also* Manning, Bradley
Spanish Guinea: An Annotated Bibliography (Berman) 159
Sparanese, Ann 75–76
special libraries 43, 157–58, 141; Occupy Wall Street movement 17, 172–73
spine length 90
Spunk 42
SRRT *see* Social Responsibilities Round Table (SRRT)
stacks access *see* closed stacks; open shelving
staff policy input *see* library staff policy input
staff reprimands *see* worker reprimands
stamp campaigns *see* postage stamp campaigns
"stand-your-ground laws" (proposed subject heading) 179
Stanford University: BALLOTS system 3
Stark, Matt 141
state governments 152
state library associations 86–87
state library systems: Hawaii 16, 18
Steinbeck, John 49; *Of Mice and Men* 72
Stevens, Norman D. 181
stigmatizing and pejorative labels *see* labels, pejorative and stigmatizing
Stink books (Megan McDonald) 138–39
"stop-and-frisk" (proposed subject heading 180, 184
street newspapers 23, 25
Strock, Adrienne L. 8
student use of libraries 66, 78
study room policies 90

Stupid White Men (Moore) 46, 52
Sturges, Jock 72
Subject Analysis Committee 11
subject headings: in conversion projects 4; HCL practices 5, 6, 7, 11; LC practices 4–5, 8, 15; "local deviation" 163; new/proposed 15, 19–22 passim 47–48, 96–97, 102–8 passim 118–19, 122, 126, 131, 138–48 passim 154–56, 163, 170, 175–81 passim 184–86; philosophy behind 89, 163; research on 77–78, 87; scope notes (public) 47, 92, 96, 104; 119, 175; subdivision 94, 117; *see also* bias in subject headings; cross-references; Library of Congress Subject Headings (LCSH)
subscription cancelations *see* periodicals: subscription cancelations
Sudan, Darfur Genocide *see* Darfur Genocide
surgeons general 144
Survival News 23
sweatshops, Haitian 174
Sweden 13, 149–50

taboo 109–10, 139–40
Taormino, Tristan 121–22
taxation 16, 36, 53, 59, 67, 135; in subject headings 186
Taylor, Arlene 77–78, 87
teachers 24–25, 37
television commercials 29–30
television "graphic images" warnings 168
television programs 133
Texaco 174
theft of books *see* book theft
Theophilus, Bishop of Alexandria 178
Thiessen, Marc 76
Tillett, Barbara 102, 103, 108, 163–64
title entries, added *see* added title entries
"toilets" (subject heading) 105
Too Much 33
topical subdivision *see* subject headings: subdivision
torture 29, 165, 168, 178
Tosaka, Yuji 169–70
transgender books, cataloging of 118
transgender people in subject headings 118, 142
transgender people's library services *see* library services for GLBT people
trials, political: Cuba 13–14, 62–64
True Stories of Censorship Battles

Index

in America's Libraries (Nye and Barco) 184
Tucson Public Library *see* Pima County Public Library
Turkey 111; *see also* Armenian Genocide
Tutu, Desmond 184
Twain, Mark 49, 72
"two-spirit people" (subject heading) 102, 108, 118, 119, 142
typewriters 6, 8
typists and typing 3, 6, 8–9

*U*N*A*B*A*S*H*E*D Librarian* (U*L) 6, 7–9, 159–60
"undercataloging": case studies 15, 47–48, 82–84 passim 88, 108, 110, 117–18, 122–23, 128–30, 142–43
underground press, G.I *see* G.I. underground press
unions 13, 159, 176; *see also* library unions
U.S. Army 159, 165–67; Special Services libraries 157–58
U.S. Congress 99–100, 105, 149–50, 151
U.S. government: executive office 147, 151; foreign relations/policy 68–70 passim 74, 75–76, 111–12, 166, 173–74; *see also* FBI; U.S. Congress; U.S. Postal Service
U.S. history 127
U.S. Holocaust Memorial Museum 112
U.S. Postal Service 162, 175
universal health care 25
university education *see* higher education
university libraries *see* academic libraries
University of California 2–3, 89, 111, 159; *see also* Institute of Library Research, University of California (ILR)
University of California Press 80
University of Kansas, Kenneth Spencer Research Library 36
University of Minnesota 3, 6
university press books 57, 80
"unprocessed" library collections 84–85
"urban fiction" (genre heading) 131–32
Urbanovic, Jackie 6n6
USA PATRIOT Act 11, 61, 86–87
user records *see* library user records
user requests *see* library user requests

videos 41; erotic/sexually explicit 109, 121–22, 139
"Vietnam War" (subject heading) 105
Voices from the Underground, Volume 2 157–58
Vonnegut, Kurt 7

Wachsberger, Ken 157–58
wage theft (proposed subject heading) 180, 185
Walker, Bill 85
war crimes 46, 74–75, 183
"war profiteering" (proposed subject heading) 176–77
Warfield, Peter 10, 29, 42, 85
Washington (DC) Public Library *see* District of Columbia Public Library
Wattenberg, Russell 59
wealth gap 21, 33
weeding of library materials 28, 35–41, 43, 46, 58–60
Weihs, Jean: *Non-Book Materials* 2
welfare and welfare consumers 23–24, 25
Welfare Mothers Voice 23–24
Wellstone, Paul 105
Weng, Cathy 169–70
West, Celeste 10, 140, 152–53
West, Jessamyn 17, 87
West Germany 157–58
West Virginia 40–41, 152
"What Have We Got to Lose? The Effect of Controlled Vocabulary on Keyword Searching Results" (Gross and Taylor) 77–78, 87
whistleblowers 17, 166–67, 173–74, 183–84
Whitehead, Fred 10, 16, 35–37
"widgets" librarianship *see* "business model" librarian-ship
WikiLeaks 166–67 passim 173–74, 183–84
Willett, Charles 15–16
Wilson Library Periodical Award *see* H. W. Wilson Library Periodical Award
Wise, Bob 40
Witter, Bret: *Dewey* 131, 133
woman librarians, murder of 178–79
women of color law school students, scholarships for 162
women's periodicals 40
Woodworth, Fred 10, 43–44, 50–51, 59
word peeves 168, 171
work-related subject headings *see* labor-related subject headings
work-study programs 159
worker policy input *see* library staff policy input
worker reprimands 53
workplace free speech *see* freedom of speech of library workers
workplace repression 52–56 passim 87
workplace secrecy 56

X-rated videos *see* erotic films and videos

"yellow peril" (subject heading) 81
Yin Yang 157–58

zines 31; cataloging of 92–94; excerpts 42, 58, 60, 158–64
"zines" (subject heading) 92